The Battle for
BRITAIN

The Battle for
BRITAIN

Interservice Rivalry between the
Royal Air Force and Royal Navy, 1909–40

ANTHONY J. CUMMING

NAVAL INSTITUTE PRESS

ANNAPOLIS, MARYLAND

This book has been brought to publication with the generous assistance
of Marguerite and Gerry Lenfest.

Naval Institute Press
291 Wood Road
Annapolis, MD 21402

Library of Congress Cataloging-in-Publication Data

Cumming, Anthony J.
  The Battle for Britain : interservice rivalry between the Royal Air Force and Royal Navy,
1909–40 / Anthony J. Cumming.
     pages cm
  Summary: "The Battle for Britain is a provocative reinterpretation of both British air and
naval power from 1909 to 1940. Anthony Cumming challenges the view that the Battle
of Britain was a decisive victory won solely by the Royal Air Force through independent
airpower operations. By re-evaluating the early stage of the Mediterranean conflict
and giving special emphasis to naval battles such as Calabria and Taranto, Cumming
argues that the Royal Navy played an equally important role in defeating Hitler's early
advances, buying critical time until the Americans could make a decisive contribution. His
argument holds that the RAF's role as an independent arm has been exaggerated and that
contemporary strategists can learn from investing too much confidence in independent
airpower."— Provided by publisher.
  Includes bibliographical references and index.
  ISBN 978-1-61251-834-3 (hardback) — ISBN 978-1-61251-835-0 (ebook) 1. Britain,
Battle of, Great Britain, 1940. 2. World War, 1939–1945—Great Britain. 3. Interservice
rivalry (Armed Forces)—Great Britain. 4. World War, 1939–1945—Naval operations,
British. 5. World War, 1939–1945—Aerial operations, British. 6. Air power—Great
Britain—History—20th century. 7. Sea power—Great Britain—History—20th century.
8. Great Britain. Royal Air Force—History—20th century. 9. Great Britain—History,
Military—20th century. 10. Great Britain—History, Naval—20th century. I. Title. II.
Title: Interservice rivalry between the Royal Air Force and Royal Navy, 1909–40.
  D756.5.B7C85 2015
  358.4'13094109041—dc23
                              2014044410
∞ Print editions meet the requirements of ANSI/NISO z39.48-1992 (Permanence
of Paper).
Printed in the United States of America.

23 22 21 20 19 18 17 16 15   9 8 7 6 5 4 3 2 1
First printing

Photos are from the U.S. Naval Institute photo archive unless otherwise indicated.
Maps created by Charles Grear.

CONTENTS

FOREWORD

A irplanes, compared with ships or armies, are relative newcomers to the battlefield. As with all new weapon systems, they were viewed with suspicion and some antagonism by the senior military officers of the day. Luckily, thanks to the pioneers of the Royal Navy Air Service (RNAS) and Royal Flying Corps (RFC) their virtues became more readily accepted, but even towards the end of the First World War there was still sufficient resistance to encourage those pioneers that only the formation of a separate service devoted to the delivery of war from the air would enable the aircraft's proper place in our national armory to be sustained and fully recognized. However, the creation of a separate service did not much change the way in which aircraft were used in support of the sea and land battles.

But with the peace and the inevitable contraction of all three services the battle for resources became the dominant factor. So it was not surprising that the doctrine of airpower was created to justify the status quo and to convince ministers that the use of the airplane in isolation could meet many of the strategic military requirements, at the time principally imperial policing.

In this book Anthony Cumming provocatively challenges the more extravagant claims for airpower. In doing so he goes out of his way to emphasize that the courage and professionalism of the Royal Air Force since its formation are not at issue, but perhaps some of the claims for the strategic achievements of airpower can be debated without for one moment disputing the selfless bravery of those who have played such a pivotal role in serving the country in World War II and after.

So with nearly one hundred years of the use of the aircraft in battle it should be possible to challenge some of the shibboleths that surround its use.

I wonder, had the admirals and generals of the first decade of the twentieth century been less resistant to the airplane's use, a fear born no doubt of which cherished weapon system it might replace on the battlefield, whether there would have been the political exasperation that led to the creation of a separate service. It is all too easy to shelter behind the "indivisibility of airpower," but the joint operational philosophy that is now so firmly embedded into our command and control structures seems to me to make indivisibility redundant. Looking to the future, when many exponents of airpower are beginning to question whether the manned combat aircraft will maintain its battlefield preeminence in the face of remotely piloted vehicles that bring less political and logistic baggage, does one really need a separate service to operate and support this capability?

I doubt whether there is the political or military appetite to address such issues for fear of where it might lead, but this book does shake the tree and allow us to see what fruit falls to the ground.

—Admiral of the Fleet Sir David Benjamin Bathurst, GCB, DL

ACKNOWLEDGMENTS

I t would have been impossible to write this book without the generous help of numerous individuals and organizations. My grateful thanks go to the staff of the National Archives, Kew; the Imperial War Museum, London; the Liddell Hart Archives, London; the Churchill Archives, Cambridge; and Torbay Council's Library Service for their courtesy and understanding on numerous occasions. I must specifically mention Simon Gough, archives officer at the Parliamentary Archives, London, who rendered invaluable service by finding and copying important government statistical information onto DVD for my use. John Vice at the House of Lords also gave me important information regarding the use of material quoted in Hansard, and I must state that this book contains Parliamentary information licensed under the Open Parliament Licence v1.0. Grateful thanks must also go to Richard Kennell (now retired) and Jill Smith at the Britannia Royal Naval College Library, Dartmouth, for their generous book-borrowing privileges and, more important, their friendship and support since the beginning of my MA over thirteen years ago. As always, I wish to thank G. H. "Harry" Bennett, associate professor at the University of Plymouth, for his continuing encouragement of my writing career and for reading the manuscript. Since publication of *The Royal Navy and the Battle of Britain* in 2010, I have had the privilege of meeting Captain Michael Clapp, CB, who commanded the Falkland's Amphibious Task Group in 1982. His vast experience, knowledge of operational command in war, and Fleet Air Arm background makes him an invaluable asset for anyone studying twentieth-century airpower and sea power. Grateful thanks are also due to PhD candidates Alexander D. Clarke and James W. E. Smith for the benefit of their considerable knowledge of military matters and for drawing important academic articles to my attention. I have also had stimulating conversations with historians David Hobbs, Richard Harding, and Andrew Lambert, not forgetting Julian Parker, OBE, and Anthony Harvey of the Maritime Foundation. David Hobbs also took time from his busy schedule to read the manuscript, point out errors, and make valuable suggestions. As ever, my gratitude goes to old friend Mark Vidler for his encouragement and support. My appreciation also goes to various academics, ex–service personnel, and members of the public who listened to my papers for the 150th Anniversary of the Devonshire Association's History Section in Exeter and the University of Plymouth's Britain and the Sea Conference during 2012. They helped me in more ways than they might imagine. Not to be forgotten are friends and family members for enduring my occasional monologues on all aspects of military power. Finally, I must also thank Adam Kane, Adam Nettina, Rick Russell, Jehanne Moharram, and all the staff at the Naval Institute Press, Annapolis, for their patience in helping me get this work into print. In this connection, Charles D. Grear's superb mapmaking skills have proved invaluable. Any mistakes that remain are entirely my own responsibility.

—Anthony J. Cumming, 2014

ABBREVIATIONS

AA	antiaircraft
ACA	Advisory Committee for Aeronautics
ADGB	Air Defence of Great Britain
AFCT	Admiralty Fire Control Table
AI	airborne radar
AOC	air officer commanding
APOC	Anglo-Persian Oil Company
A/S	antisubmarine
ASDIC	Anti-Submarine Detection and Investigation Committee
BEF	British Expeditionary Force
CAS	Chief of the Air Staff
CBE	Commander of the Most Excellent Order of the British Empire
CH	Chain Home
CHL	Chain Home Low
CID	Committee of Imperial Defence
CIGS	Chief of the Imperial General Staff
C-in-C	commander-in-chief
DFC	Distinguished Flying Cross
DNB	*Oxford Dictionary of National Biography*
DRC	Defence Requirements Sub Committee
DSO	Distinguished Service Order
FAA	Fleet Air Arm

GCCS	Government Code and Cypher School
HAC	High Angle Control
IAF	Independent Air Force
IAIAF	Inter-Allied Independent Air Force
KFRE	Kent Fortress Royal Engineers
MoD	Ministry of Defence
MoI	Ministry of Information
NAS	Naval Air Squadron
NID	Naval Intelligence Division
ORS	Operational Research Section
OTUs	Operational Training Units (RAF Fighter Command)
RAF	Royal Air Force
RDF	radar (radio direction finding)
RFC	Royal Flying Corps
RNAS	Royal Navy Air Service
SC	Sprengbombe Cylindrisch (general-purpose bomb)
SD	Sprengbombe Dickwandig (semi-armor-piercing bomb)
SFTS	Service Flying Training Schools
SIM	Servizio Informazioni Militari
SIS	Secret Intelligence Service
ULTRA	high-grade communications intelligence
WSC	Winston S. Churchill

The Battle for
BRITAIN

CHAPTER 1

A Defense Revolution

We suffer primarily not from our vices or our weaknesses, but from
our illusions.

—Daniel J. Boorstin

O n 1 April 1918, a daring and innovative concept in warfare was given
substance by the launch of a shining new branch of the British armed
forces. The Royal Air Force (RAF) was the product of a hasty mar-
riage between the air arms of the British Army and the Royal Navy. This represented the world's first serious experiment in "joined-up" airpower, a concept
that its supporters boldly announced was soon to become the paramount
expression of military conflict between the industrialized nations. The RAF
would operate independently from the older services, and though it would
provide support, the field marshals and admirals could not (except in certain combined operations situations) force it to comply with their battlefield
requirements. A little more than two decades later, the RAF was heralded as
the victor of one of the most decisive battles ever and universally recognized
as the sole instrument to have prevented a German invasion of the British
Isles in 1940. For the politicians at least, it effectively closed the book on all
questions relating to the necessity for independent airpower. Other nations,
including the United States, would eventually follow the example of the RAF
and allow "independence" for the air arms of their armies and navies.

Intended for the educated general reader but without entirely neglecting the serious student of military history, this book represents a different
perspective on the early development of airpower viewed alongside the
ongoing development of sea power. I have tried to tell the story from a perspective that does not lean on the acceptance of an arrogant view that only
an independent air force can truly understand airpower. Sadly, I have come

to believe that many of our existing ideas of the Battle of Britain and earlier airpower "successes" have over-relied on expediency, wartime propaganda, and some nebulous concepts of British national identity rather than the operational realities. The story that most of us already know is covered by countless books and TV documentaries that mostly pander to the insatiable commercial demand for military history where myth and legend get in the way of realistic historical interpretation.

It is incredible to think that in less than two decades of heavier-than-air flight and only one decade of military aviation, this new technology of the air became the basis for a third military force operating independently of the two other services. Such a dramatic outcome begs the question whether the course of British national defense strategy eventually became diverted through the unreasonable manipulation of political and public fears and the skilled promotion of public relations. For this reason, I have given particular attention to the roles of key personalities such as the "Father of the RAF"—Sir Hugh Trenchard—and the most famous politician of the twentieth century—Sir Winston S. Churchill. Indeed, Churchill's story is an illuminating thread that runs throughout the history of early twentieth-century military development, and my understanding of his influence on British military power has been greatly assisted by the works of several authors in more than one historical field. R. K. Massie's *Castles of Steel* (2007) has proved particularly valuable for its clear and detailed approach to British sea power for the period up to 1918.[1]

My short guide to early twentieth-century British air and sea power traces the origins of military airpower and examines its development alongside the continued evolution of Britain's traditional sea power. The period begins with the violation of Britain's national insularity by Louis Bleriot's lone flight over the English Channel in 1909. While the period up to the Smuts Report of 1917 saw a powerful internal British competition for resources between army and navy (and for a while, welfare), the interwar period was characterized by disputes and bitter undercurrents between the brash RAF newcomer and the Royal Navy. Sadly, the interservice rivalry over scarce financial resources had many negative outcomes for those working in the defense sphere, but politics, personalities, and diplomacy also shaped Britain's readiness for war in 1939. More than the notorious "Locust Years" of the 1930s, the problems bedeviling the armed forces at the beginning of World War II were clearly rooted in the 1920s and the earlier Smuts Report. This was reflected in the RAF's policy of imperial air control, a strategy designed to satisfy the political requirement for defense savings by policing the empire on the cheap. It may not have been as cheap and effective as was generally believed at the time.

The success of the RAF in the Battle of Britain in 1940 has come to be seen as the ultimate justification of airpower. Having already written and researched on the Battle of Britain air campaigns and the far more important Battle *for* Britain, I have summarized much of that research in two chapters toward the end of this book. Whatever one might think about the relative operational importance of air and sea in 1940, the propaganda significance of RAF heroism played a powerful part, and though largely neglected in traditional accounts, readers may be surprised to learn what an essential tool the British authorities considered this to be. Not that the Royal Navy was inactive during 1940. It supported the British Army in its continental operations, bombarded invasion ports, and fought the early stages of the Battle of the Atlantic. The Royal Navy also protected British interests in the Mediterranean against powerful Italian sea and air threats. But such actions were comparatively difficult to publicize, none more so than the controversial but nevertheless crucial Battle of Mers-el-Kébir against the French.

Unfortunately, it is unusual for the military/strategic situation in the Mediterranean Sea to be considered of much significance to the outcome of World War II. However, with Douglas Porch's expert revisionism of the importance of the Mediterranean theater in mind, I have included this as part of the wider Battle *for* Britain, as failure there during 1940 would, I believe, have had enormous consequences for the continuing survival of Great Britain as an independent nation.[2] Sea battles at Calabria and Taranto during 1940 would also demonstrate some of the limitations of land-based airpower and the clear importance of maintaining carrier-based aviation for the future.

Despite considerable criticism leveled at the Royal Air Force over the morality and operational effectiveness of the bomber offensive over Germany in World War II, the iconic status bestowed by the Battle of Britain still makes it extremely difficult to question the continuing necessity for independent airpower. While the Battle of Britain and the Finest Hour forms an important part of my narrative, this book is not just about the situation in 1940. Readers seeking to know more specific operational details for Operation Sea Lion (the German code name for an invasion of the British Isles) should read Geoff Hewitt's *Hitler's Armada* (2008) and J. Mallmann Showell (ed.), *Fuehrer Conferences on Naval Affairs, 1939–1945* (1990).[3] Also revealing, given his own experience in the RAF, is Derek Robinson's *Invasion 1940* (2005); Robinson's research as an author caused him to reevaluate some of the assumptions held during his career.[4]

But make no mistake! The heroism of the pilots ("The Few") is not in question. Indeed, RAF pilots and aircrew of all commands fought with

considerable courage, determination, and sacrifice throughout, a fact recognized by former Luftwaffe adversaries. If I have highlighted a number of
areas where the RAF is shown to be institutionally less proficient than generally perceived, then individual airmen's achievements are surely worthy of
greater recognition than usually given. I have also become aware that the
legend of "The Few" is a useful fund-raising aid for RAF charities, but it
would be nonsense to suggest (as some undoubtedly will) that these organizations have no other resources for publicizing the debt that is owed to
so many brave men and women. None of this must be allowed to cloud the
issues and deflect the writer from taking a dispassionate look at the RAF
and the airpower theories that it relies upon for its institutional existence.
Perhaps one reason why this nettle has never been grasped is the over-
compartmentalization of military history. Naval historians "do" ships and sea
power while air force historians "do" aircraft and airpower, and each group
tends not to intrude upon the other's preserve. Unfortunately, the absence
of something approaching a holistic viewpoint does a great disservice both
to military history and anyone seeking to learn lessons from the past. In my
view, only James Holland comes close to properly recognizing the efforts
of all the services, including the Merchant Navy, but even this admirable
writer sometimes overemphasizes the importance of the Battle of Britain's
air dimension.[5] For my part, it is reasonable to say that I have not given equal
coverage to the British Army here, and while the contribution of the army
to national defense was very important, my aim has been to produce a short
guide that views the period as a struggle between proponents of the air and
of the sea.

   In more recent times, the traditional story of the Battle of Britain has
proved a convenient fall-back position for those defending the continued
retention of an independent RAF or simply retaining large numbers of strike
aircraft—essential for the industries that sustain them.[6] The legend has now
become so strong it is almost unassailable, but for those who wish to look
behind the newspaper headlines of the Battle of Britain's anniversary celebrations, the following chapters will provide stimulating reading.

CHAPTER 2

The Road to War

Our country is no longer an island.

—Lord Northcliffe, proprietor of the *Daily Mail*, 1909

T he year 1909 was a landmark one in British aviation. Until then, there was little progress in British aviation despite a number of well-publicized flights by pioneers in the United States and Europe the previous year. Indeed, it was only in April 1909 that the British War Office announced it was giving up its experiments with aircraft as the "cost had been too great," having by then spent a mere £2,500. Considering the War Office would spend nearly £27 million in military defense during 1909, its attitude now seems both short-sighted and niggardly. By contrast, Germany had by then spent about £400,000 on military aviation development.[1] However, things were about to change.

From the day of Bleriot's epic flight across the English Channel in a heavier-than-air machine, it was beginning to look as if the British fleet might not be able to fulfill its traditional role as the Wall of England for much longer. If a man could cross the sea by air once, then more must inevitably follow, and what could the mighty battleship do to prevent whole armies being transported to the industrial heartlands and the very seat of government? Bleriot flew the English Channel in a flimsy contraption powered by a feeble 35-horsepower Anzani engine (thirty years later, most single-seat monoplanes were equipped with engines possessing more than 1,000 horsepower), and his aircraft seemed incapable of carrying any sort of weaponry. All the same, Britain's insularity was irrevocably breached, and there could be no looking back.

Bleriot won the £1,000 prize offered by Alfred Harmsworth, Lord Northcliffe, early pioneer of tabloid journalism and proprietor of the mass-market *Daily Mail* newspaper. Northcliffe immediately rang his private secretary and told her, "Our country is no longer an island; Bleriot has flown the channel and history is made today." He continued, "Do you realise it is the first time an entry [to Great Britain] has been made otherwise than by ship?"[2] The money was just one of a whole series of cash prizes offered by the *Daily Mail* from 1907 to 1930 for achievements in the field of aviation. Bleriot's intrepid feat inspired Northcliffe to headline the 26 July 1909 edition "We are no longer an island!"[3] It was a typical Northcliffe exaggeration stoking up already rampant invasion paranoia reflected in the numerous popular espionage/invasion thrillers that permeated British literature of the period.[4] Northcliffe had also commissioned flying enthusiast William Le Queux to produce the best-selling invasion novel *The Invasion of 1910* (1906), which was subsequently serialized in the *Daily Mail*, doing "wonders for the circulation of the newspaper."[5] The theme was echoed by H. G. Wells in the *Daily Mail* shortly afterward: "In spite of our fleet, this is no longer from the military point of view, an inaccessible island."[6] Wells had changed his tune since 1902. The Armageddon scenario of aerial warfare portrayed in his acclaimed 1908 novel *The War in the Air* now made him a prophet of new military technology, but only a few years before he had seen no immediate military use for new devices such as aircraft and his "imagination" refused to see the submarine doing anything more useful than "suffocate its crew and founder at sea."[7] Now everything was changing fast. With public awareness growing, the Air League was created on similar lines as the Navy League of Great Britain to highlight the importance of aviation to a wider audience.[8] The Air League then promoted the Air Cadet Defence Corps, a valuable source of recruitment for future pilots. Ironically, Wells would later publicly criticize the Air League for advocating a large British air fleet on the grounds that an air war between countries such as France and England would be suicidal owing to the "impossibility" of a defense.[9]

However, if 1909 was a good year for British military aviation it was less encouraging for the naval lobby. Despite official denial, the "Two-Power Standard"—a long-standing British maritime defense policy that allowed the Royal Navy to build a fleet that could match any possible fleet combination of two rival powers—was quietly abandoned, though it would be 1912 before Parliament was told that Britain was only building against one power—Germany.[10] The naval road to 1909 started in 1904 when geo-politician Halford Mackinder shocked traditional navalists by claiming that the Columbian age of maritime state supremacy was already over. Mackinder's famous "Heartland Theory" recognized that railways now enabled continental nations to thoroughly exploit their vast natural resources and diminish the influence of sea power as a primary determinant of wealth and great-power status.[11] Furthermore, public-sector finances were being squeezed because the long war in South Africa that ended in 1902 resulted in massive government debt, leading the chancellor of the exchequer to warn that the growing naval expenditure would take the nation "straight to financial ruin."[12] Sir John Fisher's appointment in 1904 as First Sea Lord owed much to his stance on increased naval efficiency with a view to "a very great reduction" in the Navy Estimates.[13]

Fisher's subsequent dreadnought warship program, aimed at making the German battle fleet technologically redundant, failed to end the naval arms race, though it gave the government a few years in which the dislocation of German naval shipbuilding caused by the dreadnoughts allowed for modest but far-reaching welfare reform, including old-age pensions paid from January 1909. This was the start of escalating demands for better welfare provision and a powerful competitor to the armed forces for public funds. In 1909, defense spending was £60.8 million (including foreign aid) against £16.9 million on welfare and pensions.[14] It is now hard to imagine a time when ordinary people agitated for increased defense spending by chanting "We want eight [dreadnought battleships] and we won't wait" at music halls.[15] After 1909, it was becoming clear to the government that Fisher's dreadnoughts had not ended the arms race and any significant future expansion in welfare provision would have to wait because of the resumption in German naval building. The naval estimates began climbing again, but if the Royal Navy was going to maintain its supremacy it could not simply expand its battle fleet with greater numbers of dreadnoughts.

At first the Royal Navy was reluctant to develop submarine warfare. However, as an early pioneer of the torpedo, Fisher had long recognized the submarines' potential and even in 1904 was toying with the idea of using them as a substitute for the battleship in the line of battle. By 1914, the undermining of battleship primacy was already under way with the increasing adoption of submarines and fast armored cruisers for imperial defense. The policy favoring an increased number of armored cruisers was a reflection of the fact that Great Britain ran a far-flung maritime empire, including 4.25 million square miles of territory, and that the link between commercial prosperity and empire was still closely appreciated. The empire had undergone considerable expansion between 1871 and 1900, meaning future national survival would have to encompass protection of trade as well as the prevention of invasion, and these factors would inevitably shape a future war at sea.[16]

Sadly, Fisher's abrasive personality and reforms split the navy, winning him
many enemies. When he retired in 1910, the Royal Navy was left with no
clear doctrine. A "continental school" within the navy foresaw war in home
waters against Germany and opposed a "maritime lobby" that wanted more
focus on the protection of trade. Nevertheless, Fisher's contacts with media
figures such as journalist W. T. Stead allowed him to effectively pressurize
the government by communicating naval requirements to a wide audience
via the national press.[17] His anticipation of unrestricted submarine warfare,
use of aircraft, and combined operations with amphibious craft made him a
visionary figure.[18]

A more junior politician influenced by Mackinder's theory was Winston S.
Churchill, a future First Lord of the Admiralty and prime minister but from
April 1908 to February 1910 president of the Board of Trade. Churchill's
personal influence on military development in the following decades would
become increasingly powerful. Mackinder's influence encouraged Churchill's
opposition to the proposed dreadnought battleship expansion program of
First Lord Sir Reginald McKenna in order to pay for the Liberal welfare
reforms that finally became the People's Budget of 1909. Despite his own
appointment as First Lord of the Admiralty in 1911, Churchill had already
broken away from some of the prevailing notions of sea power, and his reputation as an uncompromising economist played an important part in his
appointment.[19] His new position also owed a great deal to the Admiralty's poor
performance in the negotiations within the Committee of Imperial Defence
(CID) that year and to the Royal Navy's need for more dynamic political
leadership in Parliament and committee than had previously been the case.[20]
Under Churchill, the fleet began moving away from traditional coal-burning
to more efficient oil-burning engines, allowing savings in weight, manpower,
and cost in the new fast *Queen Elizabeth*–class of battleships. Furthermore,
the ability to refuel at sea would, he argued, "avoid the growing submarine
menace which will await them near their coaling bases."[21] Eliminating long
clouds of smoke from funnels would, he told colleagues, assist the new gen-
eration of warships to evade detection at sea.

Coal was one of the few natural resources the British possessed in abun-
dance, and forsaking this natural advantage was bound to enhance the strategic importance of the Middle East, making them dependent on foreign
energy imports. Without doubt, his first tenure as First Lord demonstrated
Churchill's readiness to take a risk. The decision to install new 15-inch guns
on the new battleships was accelerated without the usual lengthy testing procedures, and he had to guarantee that a reliable supply of oil for the warships
would be available in wartime. The gambles paid off as the 15-inch guns

proved successful and the British-controlled Anglo-Persian Oil Company (APOC) was set up in 1914 for the purpose of securing adequate supplies of oil.[22] One gamble that did not pay off was the decision to recall Fisher from retirement in 1914 as there was simply no room for two such monstrous egos at the top of the Admiralty tree. As First Lord and a future secretary of state for air, Churchill would subsequently play a particularly important role in the early development of airpower and its expression as the third great military arm of British defense policy. However, for the time being, Kaiser Wilhelm II's support for building German dreadnoughts and the resumption of the Anglo-German naval arms race severely limited Churchill's ability to restrain massive naval spending. The continuing need for economy was forcing the consideration of even newer (and potentially cheaper) technologies on the Royal Navy than the submarine and the fast armored battle cruiser—this meant airships and aircraft. An important characteristic that would later define Churchill in the minds of his many admirers and critics was already apparent to Sir John Jellicoe, destined to be the incoming C-in-C (commander-in-chief) Grand Fleet in August 1914. Back in 1912, Jellicoe wrote that the First Lord was "very apt to express strong opinions on technical matters" and "tried to force his views upon the [Navy] Board." Acknowledging that Churchill's considerable persuasive powers were an asset when deployed on behalf of the Admiralty in Parliament, he believed this "gift" was a "positive danger" when used against colleagues on the Board. Unfortunately, "officers are not brought up to argue a case and few of them can make a good show in this direction."[23] In subsequent years, other senior military figures would express similar views on Churchill's tendency to force unsound ideas on the chiefs of staff.[24]

The British army was in a different position prior to the outbreak of war and did not enjoy the depth of public affection traditionally given to the Royal Navy. Changes in political attitudes meant the army was to play a greatly increased role in the next few years and the mass utilization of railways, barbed wire, and machine guns would drastically change the face of the European battlefield for armies of the industrialized nations. However, these were technologies that had been in existence for decades, and no large European nation had a decisive technological advantage in these respects. Those clearly influenced by Mackinder and Wells in the years prior to World War I were Sir Edward Grey, foreign secretary (1905–1916), and Richard Haldane, secretary of state for war (1905–1912). These two men were most responsible for pushing the nation away from its traditional maritime defense policy toward a substantial land-power commitment in the form of a strong land-based expeditionary force for service in Europe.[25] Fears grew that if France was not supported by a substantial troop commitment, then Germany might triumph before the benefits of a maritime defense policy could be felt. In the process, the Admiralty and its supporters tended to disengage themselves from the discussions about the best ways of helping France militarily, and by 23 August 1911 the plans of the army had become firmly established in the CID. By 1912, Churchill had forced the Admiralty to comply with the direction of general strategical policy, meaning that by the outbreak of war there was no credible alternative to a substantial continental commitment.[26] Not that the change in policy translated into front-line strength very quickly. The snide comment of German statesman Otto von Bismarck would have seemed almost as relevant in 1914 as when he made it in 1864: "If Lord Palmerston sends the British army to Germany, I shall have the police arrest them."[27] In 1914, the British Expeditionary Force (BEF) was then just six infantry divisions and one cavalry division, and it would not be until 1916 that the new mass army of volunteers was ready to fight in any strength.[28]

For the British, the general loss of confidence engendered by Britain's difficult and costly war against the Boers between 1899 and 1902, coupled with high naval expenditure and economic problems, suggests that new ways of military thinking had long been needed. This became even more apparent when Germany tested the entente's strength in the Agadir Crisis of 1911, when French and German interests collided in Africa. Britain firmly supported France in this crisis, partly because Britain feared Germany was trying to acquire an Atlantic naval base at Agadir, and a negotiated settlement was finally reached.[29] This incident convinced Churchill of the necessity for the Royal Navy to convert the fleet from the abundantly available home-produced coal to riskier foreign oil in order to preserve naval supremacy.[30]

Haldane—best known for his army reforms and instigation of the CID—was also the founder of the Advisory Committee for Aeronautics (ACA), created only weeks before Bleriot's landmark flight in order to undertake, promote, and institutionalize British aeronautical research. This institution was quickly copied abroad. Haldane was present at Northcliffe's celebratory reception for Bleriot in 1909, though he was not particularly moved by the press baron's passionate warnings of the air threat. Haldane told the House of Commons shortly afterward that very little progress had so far been made in the field of military aviation. So far, he claimed, "the aeroplane would have to rise much higher before it can be a safe instrument for reconnoitering," but he believed Bleriot's crossing and other recent events had shown it would eventually be "capable of great results."[31] A few months earlier, he had told the House that the army "is going in for dirigibles, and the authorities are considering the best pattern," but this statement, described as "cold comfort," had not protected him from criticism in the *Times* for the lack of progress to date.[32]

The year 1909 was also the year in which the Admiralty embarked on airship development, with Captain Murray Sueter in charge of the ill-fated *Mayfly* experiment. As a future creator and wartime head of the Royal Naval Air Service and key supporter of the Smuts Report leading to the founding of the Royal Air Force, Sueter's influence on early development would grow in the years ahead. In his 1912 speech to the Aerial Subcommittee of the CID, Sueter accurately prophesied the shape of a future European air war stating that "both sides would be equipped with a large corps of aeroplanes each trying to obtain information on the other and to hide its own movements." He went on to claim that this "would lead to the inevitable result of a war in the air, for the supremacy of the air, by armed aeroplanes against each other." More controversially, he asserted, "The fight for the supremacy of the air in future wars will be of the first and greatest importance."[33] Within months the subcommittee recommended that a Royal Flying Corps be formed, including a military wing, a naval wing, a central flying school, and an aircraft factory.

It was unfortunate that, with the dangers inherent in such pioneering activities, more serious consideration had not been given to providing parachutes for aircrew. Parachutes would be issued to observers of tethered observation balloons but were rarely given to British airmen for a variety of reasons, including the incompatibility of equipment and a culture of pilots not wanting to appear cowardly by wearing one. The official view was that parachutes were undesirable because pilots might abandon their machines in circumstances where they might otherwise have put up a fight or nursed a damaged aircraft back to the airfield—an attitude that reflects credit on neither the humanity nor the logic of the prevailing military mindset.[34] Though far less sophisticated than the modern parachute, it was already an effective life-saver. These devices were demonstrated at public displays by pre-war pioneers such as the intrepid Dolly Shepherd, who retired in June 1914, albeit with the legacy of numerous jumping injuries. "You had to go where the wind took you," she recalled. Once, coming down on top of a train she described how the driver "blew the steam and just blew me off into the canal at Grantham."[35]

Despite recognition of civil and military aviation's potential by the creation of the ACA, and the Aerial Subcommittee of the Committee of Imperial Defence, competing military requirements meant British aeronautical development still lagged behind that of France and Germany. Fortunately for the British and French, Germany went much further down the dead-end route of lighter-than-air Zeppelin and Schütte-Lanz airships, yet managed to do so without completely neglecting the airplane. Of course, prior to 1914 not even Sueter could really have known where all this was headed. There were no real experts, only pioneers feeling their way, so who could really blame the cavalrymen—the traditional reconnaissance experts—for deriding the airplane and claiming it would only frighten their horses.

All the same, the higher echelons of the army might have shown a little more interest in new developments. At the British army's autumn maneuvers held on Salisbury Plain in 1910, Captain Bertram Dickson of the Royal Artillery demonstrated the potential of aircraft as a reconnaissance tool. The military were not impressed.[36] However, during these maneuvers, Dickson impressed on Churchill the importance of aviation to the military. The following year, the Air Battalion of the Royal Engineers, a unit of observation balloons, began using heavier-than-air aircraft, and this formed the nucleus of the Military Wing of the Royal Flying Corps (RFC) following discussion with the Aerial Subcommittee of the CID the following year. Thanks to the initiative of the Royal Aero Club, there was already a small naval detachment of 2 aircraft in existence, and this was promptly absorbed into the RFC as the Naval Wing of the RFC along with its Naval Flying School at Eastchurch. At the outbreak of war, the 2 services mustered 113 aircraft and seaplanes with 6 airships ready for operations. By comparison, Germany had 232 aircraft and France had 120 ready for action.[37] This then was Britain's first experiment in joined-up airpower. It lasted 3 years and 3 months. It was not, however, the independent airpower concept recognized in later years—the Royal Flying Corps existed to support the army and navy directly in reconnaissance and gun-spotting roles. However, an organization geared to the needs of the War Office was never likely to satisfy the Admiralty for long, and on 1 July 1914 the RFC's naval contingent had broken free under the banner of the Royal Navy Air Service (RNAS).

By the outbreak of war, Fisher and Churchill had played key parts in winning the Anglo-German naval race and the British retained a decisive numerical advantage in dreadnoughts with the bulk of the fleet now concentrated in home waters. Overall, the Royal Navy had sixty-two battleships to the Kaiserliche Marine's (Imperial German Navy) forty-three, with the British holding a significant numerical advantage in other main classes of warships. Allied with a French fleet that included twenty-three battleships (including fourteen dreadnoughts), the Allies possessed a very substantial naval advantage indeed.[38] But for Jellicoe, the numerical naval superiority in terms of the ships under his command versus the German High Seas Fleet in the North Sea was more slender than these figures suggest. In August 1914, the rival battle fleets in the North Sea amounted to nineteen British

battleships against thirteen German, and in the period December 1914–
January 1915, twenty-three to sixteen battleships respectively—but still a
comfortable superiority.[39] Furthermore, German dreadnoughts were, by and
large, better constructed than their British equivalents, being wider, more
heavily armored, and containing a greater number of water-tight bulkheads.
German optics for aiming the guns were also superior, especially in low-light
conditions. For Grand Admiral Alfred von Tirpitz, architect of the Kaiserliche
Marine, the most important characteristic of a warship was that it should stay
afloat, and he had them designed accordingly—a policy that would pay off in
future battles.[40] This meant German dreadnoughts could take more hits than
their British contemporaries.

Great Britain and the British Empire finally went to war with the Central
Powers in August 1914. The dreadnought, submarine, and aircraft all represented the major cutting-edge technologies of the time. Now they would be
put to the test.

CHAPTER 3

The Key to Victory

It is unfortunate, considering that enthusiasm moves the world, that so few enthusiasts can be trusted to speak the truth.
—Arthur J. Balfour, MP, letter to Mrs. Drew, 1918

In a war of this order, sea power was the key to ultimate victory so long as either party could manage just to hold their own on land.
—David Lloyd George, *War Memoirs of Lloyd George*

The War in the Air

The RNAS expanded rapidly in the early phase of the war under Churchill's and Sueter's stewardship, because of their enthusiastic support for new methods of warfare and the multiplicity of maritime roles that aircraft could play. These included fleet reconnaissance, the hunting of submarines and ships, the launching of attacks upon enemy coastlines, and the defense of the homeland against all forms of enemy attack. As the official air historian pointed out, "The navy naturally paid more attention than the army to fighting in the air." As the navy had to operate farther from the enemy on the ground, it wanted machines that were more than observation platforms, "machines that could fly far and hit hard." It was the Admiralty that "diligently fostered the efforts of the leading motor car companies . . . and so were instrumental in the production of very efficient engines of high horse-power."[1] From the outset, the Royal Navy worked on ways of operating aircraft from ships and developed the aircraft carrier—one of the most effective weapons systems in the history of warfare. On 2 August 1917, Squadron Commander Edwin Dunning became the first pilot to land his aircraft on board a moving ship—HMS *Furious*. Sadly, Dunning drowned a few days later in an attempt to repeat the feat. The carrier concept immediately proved its worth when that month an RNAS Sopwith Pup from HMS *Yarmouth* shot down Zeppelin L 23 (LZ 66) off Denmark.

At first, the airship seemed more dangerous than the heavier-than-air machine. The fear for naval and military air commanders throughout the war was that airship attacks on London, though unlikely to be of great military significance, would nevertheless result in frantic civilian demands for resources to be diverted away from the front toward home defense. This fear turned out to be well grounded. Both the RNAS and RFC had at various times been responsible for the air defense of Great Britain but were only really successful against airships when incendiary ammunition became available in 1916. The first victory came when Lieutenant R. A. J. Warneford of the RNAS stumbled across the Zeppelin LZ 37 in darkness during the early hours of 7 June 1915. Tracking it for a considerable distance he finally managed to drop his small bombs onto the 500-foot top panel. After a lengthy pause, LZ 37 ignited and the burning wreckage fell on a convent near Ghent, Belgium, killing a nun outright and badly burning several other women. The airship's helmsman had a miraculous escape jumping two hundred feet from the doomed machine, crashing through the convent roof and onto an empty bed. He was the only survivor of LZ 37, one of the luckiest men in the Imperial German Navy. Warneford narrowly escaped death from the blast of the gasbag's explosion only to die in an aircraft accident days later.[2]

Under Churchill, the Admiralty confronted the airship menace by bombing their bases. Several attempts were made, and one Zeppelin was destroyed by an RNAS aircraft in its shed at Düsseldorf on 8 October 1914. At Christmas, seven seaplanes made a dramatic but ineffective raid on the Cuxhaven sheds. This long-distance raid was only made possible because Churchill had ordered the rapid conversion of four cross-channel passenger ferries into seaplane carriers specifically for the Cuxhaven mission. This was to greatly extend the range of the seaplane bombers, representing the very first use of aircraft carriers in war.[3] By contrast, airships had limited military potential, being accident prone and vulnerable to bad weather. The Zeppelins also proved unsuitable for the direct support of Germany's High Seas Fleet as they were unable to make effective attacks on warships at sea. But as the official historian pointed out, the Zeppelins "splendidly fulfilled their primary task of reconnaissance work over the North Sea" and emphasized the British diversion of resources away from the land fighting.[4] Yet, the offensive consumed even more German resources as it took more than ten bombs to kill a man, and the military damage sustained by the British was estimated as £1,527,585 during the war—though a definitive figure is almost impossible to arrive at.[5]

As the war progressed, interservice rivalries were particularly felt in aircraft procurement. The RNAS "went private" and obtained some well-designed machines from companies such as Short Brothers and T. O. M. Sopwith—especially the agile Sopwith Pup, Triplane, and the versatile 1½ Strutter. This policy, by and large, served the RNAS well. However, the RFC was over-reliant on the state-owned Royal Aircraft Factory (Royal Aircraft Establishment by 1918) at Farnborough. Some designs proved unsuitable for air combat, and Mervyn O'Gorman, superintendent at Farnborough, has sustained considerable criticism for retarding the development of designs suitable for air combat, and obstructing the efforts of private manufacturers to produce suitable aircraft.[6] Although reasonable enough machines for 1912 and easy to fly, the B.E.2 series remained the mainstay of the RFC for far too long. A major weakness was the gunner's extremely limited field of fire from the front seat where he was caged in by struts, wires, and crucial parts of the aircraft. Unsurprisingly, the B.E.2 crews suffered when the Germans introduced the Fokker E.I monoplane. The E.I was an unexceptional aircraft in terms of aerodynamic performance but carried a devastatingly effective single machine gun synchronized to fire between the propeller blades and in the direction of flight. This avoided the inherent problems arising from having to coordinate the actions of a separate pilot and gunner. Subsequent British losses led to the B.E.2s' unfortunate press soubriquet "Fokker Fodder."

Equipped with the first real fighter, better German pilots such as Max Immelmann, hailed as "The Eagle of Lille" by the German propaganda machine, and Oswald Boelcke developed specialized tactics. In particular, they advocated building up speed by diving from superior altitudes and getting the sun behind them in order to conceal their approach.[7] "Beware of the Hun in the sun" soon became the standard advice from experienced RFC/RNAS crews used to squinting against the sun for an attacker that might kill them without warning. Aerobatics practiced by pre-war pioneers such as looping-the-loop were adapted for combat by both sides, though feature films such as *Hell's Angels* (Howard Hughes, 1930) have grossly exaggerated their use for visual effect. Looping to get upon an opponent's tail could be highly dangerous in low-performance biplanes, and inexperienced pilots were dissuaded from using it.[8] The "Boelcke Dicta" was to try and get behind an opponent to attack, and if dived upon, to turn to meet him.[9] Good shooting was paramount, and aristocratic pilots such as Manfred von Richthofen, reared on game shooting, had an immediate advantage.[10] Richthofen, the highest scoring ace of World War I, had a reputation that rested more on his ability to shoot and get in close to the target than to perform flashy aerobatics.

Neither Boelcke nor Richthofen believed in aerobatics, preferring to emphasize audacity in the face of the enemy.[11]

However, Immelmann became associated with the "Immelmann Turn."
This involved diving upon an enemy machine—preferably from out of the
sun—raking it with gun fire, then pulling into a half-roll as the fighter over-
shot and returning for a second fast attack from the opposite direction.[12] This
was only practical for a few expert pilots given the relatively fragile and low-
performance aircraft then in service with both sides.[13] Air fighting quickly
became a team affair. By the end of the war, tactical formations of several
fighter aircraft operating together were highly developed by both sides and
became the basis of those adopted in World War II. The "V" formation was
adopted with some variation on both sides, with the leader flying at the point.
Line formations involved aircraft flying side by side in pairs, and echelon formations involved layers of machines arranged on different levels.[14]

But from the summer of 1915, the problems arising from the RFC's
technical inferiority were exacerbated by the attitude of its commander, the
controversial Sir Hugh Trenchard, whose unwavering belief in the value of
the offensive was said, by newspaper critics, to have caused unnecessary
losses of aircraft and crews. Trenchard believed it was better for morale if
the RFC could make its presence visible by operating over and beyond the
enemy's front line, and there was considerable logic in this.[15] Indeed, to have
rejected the idea of the offensive would have been to question the point of
an air arm whose primary function was to support the army in the reconnaissance role. Even in the difficult circumstances of the Fokker Scourge, overall
air casualties were slight compared to those being suffered on the ground. By
forming an aerial barrage of Fokkers over Verdun at the outset of the battle
and then allowing their more aggressive pilots to hunt for French machines
over the French lines, the Germans initially gained aerial supremacy (though
the term had not been coined yet) over the battlefield, and this had clearly
not been lost on Trenchard.[16] Indeed, Trenchard's attitude to the offensive
was not significantly different from that of army commanders Sir Douglas
"Butcher" Haig and Sir John French, and indeed the majority of naval commanders who tended to stress Nelson's advice of "engaging the enemy more
closely" irrespective of odds. Yet Trenchard's insistence on being on the constant offensive was questionable during periods of relative inaction on the
ground and especially so when the enemy held air superiority. Furthermore,
his argument that the enemy would go on the attack once offensive patrols
were discontinued was something likely to resonate more with his military
colleagues than anyone else.[17] It failed to impress the commander of No.
16 Squadron, Hugh Caswell Dowding, better known as the commander of

RAF Fighter Command during the Battle of Britain in 1940. Dowding and Trenchard clashed over the need to rest pilots exhausted by non-stop action. Trenchard was alarmed by Dowding's "pessimistic" attitude and had him posted to a training command.[18] But thanks to Trenchard, during the Battle of the Somme, 1 July to 18 November 1916, "The RFC established aerial supremacy and held it regardless of cost—but the cost was frightful."[19] All he could do was use four times as many aircraft for mutual protection for each patrol prior to the Fokker Scourge—but that meant accepting a great reduction in reconnaissance information. In mitigation, many E.I pilots had been taken from their two-seater units, with an adverse effect upon German observation and artillery cooperation.[20]

Back in 1915, Trenchard had been commander of the RFC's First Wing, providing direct support to Haig's First Army. Trenchard's command had supported Haig during the Battle of Neuve Chapelle in March 1915, but the First Wing's attempts at bombing had shown little effect upon the enemy and the artillery had often ignored the information provided by the aircrews. Later battles, such as at Ypres, were unsuccessful at breaking the stalemate on the ground, but Trenchard's camera crews had provided some useful information. As a cavalryman, Haig was initially skeptical of the RFC's ability to influence the situation on the ground, and in 1911 he had written, "[F]lying can never be of any use to the Army."[21] Despite this, Trenchard and Haig soon formed a positive relationship and worked well together for the rest of the war. This was mainly because Trenchard's focus never strayed from the need to provide direct support to the army. Reconnaissance and artillery spotting remained the main activities of both the RFC and the RAF for the entire war, with bombing and machine-gun strafing of ground targets gradually emerging as secondary activities. Despite Trenchard's enthusiasm for the potential of aircraft, his appointment in 1918 as commander of the Independent Air Force (IAF), later renamed Inter-Allied Independent Air Force (IAIAF)—a multinational allied strategic bombing force—did not fundamentally alter his views on the main purpose of airpower. The IAF was an attempt to follow up earlier unsuccessful RNAS attempts at long-range deep penetration of targets inside Germany, but the war ended before Trenchard could extend his attacks far beyond German border towns, and indeed, much of the IAF/IAIAF effort was made in direct support of the army.

Although the misery of the Fokker Scourge was declining toward the end of the Battle of the Somme, the Imperial German Air Force (Deutsche Luftstreitkräfte, from October 1916) quickly reorganized its fighter aircraft into the fighter squadron system known by the pilots as the Jagdstaffeln, or "hunting echelons." Reequipped with high-performance Albatross tractor-driven biplanes that mounted not one but two forward-firing synchronized machine guns, they outclassed the "pusher" D.H.2 and F.E.2b of the RFC and achieved air superiority over their front line.[22] Allied losses peaked during April 1917 (Bloody April) as the RFC provided support for the British army during the Battle of Arras. However, losses began to fall during the summer. RNAS squadrons deploying the Sopwith Triplane already enjoyed air superiority in the far north of Flanders, but in response to urgent appeals from the hard-pressed RFC, the RNAS sent No. 10 Naval Squadron to serve under the No. 11 Wing RFC at Droglandt.[23] Another redoubtable naval unit, No. 8 Naval Squadron, was already using the Sopwith Triplane in support of the RFC. This unit claimed 298 victories between October 1916 and the Armistice and included 25 aces (pilots who scored 5 or more confirmed kills).[24] As the war progressed, 6 RNAS squadrons became attached to the RFC.[25] Mainly, perhaps because of the high quality of naval pilots and machines, the tide began to turn against the Albatross, and B Flight of No. 10 Naval Squadron (Black Flight) was to become one of the most successful units of the war. Brilliantly led by Canadian ace Raymond Collishaw, Black Flight alone scored 87 victories between May and July 1917, prompting the Germans to design their own triplane—the Fokker D.R.I made famous by Richthofen.[26] However, it was not good enough to recover the air initiative against newer Allied designs entering service, the Sopwith Camel, S.E.5a, Bristol Fighter, and later versions of the French Spad. This might not have been possible without the cooperation of the Admiralty, who ordered superior aircraft from private suppliers such as Sopwith on behalf of the RFC. Indeed, the Sopwith Camel was the first British machine to mount two synchronized machine guns firing through the propeller—a year after the German Albatross first appeared.

Smuts and the First Battle of Britain

The struggle to reestablish Allied air superiority over the western front was further handicapped by the diversion of British fighter squadrons from France to counter the German daylight bomber raids on London from June 1917. It was Germany's General Ernst von Hoeppner, the man who reorganized Germany's fragmented air services into one unified command, who was responsible for opening this new strategic dimension to air warfare. Hoeppner's plans were based on the capability of the Gotha G.IV to carry 660 pounds of high explosives and an estimate that eighteen bombers would be able to deliver the equivalent amount of destruction as three Zeppelins. So far, he pointed out, "Three airships have never reached London at one time."[27]

Around mid-day on 13 June 1917, the British sustained what was to become the worst air raid of the war. Kapitänleutnant Ernst Brandenburg's England Squadron swept over Essex and penetrated London's antiaircraft defenses from the northwest at an altitude between 14,000 and 15,000 feet. Twenty-two Gothas had originally taken off from airfields in Belgium, but owing to "mechanical problems" some had fallen out of formation and bombed ineffectually along the Thames Estuary. Thousands watched anti-aircraft shells burst harmlessly against a mostly blue sky as the German air-men wheeled about in a series of maneuvers without deviating from the need to maintain an all-round mutual defense. Down below, take-cover warn-ings displayed by police cyclists were mostly ignored by a gawking public. Curiosity overcame fear because daylight air raids were outside of people's experience as most Zeppelin attacks had been made at night. Exaggerations by witnesses abounded. Some onlookers with binoculars claimed they could make out the pilots and the black crosses of their aircraft. Others said they saw as many as thirty German aircraft in the sky, a misconception that may have stemmed from the Gothas' skillful morphing of formations.

At approximately 11:30 a.m., bombs fell on the Royal Albert Docks and East Ham, killing eight people and inflicting serious property damage. As intercepting aircraft had not yet arrived on the scene, Brandenburg took a calculated risk and extended his formation to drop seventy bombs over a one-mile area radiating out from his main target, Liverpool Street railway station.[28] Those bombs striking the station caused carnage when the waiting midday train to Cambridge was hit. The war-poet Siegfried Sassoon, on his way back to the front line, only narrowly escaped as he was about to board the train. He would later write that the situation brought about by air raids required a different kind of courage from civilians than he had witnessed from soldiers fighting in the trenches. Helpless civilians now had to face the grim prospect of being slaughtered without warning by unseen enemies lurk-ing in the sky.[29]

Many were injured and thirteen people were killed at the station alone. There was also horror at the Upper North Street School in Poplar. At least fifteen infants were killed along with thirty seriously injured when a 110-lb bomb plunged through the roof and several floors before exploding and collapsing the ground floor down into the basement. Tragic scenes ensued as distraught mothers scrabbled through the rubble to find their dead and injured children. Most of the dead were under five years of age. Up in the air and oblivious to the horrors below, Brandenburg's men easily drove off des-perate British air attacks. The defending aircraft arrived singly and proved unable to penetrate the disciplined and coordinated defensive fire from the

Gothas. Out of 92 defending aircraft, only 1 Bristol Fighter from a training squadron made a determined attack but was driven away badly damaged and with its observer/gunner dead.[30] All the Gothas arrived safely back in Belgium. The raid cost the British nearly £130,000 in damage, 162 dead, and 432 injured.[31] Casualties were worsened by the general disregard of take-cover warnings and the fact that many victims were eating luncheon in busy cafes and restaurants. This was the greatest loss of life yet sustained in a single air raid and equated to a figure "greater than three-quarters of all casualties from some twenty-three Zeppelin raids in 1915," wrote Raymond H. Fredette, "the worst year for that type of attack."[32] But it was the tragic deaths of so many small children that aroused intense public fury. The subsequent funeral was widely reported by the press. King George V and Queen Mary sent a message of condolence, and many of the floral tributes read, "To our children murdered by German aircraft."[33] Another raid against London on 7 July managed to kill 54 people and injure 190 for the loss of 1 Gotha shot down on the return flight by the RNAS.[34] According to the Press Association, 20 unchallenged enemy bombers provided "an unbelievable spectacle as in stately procession it moved slowly . . . daringly low." [35] The *Daily Mail* compared the raid with the disastrous national humiliation of 1667, when the Dutch burned the English fleet in the Medway.[36]

While the Germans celebrated, the British government was at its wit's end. Previous outbreaks of rioting aimed at "foreigners" in the aftermath of Zeppelin raids had already provoked nightmares. Zeppelin LZ 38's raid on London's East End on the night of 31 May 1915 resulted in seven people killed and an estimated property damage of £18,500, but it was a poor material return for the German efforts. Nothing could be done to prevent foreign correspondents reporting the incident in lurid terms, but the British people were generally unable to read their reports and the impact of the raid appears to have died away quickly.[37] There had been no marked public reaction to the occasional nuisance raids by aircraft on the Kent coast since the beginning of the war, but a heavy daylight raid on Folkestone on 25 May 1917 heightened fears and caused alarm among the public and within the government itself. Brandenburg's raid of 13 June 1917 on the capital city caused panic, but this was mostly confined to the government itself. If there was a remarkable absence of panic on the street there was plenty within the government. Chief of the Imperial General Staff, Field Marshal Sir William Robertson remarked at one Cabinet meeting, "I could not get a word in edgeways. . . . One would have thought the whole world was coming to an end."[38] Sadly, the key decisions about to be undertaken would be made in panic, not calm deliberation.[39]

Goading the government into action was the national press. Following the attack on Folkestone a few weeks earlier and prophesying the essence of air policies popularly known in the 1930s as "the bomber will always get through," the *Times* thundered: "The only means of coping effectively with this prospect is by an aggressive aeroplane policy of our own. . . . In the air, far more than in any other sphere of modern fighting, the overwhelming advantage is always with the attack." A thorough overhaul of the system of intelligence, observation, and communication upon which early warning depended was also demanded.[40] A few weeks later the *Times* claimed "it is the absence of evidence to expand . . . to meet the increasing menace from the air which causes public disquiet." The "main question is whether the Government can improve and increase the system of aerial defences in this country without detriment to the paramount requirements of the armies." Many "consider that one great defect . . . is that the air defences are under the dual control of the Army and Navy. . . . Whatever be the merits of the case for a unified control . . . in the past the cooperation between the two Services has not been sufficiently close." The real origin of the intense interest now being shown in air warfare was "the distinctive recognition that aircraft are rapidly becoming a primary means of gaining ultimate victory."[41]

This was not the first demand for major reform of the air forces. Zeppelin raids in 1915 brought forth press demands for a "Ministry of Aeronautics." As a recognized aircraft exponent, Churchill was put forward "as a suitable air minister."[42] Later raids led to renewed calls for a separate ministry, and the creation of succeeding organizations all fell short of this demand. Lord George Nathaniel Curzon, president of the Air Board, also informed the House of Lords of his aspiration for leading a single service. This was opposed by the *Times*, who told him publicly that the air post "was not a job for a politician, however eminent." Curzon was also opposed by the war minister, Lord Horatio Herbert Kitchener, and by First Lord of the Navy Arthur Balfour. Balfour then told Prime Minister Herbert Asquith, that "a fighting Department should . . . have the whole responsibility for the instruments it uses." It was necessary that "the Navy should be autonomous." Disgruntled, Churchill then attacked the Air Board in the House of Commons as an attempt to evade forming an Air Ministry and lambasted the government for indecision and taking the easy way out. Annoyed that the Admiralty had recently secured £3 million of public money for aircraft and engines without consulting him, a frustrated Curzon complained to Asquith of naval intransigence and repeated his call for unification "but not while the war is still proceeding, and in the face of the dislocation that might be caused." But for now, Curzon wanted complete responsibility for the supply, design, inspection, and finance of military aircraft. Balfour bluntly rebuffed this, and the situation remained unresolved until Asquith fell in December 1916. Change came quickly under Asquith's successor, David Lloyd George. The organization and supply of aircraft was then passed to Lord Cowdray, who succeeded Curzon at the Air Board, and by late spring 1917 even the *Daily Mail* was happily reporting that "aeroplanes are fluttering out of the factories like butterflies in June."[43] The change initially upset the Admiralty—the army having little to lose with its existing ties to the unsatisfactory Royal Aircraft Factory.

As a response to the press clamor for action in the wake of the Gotha raids, the War Cabinet appointed a committee including the prime minister and the famous Boer leader Lieutenant General Jan Christiaan Smuts to find a solution. However, because of ill health and no doubt because of a great number of other matters competing for his time, the prime minister left the committee to Smuts. A skilled academic and lawyer, he seemed well suited to an investigation of this nature. He had a strong reputation from the Boer War as a master of hit-and-run guerilla warfare, of which, it might be argued, this new war in the air was merely a variant. He was also popular with the British public and available for work. Having been invited to participate in an Imperial Conference during the spring of 1917, Smuts was asked to stay in London as a member of the War Cabinet.

The first report of the Committee on Air Organization and Home Defence against Air Raids followed the War Cabinet meeting of 11 July 1917. Smuts' report examined "arrangements for Home defence against air raids" and acknowledged London's peculiar position as the imperial "nerve centre." He claimed "London might through aerial warfare become part of the battle front" within the next twelve months and recommended that the capital should "have the first call upon our output of aircraft and anti-aircraft guns" as long as other military operations would not be unduly prejudiced. He blamed most failures on having to organize a defense against the night attacks of Zeppelins. These failures included the use of older, slower interception aircraft flying singly rather than in formation and operating from a variety of scattered airfields. Antiaircraft guns were not concentrated in front of the defended areas, and no system of unified command in the air existed. Furthermore, there were many defective antiaircraft shell fuses, and some aircraft were grounded because of a shortage of spare parts. There was also little coordination between the RNAS, the Observation Corps, and the London antiaircraft guns. Because of the fragmentation of command and the importance of London, the report recommended appointing a senior officer of "first-rate ability and practical air experience in charge of the non-naval constituents of executive command of London's air defences."[44]

The German daylight bombing campaign was abandoned shortly after Brigadier-General E. B. Ashmore's appointment as head of London's air defenses, and the official historian attributed this partly to "improvement in the defences of London." But as one revisionist has pointed out, all of the three daylight raids made after 7 July were strictly coastal attacks.[45] Some of these coastal attacks were seen in Britain as attacks intended for London that had been frustrated by the air defenses. Certainly, the Gotha attack on the naval base at Chatham during 12 August was perceived that way, as RNAS aircraft drove the bombers away from Chatham and toward Southend-on-Sea, where bombs caused many casualties. One Gotha was shot down far out over the North Sea by a pursuing Sopwith Pup. This was the last "successful" daylight Gotha raid on Britain. By 22 August, nineteen Gothas had been lost or seriously damaged—ten on 18 August alone.[46] The losses attributable to the air defenses were gradually increasing, but the real reason for abandoning daylight attacks given by one author was the wastage of machines and pilots caused by pilot exhaustion and overworked aircraft.[47] The German Army High Command officially concluded that the experiment in daylight bombing had failed, and henceforth raids would be made at night. But as David Divine states, they had "unknown to them achieved results quite disproportionate to the damage and casualties effected," and had started a sequence of events in Whitehall.[48]

Smuts continued with his inquiries. Most were conducted informally and in private by a series of interviews at the Hotel Cecil, London, where he consulted Sir David Henderson—a former general officer commanding, Royal Flying Corps, and now director general of Military Aeronautics; William Weir, Scottish industrialist and member of the Air Board since December 1916; Major-General Sefton Brancker, deputy director general of Military Aeronautics; Commodore Godfrey Paine, Fifth Sea Lord and director of Naval Aviation; Rear Admiral Mark Kerr, seconded to the Air Board in August 1917; Winston Churchill, minister of munitions; Lord Cowdray, president of the Air Board; Lord Curzon, Cowdray's predecessor as president of the Air Board; and Lord Derby, secretary of state for war, together with a number of others. Only three written papers submitted to Smuts appear to have survived, and these came from Cowdray, Henderson, and Kerr. A memorandum from Cowdray submitted after 11 July complained that the Air Board could not fulfill its function without an adequate Air Staff. On 16 July, he informed his colleagues at the Air Board that Lloyd George had subsequently sent him an extract from the War Cabinet meeting of 11 July at which the Committee on Air Organisation and Home Defence had been decided upon. On receipt of this extract, Cowdray asked the prime minister for an interview with Smuts, and this was granted shortly afterward. Cowdray told Smuts that he had originally thought the Board's powers were adequate but had since changed his mind "and come to the conclusion that the Board should be permanently established with fresh powers." He then sent a further memorandum in which he explained why he had not recommended "an independent aerial service" at the time the Air Board's draft charter was written. His present view was that the current "administration of the Naval and Military Air Services as at present exist, or will exist when their imperative needs are satisfied, should not be changed."[49] From this it becomes clear that Cowdray's request for an enlarged Air Staff was intended to facilitate plans for a unified service *after* the war had ended.[50]

Henderson's memorandum had much more impact upon Smuts. This advocated a department "with full responsibility for war in the air." Part of the air force would have to be "an accessory to the Navy and to the Army," but the personnel should be neither soldiers nor sailors, as this "would only prolong the situation of divided responsibility." An independent central force could not be created until "the immediate needs of the Navy and the Army can be supplied"; however, he thought these would be met in early 1918 when "a considerable force of bombing machines will also be available." Cowdray's memo took this force for granted when it asked which ministry should administer the surplus aircraft fleet as if the surplus fleet was already an acknowledged entity.[51] However, the assumptions regarding the availability of a large bomber force were based solely on forecasts for aero-engines, and in September 1917 it was estimated the six main types would total 15,914 engines, allowing approximately 3,302 engines more than anticipated requirements.[52] It appears these figures were given to Smuts by Weir the previous month. A third memorandum was submitted by the former naval C-in-C of the British Adriatic Squadron, Rear Admiral Mark Kerr. This played a more important role in the Smuts Report than generally understood. The first British flag officer to gain his pilot's license and an early proponent of the aircraft carrier, Kerr had considerable aviation expertise for the time. His "bombshell memorandum" accurately reported that the Germans were building a new heavy bomber, though he overestimated the aircraft's bomb-carrying capacity and the German ability to build such a huge fleet within the foreseeable future. From intelligence sources in Italy, he reported that Germany was building four thousand of these to destroy large tracts of southeast England, and Kerr wanted a bomber force of two thousand heavy bombers under a powerful Air Ministry in order to counter the threat.[53]

The second Smuts Report regarding the future direction of airpower was submitted to the War Cabinet toward the end of August. Both Henderson's and Kerr's contributions were clearly discernible. Indeed, Cowdray may well have persuaded Smuts to leave amalgamation until after the war but for Kerr's intervention. The Admiralty was particularly criticized for "jealously" retaining the roles of RNAS training, personnel, and supply of lighter-than-air craft as "its special perquisites." Paragraph 5 stated: "The time is however rapidly approaching when that subordination of the Air Board and the Air Service to the older services could no longer be justified." As recent attacks demonstrated, air fleets can "conduct extensive operations far from, and independently of, both army and navy." In a sentence destined to be endlessly repeated by the prophets of airpower, "[A]nd the day may not be far off when aerial operations with their devastation of enemy lands and destruction of industrial and populous centres on a vast scale may become the principal operations of war, to which the older forms of military and naval operations may become subordinate." Given the rapid march "of events during the war . . . there is every reason why it [the Air Board] should be raised to the status of an independent Ministry in control of its own war services." The previous shortage of aero-engines had been replaced by a situation in which a surplus was anticipated for the spring and summer of 1918, which would require the creation of an Air Staff for planning and directing independent air operations. Already rampant War Cabinet fears were manipulated with a request that it use "some imagination" and envisage a situation in the summer of 1918 whereby the army was advancing in Belgium at a "snail's pace" while air battles raged behind the Rhine and against German industrial centers and lines of communication. The enemy was making "vast plans to deal with us in London if we do not succeed in beating him in the air and carrying the war into the heart of his country." It was also pointed out that the combatant nations' declining manpower must foster a greater reliance on arms and machinery, and therefore "the side that commands industrial superiority and exploits its advantages in that regard to the utmost ought in the long run to win." The rest of the report was concerned to consolidate the above arguments and rule out any possibility of the army and navy retaining their own services in addition to the new air service now being proposed, as it would only make for confusion.[54]

The second report was approved in principle. Now chairman of a new Air Organization Committee of the War Cabinet with Henderson as his chief assistant, Smuts had the enormous task of implementing his recommendations. RFC/RNAS amalgamation was now the dominant view of politicians and airmen and was unopposed by the Admiralty. With the German air raids intensifying and the British army's latest offensive stalled in the mud of Flanders, a feeling of urgency gripped the government, and Smuts' sharp lawyer's mind rapidly assimilated the details and exploited the government's panic in his demands for wide and sweeping powers. As the expansion plans rested heavily on the anticipated surplus of engines and aircraft geared to provide the means to independent strategic operations, Smuts managed to turn the Air Organization Committee into the War Priorities Committee, with unprecedented powers over British industry. Now there was an instrument of military aviation policy capable of resolving all the competing claims of service organizations upon British industry, including factory space, raw materials, and manpower. In practice, power was successfully devolved through a system of subcommittees that gave Smuts the time and energy to concentrate on "essentials." His biographer admitted that Smuts had briefly taken the view that "the root and branch reorganization of British airpower might well be left until after the war," but with the deteriorating military situation "he felt it was now or never."[55]

Merging the air wings of two separate services together into an independent Royal Air Force by 1 April 1918 was a great achievement, but Smuts' decision to recommend amalgamation was taken too quickly. Smuts had taken evidence and delivered his recommendations in just two months, having made them on the back of some staggering assumptions. According to one committee member, Lord Hugh Cecil, "I thought the bombing plans rather visionary; but I did not pour cold water as I felt a change was needed."[56] The central assumption of Smuts' second report—that the day may not be far off when air operations may become the main operations of war and to which the older forms of naval operations may become subordinate—was nothing less than a rejection of Britain's traditional maritime defense strategy and an extraordinary statement given the then-precarious situation at sea and its relevance to the outcome of the war. To base national defense on an offensive aerial strategy without regard for the nation's vulnerability to economic blockade was extremely foolhardy, especially as it was Great Britain that was most geographically vulnerable. It only takes a quick look at a map to realize that the distance from the England Squadron's airfields in Belgium to London was approximately 175 miles, and once the Gothas had braved the hazards of crossing the North Sea they only needed to follow the contours of the Thames Estuary to find the London sprawl. However, for the British, the possibility of a preemptive strike or retaliation was massively complicated by the distance involved. The distance from the IAF's airfield at Nancy to Berlin was approximately 410 miles, or Nancy to the Essen industrial complex, 194 miles. Had the Ludendorff Offensive succeeded in 1918 the British position could have been much worse, as the IAF would have flown from British bases, meaning the distance to Berlin would have been around 577 miles and to Essen 305 miles.[57] With or without a continental air base, Essen at least was still within the range of the Handley Page Type O bomber in 1918, but the distance was bound to make retaliatory strikes far more difficult because of greater navigational problems and the longer warning time given to the defenses caused by the long land approaches. The war at sea was far more important, because if a continental opponent could cut off Britain's seaborne oil supply—as the U-boats were close to doing in 1917—then the air battle would be won, because no British bomber would be able to fly. Bearing in mind Britain was to come within days of starvation, it was the ship and the ration book rather than aircraft determining whether the war was to continue.

A further assumption was the anticipated surplus of aircraft engines. Here Smuts was totally misled by the information given to him by Weir. In the event, the British aircraft industry failed to meet the services' air requirements, far less produce a surplus of 3,302. In fact, the figures were "totally fallacious."[58] This does not necessarily mean Weir was deliberately disingenuous, but he had probably been informed of Kerr's memorandum about German intentions and in all probability had become infected with the bug of air exaggeration—a disease affecting many airpower proponents up to the present day. An early advocate of strategic bombing, Weir was an imaginative, hard-working entrepreneur with "an instinct almost of adventure," and it was entirely in keeping with his personality to drive through an innovative and untried concept such as an independent bomber force.[59] In September 1917 the massive Zeppelin-Staaken R.VI bomber (an example of the Riesenflugzeuge R-plane known as the Giant) made its first raid on England and hit the Royal Hospital Chelsea with the first 1,000-kg bomb to be dropped on English soil. The Staaken Giant had a wing span almost as large as the later Boeing Superfortress. Fortunately for the British, far from a fleet of four thousand, only eighteen were ever built. The German night (or moonlight) attacks on England began in September and were a mixture of Gothas and Giants. The first attack was on Dover, but three separate attacks were made on London during the fourth and fifth nights of the campaign. The harvest moon period of 24 September to 1 October enabled the Germans to bomb most nights, and every attempt at night interception failed to bring down any bombers. At night, railway arches and factories were occupied by thousands of frightened Londoners, fully dressed and waiting for the alarm. One witness writing in 1937 recalled, "The 'stop-the-war' cry was heard more frequently than was pleasant or flattering to our belief in the sticking-to-it qualities of our people."[60] Dispossessed families with bedding, pets, and food baskets pushed their way into already crowded underground railway stations. Sanitation broke down, and the Tube system stank with excrement and urine. Sometimes panic broke out with people trampled in the crush and competition for space resulting in fist fights. One witness even recorded soldiers home on leave fainting upon entering the Tube and claiming that it was better to be in the trenches than face the ordeal of an air raid where the dangers were unseen and unknown. A million Londoners were now sleeping in the Tube or other public buildings, with thousands of others sleeping rough in parks and in fields on the city's outskirts.[61] Clearly shaken, Lloyd George summoned newspaper editors to a meeting and ordered them to stop publishing photographs of bomb damage and to tone down their graphic descriptions of the bombing. Legislation was rushed through Parliament, and owners of bombed-out buildings were required to erect hoardings to hide them from the public. London was now being paralyzed by a small number of aircraft—in one week, only twenty bombers reached London.[62]

The End of the Air War

Despite the introduction of the superb Fokker D.VII fighter in the summer of 1918, the Luftstreitkräfte never again achieved the high level of superiority they experienced back in April 1917. Ultimately they were hamstrung by a lack of essential war materials, shortages of aviation fuel, and German industry's failure to develop aero-engines beyond the six-cylinder-in-line and some inferior copies of French rotary engines.[63] By reorganizing their best Jastas into larger wings, or Jagdgeschwaders (known to the RFC as "The Flying Circus"), and moving these around the front on railway flat cars, the Germans still mounted effective challenges to Allied air superiority in vital sectors (a condition sometimes known as air denial) during crucial periods of the land battles. This did not always mean the entire Jagdgeschwader (four Jastas, or up to approximately sixty aircraft) aloft at the same moment, as such large and unwieldy formations proved difficult to control without radio and could not always guarantee a satisfactory casualty exchange ratio. A grittily determined Canadian fighter pilot once ran into the full strength of Jagdgeschwader 3 after shooting down a Rumpler observation aircraft. Facing what must have seemed certain death, Major William Barker audaciously flew through the enemy formation, shooting down two Germans in the process. His Sopwith Snipe was then attacked in turn by clusters of five from different directions, wounding him several times. Barker then fainted from loss of blood and almost spun into the ground, yet came around and shot another down. He passed out again, but somehow Barker survived the 90-mph crash. Subsequently awarded a well-deserved Victoria Cross, he suffered from the legacy of multiple wounds for the rest of his life. Four aircraft destroyed in forty minutes became the record score for the highest number of aircraft destroyed in the shortest time during World War I.[64]

But in general, the air situation over the western front was a private war between air forces that made no significant difference to the situation on the ground. When Germany launched its initially devastating Ludendorff Offensive in March 1918, the RFC had already given ample warning of the German buildup, had concentrated aircraft in readiness for the expected attack, and had even launched extensive bombing raids on tactical targets behind the German lines. The RFC did not even prevent the German attack from achieving tactical surprise when it broke through the British line on 21 March 1918, and had not prevented the prior buildup of German troops. The Germans were not delayed by bombing raids, and desperate attempts at ground strafing had only delayed the attacks temporarily and in certain places. Neither is there any real evidence that the Luftstreitkräfte, despite their temporary numerical superiority in the first days of the attack and the extensive use of aircraft in a ground-attack role, significantly influenced the land battle in Germany's favor.[65]

The naval blockade of German ports meant the Luftstreitkräfte's effectiveness was much reduced in the final weeks of the war, owing to a shortage of aviation fuel depriving them of the means to train new pilots and mount patrols. Their fuel allotment, which needed to double in 1918 to 12,000 tons, shrank to a mere 1,000 tons in November as Germany's land and sea oil routes were severed by the war.[66] Superiority at sea therefore meant a rapidly increasing Allied numerical superiority of aircraft and pilots—many now coming from the United States. To begin with, the inexperienced American airmen posed little problem to the battle-hardened Jagdstaffeln. As late as September 1918, Jasta 12 virtually obliterated an American D.H.4 bomber squadron in just two engagements. These losses—thirteen large machines and twenty-six men—were equivalent to two Fliegerabteilungen (flier detachments) and would have been devastating to any of the other combatant air forces.[67] However, the Americans could absorb these losses and their combat effectiveness would improve over time. In the long term the ongoing German fuel shortages could only mean a steady deterioration in the quality of German aircrew as the ability to provide effective aircrew training programs evaporated.

Ultimately, the bombing of London was another German failure. The night air defense had gradually improved, and on 19 May 1918 it helped eliminate six Gothas. Henceforth—and with the failure of the last German land offensive in the west—the Gothas and Giants were only used on tactical targets in France.[68] As a war-winning strategic weapon, the England Squadron had failed but it had been worth the effort in terms of incurring around £2 million worth of damage, much disruption, and diversion of resources from the battlefront to home defense, but "while this was not inconsiderable, this factor was in no way decisive."[69]

The War at Sea

From the outset, Jellicoe needed a strong numerical superiority against the High Seas Fleet if he was to satisfy press and public expectations of a crushing "Trafalgar" victory against Germany.[70] In practice, strength would fluctuate almost on a daily basis as a portion of the fleet would always be required outside of home waters. If too many ships were detached from the Grand Fleet—for example, to avenge Admiral Sir Christopher Cradock's defeat off Coronel in the South Atlantic—then it would cause tremendous anxiety to the Admiralty and C-in-C, lest the Germans seize the opportunity of confronting a temporarily weakened Grand Fleet.[71] Furthermore, the introduction of torpedoes and mines in naval warfare forced the abandonment of the Royal Navy's traditional policy of closely blockading enemy ports. Indeed, the German strategy envisaged their ports being closely blockaded from the outset, and the Kaiserliche Marine looked forward to exacting a heavy toll of warships when the British made their move. Instead the Admiralty opted for closing the North Sea to German shipping at its northern and southern exits. These exits were the English Channel, approximately eighteen miles wide at its narrowest point, and the two-hundred-mile gap between northern Scotland and Norway. Strong net barriers were stretched across the English Channel, and a fleet of miscellaneous craft was deployed from Dover aiming to deter U-boats from taking a shortcut into the Atlantic. This forced them to take the more hazardous and less economic route north.

Maintaining distant blockade required the use of a great many ships for patrol duty, especially destroyers. Naturally, statistics do not tell the complete story, and the Germans had one substantial advantage with their numerical superiority in destroyers. These were key ships used by both sides to screen and protect the massive dreadnoughts and to threaten those of the enemy with deadly torpedoes.[72] Destroyers were also the primary British defense against U-boats for most of the war. Though essentially weapons of ambush, U-boats were far less susceptible to blockading than any other type of vessel and were a potent threat to large surface ships in some situations. This was graphically demonstrated by the early sinking of three old but large armored cruisers by submarine U-9, all within quick succession. That so many had been sunk in one incident was the result of desperate attempts by the British captains to rescue survivors. After this disaster, warships were ordered not to hang about in areas where U-boats were believed to be lurking, even when survivors required rescue. This inevitably placed captains in an invidious position. As Admiral R. H. S. Bacon was later to write, "You can inveigh about the loss to the country and admonish, but at the same time it is impossible for any sea officer . . . to condemn such deeds."[73] This new fear of underwater weaponry would have an inhibiting effect upon future strategy and tactics.[74]

Jutland, the only major set-piece sea battle in home waters between rival surface fleets, was a German tactical victory of sorts. It exposed several defects in the British Grand Fleet, of which the failure to deploy aerial reconnaissance was just one of many shortcomings brought to light. Poor ammunition handling practices meant that flash from turret hits allowed fires to rapidly spread to the ship powder magazines. British armor-piercing shells often failed to pierce German armor because of faulty fuses, meaning that shells exploded on contact with armor rather than within the ship.[75] Signaling errors contributed to communication breakdowns within the British fleet and key intelligence information from the Admiralty was withheld, adding to Jellicoe's difficulties during the action. Controversially, Jellicoe was accused of allowing the enemy fleet to escape after Admiral Reinhard Scheer's sudden turn-away from a head-on confrontation with his dreadnoughts. Jellicoe then turned his ships away from pursuit and into a defensive formation because Scheer had covered his escape with a screen of torpedo boats and the British admiral was loath to expose his dreadnoughts to this danger. However, it must be emphasized that the danger to capital ships represented by torpedoes was recognized by all the main naval powers of the day, and Jellicoe had earlier made it clear to the Admiralty that he would not risk his ships in this type of situation—a move endorsed by the Admiralty without reservation.[76] But in the end and despite higher British losses, the British could absorb these better than the Kaiserliche Marine and would find it easier to replace them.[77] German claims that the High Seas Fleet had won a great victory were initially believed, but it soon became apparent they were forced to withdraw and the battle had not achieved the aim of substantially weakening British sea power. Unfortunately, the "Jutland Controversy" raged fiercely until 1927, with the popular press fanning the flames of debate. The dispute between the two principal British commanders, Jellicoe and Admiral Sir David Beatty, centered on the failure to turn the battle into a decisive action. Beatty resented what he saw as the under-representation of the achievements of his battle-cruisers, and Jellicoe defended himself from charges of undue caution.[78] As his biographer admits, Jellicoe was not the second Nelson that had been anticipated, but was still a "fine officer of outstanding ability," and it seems unlikely that anyone else could have achieved more.[79] Had Jellicoe actually lost the battle, rather than failing to make it decisive, he really would have been the one man that lost the war in a single engagement.

The consequences of a British defeat whereby a large part of their fleet had been destroyed would have had catastrophic consequences for the Allied cause. Not only would the Allied blockade on the central powers have been broken, but it would have been the means by which the Germans could have massively strengthened the blockade of Great Britain without resorting to the high-risk strategy of unrestricted submarine warfare. It was the ruthless pursuit of this policy—involving the deaths of many U.S. citizens—that played a major part in bringing the United States into the war. The consequences of Jutland were far-reaching, but it is not true to say that the High Seas Fleet never came out again. In fact, the German High Seas Fleet came out on three subsequent occasions, still hoping to isolate and destroy a portion of the Grand Fleet. Nevertheless, thanks largely to the British code-breaking activities of the Admiralty's Room 40, the intelligence initiative was always with the British, and the High Seas Fleet under Scheer would not risk a direct en masse confrontation with the undiluted strength of the Grand Fleet. This allowed the Royal Navy continuing dominance in the North Sea.[80]

Jutland had still been a great disappointment, and the Admiralty's failure to put its case to the media before the German claims of victory had a depressing effect on public morale. Only by asking Churchill to write an upbeat press release from the official dispatches was public gloom finally dissipated.[81] Perhaps more might have been achieved had Churchill remained at the Admiralty, but the failure of the first major amphibious operation in modern warfare had already cost him his job. The Gallipoli campaign of 1915–16 against the Ottoman Empire was an attempt to force the Dardanelles with warships and then troops. Despite its failure, it was later studied by British planners for the D-day operations in Normandy. Some of its features included an aircraft carrier (or seaplane carrier), aerial reconnaissance, and photography. Bitter arguments with Fisher over the conduct of this campaign led to Fisher's resignation, which forced Churchill's resignation also.[82]

The comparative irrelevance of the air situation over land in 1914–18 contrasts strongly with the situation at sea. Despite U-9's hat trick of sinking three armored cruisers in September 1914, U-boats had not achieved much success in reducing the Grand Fleet because Jellicoe and his successor were wary of German attempts to lure them into a submarine ambush. It soon became clear that the U-boat's strengths lay in another direction. The sinking of oil tankers by U-boats restricted naval operations because the Royal Navy's newest dreadnoughts, its light cruisers, and its destroyers all used oil. At one stage the British oil reserves slumped from six months to a mere eight weeks. But it was the food situation that was to prove critical for both sides.[83] Issues of morality and American displeasure ultimately failed to restrain the Kaiser and his advisers from unrestricted submarine warfare. German military leaders saw nothing but hypocrisy in American protests about the killing of unarmed civilians at sea because America seemed prepared to tolerate the slow starvation of German women and children brought about by the Allied blockade.[84] For their part, German strategists had recognized the vulnerability of the British Isles to submarine blockade, and the failure of world harvests in 1916 seriously endangered Britain's survival by early 1917. U-boat sinking in the first months of that year easily met the German target figure of 600,000 tons per month. As the RFC suffered its worst ordeal above Arras, the British Merchant Navy was experiencing a "Bloody April" of its own, as U-boats were sinking 860,000 tons of shipping and shrinking British wheat stocks to a mere six weeks during that month. Just in time, the Admiralty introduced the convoy system, dramatically reducing the number of available targets as large convoys could hide as easily in vast oceans as single merchant ships. Even so, it would be several months before the benefits could take full effect.[85] The convoy system would not have averted defeat by itself had the government not introduced food rationing during the first half of 1917. Had the U-boats succeeded in their aim of starving Britain into peace negotiations, then the psychological blow to France, Belgium, and Russia of a British defeat and the loss of British financial services would surely have led to complete Allied collapse during 1917. As it was, and despite the American declaration of war against the Central Powers in April 1917, the period marked a low point in Allied fortunes, with battlefield reverses and Russia's internal problems that would eventually remove Russia from the side of the entente powers. But if the Germans seemed to be doing well, they needed to do far more in the months to come as the Allies were far better placed to win a lengthy drawn-out contest.

As the Admiralty started to trial the convoy system, the RNAS stepped up its anti-U-boat offensive. In this campaign, the air dimension at sea at last began to prove its worth. Increased merchant ship production, convoying, new weapons such as the depth charge and hydrophones, and the successful application of aircraft and airships against the submarine all played their parts. Virtually all basic air/sea war techniques used in future wars were developed by the RNAS between 1914 and 1918, with the exception of those based around missiles, electronics, and radar.[86] In fact, helping to defeat the U-boat was the greatest achievement of the RNAS during the war. Bombing attacks by aircraft against U-boat facilities, in support of other naval forces at Dunkirk under Commander Charles Rumney Samson, had not been successful. Neither had attempts at spotting for naval bombardments against canals and sea-locks, and if some improvements to spotting and bombing techniques were noted after 1916 they did not justify the resources put into them. Air cooperation with the fleet at sea—something markedly lacking at the Battle of Jutland in 1916—also made little contribution to the war between surface fleets.[87] But on 10 May 1917, Seaplane 8663 sank submarine UC.36 by bombing, followed by a further five submarines sunk by other seaplanes between then and September 1917.[88] While statistically this was a modest achievement, it nevertheless forced changes upon the U-boat fleet that restricted its activities. The U-boats reduced their average time in target areas from seven days to five, since they could no longer operate on the surface during daylight because of the danger posed by aircraft, and their potential targets would now be increasingly dispersed throughout the ocean. However, the use of these techniques in isolation from other developments did not end the critical period. Eight new U-boats entered service in May and sinkings rose again in June, only to steadily decline over the next few months. By the end of the year, more than 90 percent of British shipping traveled in convoy, and during 1918, 92 percent of Allied shipping was convoyed, with a loss rate of only 0.5 percent.[89] Ultimately, it was the survival of merchant shipping that became the most important factor, and from April 1918 the British and Americans were building more ships than the Germans could destroy.[90] For their part, the RNAS and later the RAF sank no U-boats alone during 1918 but shared 8 sinkings with surface vessels. During the course of 7,010 convoy escort sorties, only 3 vessels traveling in convoy sustained U-boat attacks, and between June and July 1918, 500,000 American servicemen were successfully transported across the Atlantic.[91] Only 1 transport filled with American soldiers bound for France was torpedoed and sunk. The *Tuscania* was sunk on 5 February 1918, resulting in the deaths of 166 National Guardsmen. U-boats also managed to sink a few ships returning to the United States. While these sinkings sometimes led to the drowning of homeward-bound wounded soldiers, these deaths could not alter the situation developing on the battlefields.

What eventually determined the battlefield situation was the wider state of affairs arising from the tightening grip of the Allied naval blockade. Unfortunately, this took a long time to develop, and when it began to influence the German war effort it was manifested in the painful starvation of women and children in the streets of Vienna and Berlin—sufferings the German High Command seemed determined to ignore. As the war progressed the definition of war materials expanded from munitions to include food and fertilizers. The poor quality of German soil necessitated large quantities of

potash, phosphates, and nitrates from America that were no longer available.[92] In consequence the winter of 1915–16 came to be known as the "tur-
nip winter" as there was little else to eat.[93] The brunt of the food shortages
fell on the civilian population rather than the armed forces, but even military
rations were heavily cut toward the end. The effects of the British blockade
were therefore felt in Germany in terms of shortages of a wide variety of war
materials over a long period. All of these hardships had a cumulative effect,
adding to the atmosphere of revolution that brewed in Germany during the
final stage of the war.

   To begin with, the British blockade threatened to have serious consequences for relations with neutral powers, especially with the United States.
After all, the clumsy British implementation of the blockade during the
Napoleonic wars had been a major cause of the war between Britain and
the United States in 1812. This was of serious concern while the Americans
remained neutral as the Allied cause was so heavily dependent on money
and other imports from the United States.[94] The British had stop-and-search
procedures for neutral ships heading to German and other continental
ports, and neutral cargoes thought to be ultimately bound for the enemy
were often impounded. Despite diplomatic protests centering on the "free-
dom of the seas" principle, such actions did not generally endanger human
life. Meanwhile, the Allied fleet was getting stronger. From 1917, the Royal
Navy's numbers were augmented by American ships under Admiral William
S. Sims and placed under British control rather than operating as a separate fleet. Working directly under British command from bases in Ireland,
American destroyers played an important role in defeating the U-boats, and
their dreadnoughts were integrated into the Grand Fleet and trained up to
British gunnery standards.[95]

   However, the Allied navies were not content to merely continue their
blockading actions, and three events in the summer of 1918 pointed to the
future direction of maritime airpower. The first was the highly successful raid
on the Zeppelin base at Tondern in July, where Sopwith Camels launched
from the makeshift aircraft carrier HMS *Furious* destroyed two airships and
their sheds. In August, four German seaplanes and six fighters destroyed a
flotilla of six British fast coastal motorboats in approximately fifteen minutes
off the Heligoland Bight. This was the fastest sea battle yet recorded and the
first time that aircraft had wiped out an entire naval force. While this was
going on, a Sopwith Camel launched from a lighter engaged and destroyed
a Zeppelin shadowing a force of Royal Navy cruisers and destroyers operating near Heligoland.[96] Though it was never implemented, Admiral Beatty
formed an ambitious plan to sink the German fleet at Wilhelmshaven in

mid-1918 with a mass air-strike using Sopwith Cuckoo T.1 torpedo bombers—plans predating the famous battles at Taranto and Pearl Harbor more than two decades later.[97] The Royal Navy had made enormous advances since Jutland in its appreciation of airpower at sea with the *Argus*, an aircraft carrier in service plus a further three under construction or conversion, making Great Britain, for now, the leader of the field.

The end of the war saw the Royal Navy's ultimate triumph as the German High Seas Fleet sailed into the Grand Fleet's main base at Scapa Flow to surrender. The subsequent peace treaties forbade Germany to possess a fleet larger than necessary for coastal defense, or to have an air force. For years it was mandatory for military planners to dismiss the German military from future calculations, and the future was uncertain, not just for the Royal Navy but for the RAF in particular. Indeed, the RAF may not have survived at all but for the volte-face of Sir Hugh Trenchard. It is largely his story that will be told in the next chapter.

CHAPTER 4

The Savior of the Royal Air Force

We want the man of initiative and the man of action, the methodical man, and even the crank. We open our ranks widely to all.

—Sir Hugh Trenchard, speech to the Cambridge
University Aeronautical Society, April 1925

More than anyone else, the title "Father of the Royal Air Force" is attributed to Hugh Montague Trenchard, first Viscount Trenchard. An alternative candidate for the title might equally have been Trenchard's own nominee, Sir David Henderson, the officer drafting the Smuts Reports leading to the formation of the Royal Air Force. Both Lloyd George and Smuts may have similar claims. In fact, Trenchard disliked the epithet—he would probably have preferred "Savior of the RAF," a far more apt description of this formidable man.

What sort of man was Trenchard? As a young army officer he was an "inarticulate, prickly young man, socially inept and without money." This and his teetotaler habit earned him his nickname "the Camel," an unfortunate title that must also have owed something to a small jutting head and long neck. As a child he was a poor scholar and mentally scarred by the public disgrace that resulted from the bankruptcy of his father's solicitor's practice. His saving grace was a proficiency at sports, especially equestrian pursuits, and he demonstrated a sound ability to organize sporting teams and tournaments. Initially rejected by the Royal Navy and the army, he finally staggered through the undemanding militia entrance exam and was posted to the Royal Scots Fusiliers. Trenchard took part in the Second Boer War (1899–1902) and showed promise as a captain of irregular cavalry, but a severe bullet wound in chest and spine left him with lung damage and mobility problems. An intense program of winter sports in Switzerland and a bobsleighing accident jarred his spine into place, bringing about a remarkable recovery and a return to active duty. His subsequent service "enhanced his reputation as a man of formidable personality who never hesitated to criticize all and sundry in the bluntest terms." He was promoted to lieutenant colonel and received the Distinguished Service Order, but by 1912 his career had stalled being "too 'unclubbable' [and too poor] for high rank." Nevertheless, at nearly forty, Trenchard learned to fly, and with two weeks of tuition and approximately one hour in the air, he received pilot's certificate no. 270 from the Royal Aero Club. No natural pilot, his success in learning to fly in such a short time was a tribute to his bravery and determination. Seconded to the newly formed RFC in May 1912, he became the assistant commandant at the Central Flying School at Upavon, an establishment for training naval and army flyers. Here, his bawling voice earned him the nickname "Boom."

In 1914 and with the outbreak of World War I, Trenchard took command of the Military Wing of the Royal Flying Corps remaining in Britain. Along with Sefton Brancker at the War Office, his job was to expand the RFC by building new squadrons and providing pilots and machines to replace those lost in action. His autocratic and abrasive manner—harsh even by 1914 standards—was then considered a virtue in running an organization attracting so many "free-spirits."[1] In August 1914, Trenchard, now a brigadier-general, succeeded Sir David Henderson as General Officer Commanding, Royal Flying Corps in France and inherited a priceless legacy from Henderson in the shape of Maurice Baring, poet, author, and former foreign correspondent. It was Baring who gave Trenchard a coherent voice that could be heard and understood in the corridors of power. "I can't write what I mean, I can't say what I mean, but I expect you to know what I mean," he once said.[2] Baring was also a natural diplomat, reducing the negative impact of Trenchard's overbearing, tactless manner, and his fluent French enabled good relations with the French Air Force. Marshal of the Royal Air Force, and one of Trenchard's disciples, Sir John Slessor confirmed this lack of articulation but felt "he had a flair, an instinct, for getting at the really essential core of a problem."[3] His biographer stated: "[H]is main concern, formulated during 1915, was to develop an unflinching spirit of constant aggression among pilots and observers," and as previously described, he controversially demanded his men maintain offensive action at all times.[4] Trenchard also believed the purpose of the air arm was to support the army and was therefore able to establish a good working relationship with Field Marshal Haig. This focus on tactical support of the army meant that Trenchard and Haig strongly opposed sending squadrons away from the battlefront to home defense when the German Gothas bombed London in daylight during the summer of 1917.

Shortly before the new Royal Air Force came into being, Trenchard reluctantly accepted the new post of chief of the Air Staff (CAS) under the first air minister, the scheming newspaper owner Lord Harold Rothermere, brother of Lord Northcliffe and a political ally of Lloyd George. Desperate to escape Rothermere and Lloyd George's constant intriguing against Haig, and following a series of petty squabbles, he resigned after a few months. Nevertheless, his brief tenure at this important time made him a central figure in the merging of the RFC and RNAS despite his previous arguments against the independent Air Ministry. He later reluctantly agreed to lead the new Independent Air Force (IAF), a small unit created for the purpose of bombing targets in Germany. Despite this and his enthusiasm for the potential of military aircraft—given the available resources and technology—he preferred instead to concentrate on directly supporting forces on the ground. Trenchard's bombing enthusiasm would only emerge coherently after the war had ended. Toward war's end the IAF became the Inter-Allied Independent Air Force (IAIAF), still led by Trenchard but now including Allied components, including the future American bombing proponent William "Billy" Mitchell. "A more gigantic waste of effort and personnel there has never been in any war," Trenchard wrote as hostilities drew to a close.[5] He was probably right. The official history estimates that from 675 Anglo-French strategic raids for the period 1915–18, twenty-four million marks of damage (or around £1,200,000) was inflicted, about half of which was achieved in 1918. The IAF/IAIAF therefore *shared* in £600,000 worth of damage but lost 352 aircraft—heavy losses that indicated Trenchard had driven the crews of the IAF/IAIAF as hard as he had driven the unfortunate B.E.2 crews during the "Fokker Scourge." A Handley Page cost £6,000 and a D.H.4 £1,400, so along with the unspecified costs of airfield construction and maintenance it is unlikely the IAF/IAIAF was ever cost-effective.[6]

Nevertheless, Trenchard has also been recorded as saying that the evidence of these raids "convinced him that, in any future war with Germany, a systematic campaign of heavy bombing would shatter the morale of its people."[7] The evidence available from intelligence sources suggested "an excellent moral effect" such as the panic created by bombing Cologne.[8] A frightened delegation of Rhineland town mayors traveled to the headquarters of the German High Command to deliver a petition for the bombing of London and other cities to be stopped, only to receive a curt dismissal from Field Marshal Paul von Hindenburg.[9] However, German civilians were war-weary from four years of war, suffering extreme hardships resulting from the potent combination of severe agricultural failures and the British naval blockade. This new terror of day and night bombing raids was undoubtedly the last straw for those unlucky enough to be within range. By late 1918, German society was disintegrating, but this was not confined to the areas being bombed. Trenchard may have noted the panic created by air attacks upon already defeated Turkish, Bulgarian, and Austro-Hungarian troops in 1918—something given peculiar emphasis by Slessor in the 1930s—but there is no indication he took this into account at the time.[10] Many years later, Slessor defended Trenchard's apparently inconsistent attitudes by claiming they were correct "at *that time and in those circumstances*," given the equipment limitations of the period.[11]

When peace finally came in 1918, the reputation of the traditional services emerged in tatters. Victory, according to some of the returning soldiery, was achieved by attrition rather than inspired leadership—the sort of futile incompetence portrayed by the war poets of the day and more recently lampooned in the popular British television series *Blackadder Goes Forth* (1989).[12] The Royal Navy's "failure" to achieve an outright victory at Jutland and friction between Lloyd George and the Admiralty over the convoy system did nothing to inspire public confidence in the senior service either. On the other hand, the Royal Air Force seemed to come out of the conflict comparatively well. According to one author, "[T]he realities of the air effort were, in fact, lost in a cloud of admiration for the personal heroism of pilots and the self-sacrifice of air crew." An image of "chivalry and the potential of air warfare had been created . . . partly by a masterly exercise in public relations."[13] War poet Siegfried Sassoon was taking a swipe at the British press when he wrote, "Editorial Impressions" in 1918, but a description of the British airmen in his poem suggests the aviator was receiving some sympathetic media treatment. "By Jove, those flying-chaps of ours are fine!" Sassoon wrote, but whether the wider public felt the same way is hard to determine.[14] Of course, none of this was factually demonstrable, but war-weariness resulting from four frustrating years of war was bound to create a cynical attitude toward the leadership and a nostalgic longing for the noble virtues of the past.

Against this background, the postwar future of airpower was under discussion well before the armistice, and two competing plans were placed before the politicians. Major General Frederick Sykes, chief of the Air Staff, submitted a recommendation that the Air Staff be expanded into an Imperial Air Staff controlling an Imperial Striking Force with bases throughout the British Empire. However, his detailed proposals did not emerge until December as the *Memorandum on the Airpower Requirements of the Empire*. The RAF would have sixty-two service squadrons and ninety-two cadre squadrons. Eight squadrons and fifteen cadres would remain in the UK, with nine going to the Mediterranean and Pacific. This involved the construction of airfields in the Azores, Newfoundland, Gulf of St. Lawrence, West Indies, and Bermuda plus single-squadron bases at North Borneo, Singapore, and Hong Kong. Resources for the army in Britain, India, Egypt, and Mesopotamia were also included. Other proposals included establishing central flying schools and constructing strategic air routes for commercial flying. Indeed, military and commercial aviation issues were still heavily entangled. Sykes estimated this would cost £21 million for a service approximately one-third of wartime strength, but his proposals were too expensive to be favorably received by a postwar government intent on slashing defense expenditure to the bone.[15] An interesting feature of Sykes' visionary plan was a proposal to use civilian aircraft for military purposes in order to replace combat losses.

Despite the potential for maintaining a high level of offensive power at minimal cost, Lloyd George did not wish to rely upon the conversion of civilian aircraft in this way.[16] Despite his role in helping create the RAF, he now seemed to have lost all interest in the Air, telling Churchill: "Make up your mind whether you would like to go to the War Office or the Admiralty. . . . You can take the Air with you in either case. I am not going to keep it as a separate department."[17] Churchill took the Air with him to the War Office and subsequently invited Trenchard to replace Sykes as chief of the Air Staff in early 1919. At Churchill's request, Trenchard drew up a cheaper alternative to the "Sykes Memorandum," with a simplified Air Ministry and a small RAF that could be controlled by a handful of officers. It included recommendations on training, interservice relationships, and recruitment. The advantages lay in its simplicity and a basic structure that could be adjusted to whatever financial level the Cabinet wanted.[18]

The period of 1919–20 seems to have been the most vulnerable for the independent Royal Air Force as criticism over misspending on administration, new buildings, and bureaucracy mounted. However, Trenchard and Churchill worked well together and gained Cabinet approval for a scheme to include forty service squadrons plus forty-two for training at a cost of £17 million. This was significantly cheaper than the earlier Sykes plan but offered far less proportionally in terms of squadrons.[19] The next step was to formulate a more convincing raison d'être for the RAF and prove its value as an independent force by demonstrating value for money. In late 1919, Churchill announced Trenchard's "Charter of the RAF," telling the House of Commons that the first duty of the RAF was to garrison the empire.[20] At about this time, Churchill and Trenchard met the chief of the Imperial General Staff, Sir Henry Wilson, to discuss a coming campaign in Somaliland by the Air Ministry and Foreign Office. Wilson, aware of heavy military commitments elsewhere, finally agreed on the proviso that he would not be asked for troops.[21] The following year the RAF used its bombers against the so-called Mad Mullah in Somaliland and ended his rule. The campaign was later to be described by future colonial secretary Leo Amery as the "cheapest war in history."[22]

However, this was still in the future. Aware of his vulnerability to criticism from the other services, especially the forceful and charismatic First Sea Lord David Beatty and the "cynical" but highly intelligent Wilson, Trenchard took the unusual step of calling on Beatty at the Admiralty in December 1919 and asking for a twelve-month truce to get the RAF firmly organized. A letter from Trenchard to Beatty shortly before the meeting sets out his arguments more clearly than witness accounts of the meeting itself. Trenchard's vision was of a three-part air service to include small portions trained to work specifically with the other services. All would be trained and supplied by the Air Ministry, and the "Independent" portion might become larger than the others put together. This had already been adopted in principle by forming a Coastal Area, but this could not be immediately implemented because of the need to build "an Air Force Spirit" so as not to return to the previous system of separate services. Trenchard also pointed to "the large numbers of Naval and Army officers and Members of Parliament" favoring RAF dismemberment and creating delay in the building of the Air Force by "endless discussion" in Cabinet, Parliament, and press. Splitting the vote for Air Estimates would now be "impossible" because of the administrative complications in paying for facilities common to all three services and other problems. Trenchard also emphasized the need for a period of stability as past political changes resulted in policy changes, waste, and insecurity among the staff and reiterated the need for the Air Ministry remaining "as a separate department entirely responsible for its own estimates." Appealing heavily to Beatty's perceived sympathy for "the principle of an Air Service," he claimed that the unrest created by the RAF's opponents at this time could "mean the end of it" if Beatty was seen to side with them. It concluded by stressing the importance of the "personal elements" in fermenting a feeling of unrest among subordinates.[23]

Why Beatty even agreed to the meeting is a mystery, since he was firmly committed to recovering RNAS control from the Air Ministry despite a warning from his predecessor that the Cabinet would be against it.[24] Trenchard may have thought Beatty would be sympathetic as he was a supporter of the Smuts Reports at a time when Trenchard had been against an independent Air Ministry, and Beatty was credited with swinging the Admiralty behind the Smuts plan in 1917 "believing that it was then in the national interest."[25]

Beatty's motive for supporting these reforms seems to have been a desire for a single Ministry of Defence with a single secretary of state and a Chiefs of Staff Committee dealing with all operational aspects of defense, and he was to play a leading role in the creation of this committee, becoming its first chairman.[26] An independent Air Ministry and a larger joint defense committee was a step in this direction if air operations became the dominant mode of warfare. No doubt Beatty thought that within a short time he could recover the air units supporting the fleet at sea. If so, he was surprisingly naïve, but it might also be said that Beatty was a man ahead of his time and ready to take a risk in the national interest. But as Jutland showed, he was also headstrong and impulsive and was now about to take a huge risk.

Trenchard's recollection of the meeting was that Beatty and Wilson firmly rejected his doctrine. "[T]he air is one and indivisible . . . the heart of his case for RAF control of squadrons over land and sea" despite the CAS's assurance that "apart from its own strategic role, the air force existed to cooperate with both army and navy" and the details were for the chiefs of staff to work out. Only then did he fall back on an appeal to fair play. Surprisingly, Beatty agreed and equally surprisingly, Wilson went along with it.[27] A major problem from this meeting was an alleged offer to Beatty of locating Air Ministry personnel dealing with naval aviation at the Admiralty, along with other naval aviation assets. Despite having declined the offer, Beatty was offended when no transfers were subsequently made.[28] This may well have been a genuine misunderstanding stemming from Trenchard's verbal inability to express his thoughts clearly, but it soured future relations. It is hard to avoid the conclusion that Beatty lost the Royal Navy its best chance of regaining its aircraft before naval aviation incurred significant damage from RAF control. Neither can it be considered ethical for senior military commanders to make such "private arrangements detrimental to the national interest."[29]

The subsequent White Paper of December 1919 resembled Trenchard's letter to Beatty and was probably drafted by his new "English Merchants," who may have lacked Maurice Baring's knack of interpreting Trenchard's "mysterious thought-processes."[30] The references to small, specially trained portions working with the other services common to both documents soon became the focus of countless accusations of "breach of faith." This was because the charter now included a sentence about these portions "probably becoming, in future, an arm of the older service." No guarantees were given to the traditional services about meeting their requirements, and the document essentially restated within different wording the overoptimistic and central assumption of the 2nd Smuts Report that the RAF would "grow larger and larger and become more and more the predominating factor in all types of warfare."[31] Nevertheless, the White Paper received substantial criticism and the Air Force Estimates for 1920 were reduced by £2 million, with service squadron strength slashed from forty to twenty-five and a half, most of these subsequently being deployed to the empire.[32] All the same, the White Paper was a substantial achievement given the climate of public-sector cutbacks and criticism.

Churchill left the Air Ministry in March 1921, but shortly before departing he gave Trenchard a golden opportunity to consolidate the RAF's position by sending him to a Middle East conference. He reluctantly accepted but in going, Trenchard was to find the means by which he could build on the RAF's success in Somaliland and fight off Admiralty lobbying and parliamentary criticism. A revolt had broken out in Mesopotamia (Iraq) causing the chief of the Imperial General Staff, Sir Henry Wilson, to fume, "They [the Cabinet] had decided to remain in Mesopotamia and Persia against every advice and remonstrance on my part," and a large deployment of four and half divisions was tied down there at the end of 1920. In a period of press demands for financial entrenchment, "the Cabinet were at their wit's end as to how to effect savings" given the scale of international commitment the Cabinet had already agreed to.[33] However, to the delight of the Cabinet, the campaign was conducted at a fraction of the costs estimated by the army as Trenchard used bombing to achieve his end. "Control without occupation," as Secretary of State for Air Sir Samuel Hoare would put it.[34]

Nevertheless, there was an inevitable and unpopular human cost to this campaign, something Trenchard dismissed as "M.P.s [working themselves] into a lather of indignation at Question Time in the Commons." Trenchard's policy of bombing was also notably opposed by Air Commodore Lionel E. Charlton, a brave and skilful aviator from World War I but now chief staff officer to Air Vice Marshal John Salmond, Air Officer Commanding, Iraq Command. Appalled by the civilian suffering he personally witnessed, Charlton openly criticized the bombing policy and resigned his post. Henceforth, Charlton was banned from any further postings in the Middle East while the bombing policy was in force but did not otherwise seem to have been discriminated against.[35] In more recent years, Charlton has become a hero for those who opposed the later British military participation in Iraq.[36] The bombing was ruthless and one-sided. Doubts have recently been raised over the use of poison gas in this campaign, but not in dispute is Churchill's forceful advocacy of using it against "uncivilised tribesmen," perhaps the real reason behind the belief that gas was deployed in this region.[37] Be that as it may, 97,000 tons of ordnance were used against Iraqis, killing 9,000 in exchange for 9 soldiers.[38]

But operations could be stressful for aircrew because navigation was achieved by following furrows in the sand between the main centers of habitation. These were ploughed specifically for this purpose, but sandstorms could sometimes obliterate the furrows. If the pilot was unable to pick them up again he might have to make a forced landing, meaning he and his crew could fall into the hands of tribesmen inclined toward the practice of castrating prisoners. However, that problem was largely solved by paying the headman in gold for the return of "intact" prisoners. A more modern navigation system would doubtless have been appreciated by aircrew, but the furrows worked well enough so there was no overwhelming need to spend scarce resources on expensive navigation aids. There was also no air opposition in Somaliland, Iraq, or anywhere else in the empire the RAF had to police over the next two decades. Targets were mud huts rather than industrial complexes and modern cities, and the only antiaircraft fire came from blunderbusses and gas-pipe guns. The bombing of tribesmen therefore required no modern designs for aircraft and bombs or the development of sophisticated bomb-aiming techniques.[39]

Trenchard's lack of belief in the efficacy of bombing toward the end of 1918 has already been noted, but by early 1921 he changed his tune completely. However, none of the "morale" factors given as reasons for changing his mind were considered by Trenchard in 1918.[40] "The primary function of the air force in the future," he wrote in early 1921, "will be the defence of these islands from invasion by air from the continent of Europe." "This defence," he concluded, "would largely take the form of counter-offensive from the air, assisted by a ground organisation which should be co-ordinated by the Air Ministry."[41] His ideas were now rooted firmly in the Smuts Reports of 1917, and the assumption repeated by later politicians that "the bomber will always get through" stems from this. Imperial policing by air would continue into the 1930s, but the focus was now changing. This marked the beginning of the RAF's obsession with strategic bombing, but one writer points out it was more complex than that, and Trenchard did not go as far as some U.S. Army Air Corps theorists who by the late 1920s were asserting that "the strategic employment of bombardment in aviation forms a basis for the employment of the air forces as a whole."[42] But Trenchard had still not recognized a basic flaw in the Smuts Report—that a surge in technology favoring the attack is invariably countered by improvements in the defense. Furthermore, while some American bombing proponents such as William Mitchell were even more vociferous than Trenchard, the Americans had been far more cautious about accepting the unverified claims of airpower theorists—so much so that their independent air arm did not come about until 1947 with the formation of the United States Air Force. Unlike the British, the Americans had not conducted their investigations behind closed doors and formulated sounder policies as a result—policies that would later paralyze the German oil industry and severely handicap the operations of the German Wehrmacht toward the end of World War II. In fact, the Dwight Murrow Aircraft Board in 1925 "flatly rejected" the bombing visions of General Giulio Douhet and Trenchard.[43]

In 1923, Beatty made a determined attempt to regain the RNAS, and relations between the chiefs of staff reached a crisis point. Beatty gave Prime Minister Andrew Bonar Law an ultimatum that he would resign if the RNAS were not returned. Trenchard responded by also threatening to resign, and it is said that since Trenchard had offered to resign so frequently the prime minister dryly remarked that as Trenchard was an expert in resigning he would be grateful for his advice when his own turn came. Sadly, Bonar Law found himself in an impossible position that may have contributed to his retirement in May 1923 and early death in October of that year. His successor, Stanley Baldwin, then faced the threat of the Admiralty resigning en masse over the issue, but his board of inquiry (initiated by Bonar Law and headed by Lord Salisbury) came down in favor of continued RAF control.

A planned expansion in the size of the French Air Force and a belief that France was still Britain's traditional enemy seem to have been the main factors in the decision.[44] Fanning the flames in the wider arena of debate was the writing of former RAF staff officer Percy R. C. Groves, who since the beginning of 1922 had written a series of articles in Lord Northcliffe's *Times* expounding the idea of a devastating knockout blow from the air. Groves drew public attention to what he saw as French and German military air expansion under the cloak of increased civilian air development. His views were not all shared by former superiors, but Groves was now an influential media figure.[45] Even so, it was a ridiculous situation given that Britain and France had not fought each other since the Battle of Waterloo in 1815 more than a century before, had fought as allies in the Crimean War (1853–1856), and had only recently fought shoulder-to-shoulder in a major conflict against Germany. Furthermore, having suffered heavily in the latter conflict, France had far more pressing concerns over the possibility of a resurgent and militant Germany, a nation that shared a frontier with France and would not formally recognize her western border until the Treaty of Locarno in 1925. Instead of taking these realities on board, the committee seems to have been mesmerized by doom-laden forecasts of what the French Air Force might do against Britain if this expansion remained unmatched. The naval representatives challenged Trenchard's assertion that the fleet was vulnerable to land-based airpower, but using Mitchell's recent controversial and unrealistic experiments sinking old, static, and undefended battleships by bombing, Trenchard turned Salisbury against Beatty's arguments.[46] Trenchard's "definitive" biographer asserted that Trenchard disapproved of Mitchell's use of publicity, considering it a "boomerang weapon." However, the CAS had been happy to deploy public relations (PR) in order to prove the effectiveness of the RAF to a wider audience.[47]

Back in 1920, Trenchard had introduced the first air pageant at Hendon (Empire Air Day from 1925). "It would be his way of reintroducing the RAF year by year to those who paid for its upkeep."[48] It was a great success and even Beatty congratulated him for a display that "exceeded his expectations."[49] The event brought in thousands of spectators "awed by the sight of bomber formations hitting their targets in the centre of the airfield with precision." Few of the excited watchers seem to have realized that ground technicians were exploding the sham-level crossings with dynamite, and that the bomb whistles came from recordings relayed over the broadcasting system. All this helped to popularize the new service, but having to train for the display did no favors for the pilots. According to one former RAF officer, nine months of the year were set aside for air display training at the expense of training for war. The close-formation flying that looked so impressive at Hendon was no preparation for countering the more effective and looser Luftwaffe fighter formations used in the Battle of France and the Battle of Britain.[50] But the PR expertise the RAF built up at Hendon and having to fight for its survival as an independent service helped the RAF enormously in the years to come. Working alongside bodies such as the Ministry of Information and His Majesty's Stationery Office, by 1940 the Air Ministry had built up a glamorous image of the RAF that could be sold to American opinion in the campaign to involve the United States in the fight against Nazi Germany.

Trenchard did not get everything his way. In 1924, the Balfour Award (the result of the Salisbury Commission, 1923) found in favor of keeping RAF control of squadrons working with the fleet, but it also demanded that new administrative reforms be put in writing. Trenchard fought this because he and Beatty were firmly entrenched in their respective positions. The Lord Chancellor, Richard Haldane, then insisted they establish a working relationship within three months in order to get the Committee of Imperial Defence working again.[51] Only when Beatty's deputy, Admiral Roger Keyes, took the initiative was progress made on a compromise. An agreed report was finally submitted to the Cabinet, but as Paul Halpern states, "the agreement, however, proved only a truce in a long struggle."[52] Nevertheless, this agreement represented dual control of the Naval Air Service, and it lasted until 1937.[53]Arguments raged on, and the continued existence of the RAF was further questioned during a Cabinet review of defense spending in 1925 but confirmed by the Colwyn Report in early 1926. The report hoped for "greater savings which we hope will be secured by the extended substitution of air power."[54]

By 1926, Trenchard had won his battle for keeping the Royal Air Force as an independent service. He gained the support of Sir Samuel Hoare, now secretary of state for war, who in turn told the House of Commons, "The existence of an independent Air Ministry and an independent Air Force to carry out the Air needs of the country is an established part of the programme of every party." Hoare concluded by asserting that "the longer the idea remains in existence that the question is an open one the worse it is for the relations between the three services."[55]

Not satisfied with this achievement and aware that his time as CAS was drawing to a close, Trenchard tried to eradicate a major area of contention between himself and the older services. This was the relevance of airpower to traditional military doctrine as espoused by Prussian military theorist Carl von Clausewitz. Trenchard had been "provoked" by a suggestion from Admiral Herbert Richmond that the principles of war should be set down identically in the war manuals of each service. These principles had been accepted by all three services because of the need for a commander to "cling to something clear—cut to condition his actions and maintain his military logic." In his memorandum, Trenchard wrote that the navy's manual stated: "The military aim of a Navy is to destroy in battle or to neutralize and weaken the opposing navy including its directing will and morale." The army's manual stated: "The ultimate military aim in war is the destruction of the enemy's main forces on the battlefield." In the view of the Air Staff, "the object to be sought by air action will be to paralyse from the very outset the enemy's productive centres of munitions of war of every sort and to stop all communications and transportation." All services had the same objective insofar as it was the enemy nation that had to be defeated. An army must usually defeat an enemy army to do this, but an air force can pass over the enemy armies and navies to directly attack the centers of production, transportation, and communication on which the enemy is dependent. It therefore follows that the strongest side will force the enemy onto the defensive and gain aerial superiority "not by direct destruction of air forces." Trenchard went on to state: "The gaining of air superiority will be incidental to this main direct offensive upon the enemy's vital centres and simultaneous with it."[56]

This may sound reasonable enough, but it raises several problems. Trenchard assumed that Britain and the RAF would be more powerful, but the power of an air force is dependent upon industrial and physical geography, in which case Germany was already stronger in this respect because of its size and "more effective industrial base." Neither was there any recognition of the crucial fact that essential British supplies for the air offensive would have to be imported in merchant ships that would in turn require air support from the RAF. Furthermore, if the army was evicted from the Continent by an enemy army assisted by its air force, then that air force would become more powerful because it would then be able to operate against Britain at much shorter ranges. In addition, all the assets of the conquered territories in terms of production centers, communications, and transportation would increase enemy airpower manifold. Having achieved its initial objectives by land power assisted by airpower, the enemy could then launch an overwhelming concentration of airpower, in which case Britain would be vulnerable because Trenchard only believed in minimal air defenses. A further flaw was Trenchard's assumption that airpower could paralyze all communications and transportation with bombs up to 500 lbs. But as Germany and France were well served with good roads, canals, and railways, this was unrealistic as these networks were only vulnerable at certain points. He also assumed that no significant air defense was possible, and while there was little speed differential between biplane fighters and biplane bombers in the 1920s, it should have been anticipated this might well change. Even Field Marshal Haig—an officer not noted for much technical prescience—remarked in 1917, "[M]ight not the arts of air defence keep pace with or even exceed the arts of offence by bombing?"[57] Finally, hidden in Trenchard's statement about defeating "the enemy nation" is the "inner intent: to crush civilian morale by bombing—to take war to the family hearth." It was his often-stated belief that "the effects on morale of bombing were in the proportion of twenty to one compared with the physical destruction actually wrought."[58]

First Sea Lord Sir Charles Madden's case was based on firmer ground. Pointing out that Trenchard had provided neither a clear military objective nor any supporting evidence, Madden wrote: "[T]here is danger of dissipation of effort in the operations of the Air Force." This means that "the important principle of concentration on the object will be neglected."[59] Equally emphatic was the chief of the Imperial General Staff, Field Marshal George Francis Milne. "In war, concentration of effort alone," he wrote, "can bring about success, and my main anxiety, after studying the Air Staff memorandum, is lest the acceptance of the views advanced may lead us in exactly the wrong direction."[60] How right they both were! Government defense policies in the 1920s had been rigidly determined on cost grounds and conditioned by the infamous Ten Year Rule.[61] Politicians did not see the flaws because they believed the air hype and were well disposed toward Trenchard because of his reputation as an economizer.

Another doctrinal clash occurred over the defense of the naval base at Singapore, with Trenchard insisting that the base would be better and more cheaply defended with land-based aircraft than trusting to coastal defenses. However, Trenchard was assuming that bombers had reached a point of development at which battleships could be sunk from the air. As Mitchell had shown, if the battleships were neither moving nor conducting an anti-aircraft defense, and the visibility was fine, then it could be done. But this was not the reality of war at sea, and the RAF failed to sink a single moving German or Japanese battleship with free-falling bombs in World War II. War experience would eventually show that, except for dive-bombing, the bombing techniques used against smaller ships would not yield very great results either. Nor, despite the great efforts of the Royal Navy toward the end of World War I, can it be said that the torpedo bomber had reached a sufficiently high level of development. Indeed, it may never have done so at all had the Fleet Air Arm remained under the sole management of the Air Ministry. Even without this useful hindsight it should have been obvious that Trenchard's specious arguments on the relative costs of aircraft and battleships had no relevance to this particular situation.[62] In the event, Singapore fell to the Japanese army and the coastal batteries proved useless, but British airpower also proved woefully inadequate in this campaign and the base fell to Japanese land power.

In 1929, Trenchard retired as the senior member of the Chiefs of Staff Committee, having secured the RAF's position as an independent service. He held considerable expertise having served on the committee for more than nine years, and would continue to fight the case for independent airpower from his seat in the House of Lords for a long time to come. In fairness, Trenchard, Madden, and Milne possessed no crystal ball and could not have known the direction that warfare would take by 1939. But Trenchard's airpower case still rested on pure untested theory, while his two colleagues made their counterarguments on the tried and trusted principles of war and had put them into practice during their careers.[63] Yet of the three, only Trenchard's legacy would exert a powerful influence and be widely remembered into the next decade and beyond. Before we consider this further, the British policy of Imperial Air Policing merits some closer examination.

CHAPTER 5

Imperial Policing

I am strongly in favor of using poison gas against uncivilised tribes.
—Winston Churchill, secretary of state for war, 1919

T he reputation of the Royal Air Force and hence the institutional existence of that organization in the 1920s had come to depend upon
its perceived ability to carry out military operations at substantially
less cost than the army and navy. From a promising beginning in British
Somaliland in 1919–20, where a handful of aircraft drove Mohammed bin
Abdullah Hassan's "Dervish State" out of British territory into Ethiopia, the
Air Ministry and British Foreign Office and Colonial Office quickly moved
on to fight a full-blown rebellion in Iraq (Mesopotamia), with features akin to
"a fairly large conventional war."[1] Subsequent actions in places such as India's
North-West Frontier were intended to "pacify" and "civilize" warring tribes
and enforce tax collection.

Predictably perhaps, none of this impressed certain senior army and
naval officers. Reviewing the first ten years of air control, Admiral Beatty
wrote to the *Times* in 1930 contesting Trenchard's further proposed exten-
sion of "air control" against a background of parliamentary debate over the
Air Estimates. "The most advertised example of air control and the financial savings made by its adoption was," he wrote, "the operations in Iraq in
September and October 1924." Listing the forces as "[t]wenty-four aeroplanes, 12 armoured cars, eight guns, 3,630 men, cavalry, infantry, and artillery," he suggested that a more accurate description of the policy should have
been "military control." The RAF officers commanding had military back-
grounds, having started their careers in the older services and therefore "*were*
soldiers." It was not "air control, any more than armoured car or artillery

control." In future, he claimed, RAF officers under the "present regime" will not have a soldier's training and experience.[2] Another letter by Major General Sir Frederick Barton Maurice was equally skeptical. Maurice had served in several imperial wars and held senior military appointments during World War I. He was also fearlessly outspoken, having once publicly accused Lloyd George of making false statements about the strength of the BEF to justify withholding troops from Haig. This accusation ended Maurice's military career and not for the first time raised questions about how far a military commander should publicly challenge democratically elected politicians— something that remains irresolvable to the present day.[3]

"[T]he Royal Air Force," Maurice observed, "had to a great extent diminished the probability of the outbreak of small wars." He further conceded that "[a]ircraft can appear at once over a tribal gathering . . . can strike swiftly . . . need neither roads nor railways, [and] have no convoys to be raided." The possession of aircraft, had they been available in 1883 against the Mahdi, may also have prevented the "painful process" of reconquering the Sudan. However, Maurice was skeptical about their effectiveness in mountainous terrain, citing the problems of French airmen against the Moroccan Riffs [sic], and he believed Trenchard's example of air operations against the Mohmands of the Indian North-West Frontier to be "isolated" and "unconvincing." Maurice also criticized an RAF statement referring to its bombing of the Nubans in 1929. Because the tribesmen were cave-dwellers they were completely protected from the bombs. Success was obtained because the bombs kept the Nubans in the caves, allowing the infantry to approach without loss. It was therefore an example of "successful cooperation" rather than the independent air action claimed by the undersecretary of state for air. Maurice blamed Sir Samuel Hoare for exaggerating the RAF's latest claim to a greater share in imperial policing on the basis of the results obtained in Iraq, specifically criticizing Hoare's claim that the annual costs of garrisoning Iraq had been reduced from £20 million to £1.5 million.

Lord Lloyd (High Commissioner to Egypt George Ambrose Lloyd) had already pointed out that before the RAF took responsibility for the area there were already very serious disturbances in Iraq and a border dispute with Turkey, meaning that defense expenditure was unusually high. Once the League of Nations managed to resolve the dispute the army had already succeeded in pacifying the country and "already arranged for very large reductions in the garrison before defence was handed over to the Royal Air Force." The RAF succeeded in quelling minor disturbances with considerable numbers of Iraq levies, "but its capacity to protect the country in such a situation as existed 10 years ago has not been tested." He accused the RAF of "definitely" failing in Palestine, because when the disorders broke out it was impossible to bomb Jerusalem or other places with "sacred associations" and soldiers had to be rushed to the country. This "slender evidence" was the basis of Trenchard's case for the transfer of the defense of the North-West Frontier of India from the army to the RAF. The only real solution to the North-West Frontier, Maurice believed, was to open the area up to "civilization," in other words improving roads and other transport links, citing the pacification of the Waziris, who "are now abandoning the practice of raiding each other and our plains, and are seeking work in order to save money to buy Ford cars."[4]

Trenchard's riposte did not dispute Maurice's comments regarding the limits of imperial air control except in the case of Palestine. The Air Ministry controlled this area because its defense was "linked up with that of Transjordan which is peculiarly suitable for air power." The retired CAS disliked the implication that "Air Force methods" were of a transitory or "tip and run" nature, citing the advantages that the "political officer" enjoys from seeing the situation from the air. Turning Maurice's notion of "civilisation" against him, Trenchard wrote: "Air is the greatest civilising influence these countries have ever known." Air communication enabled both the tribal chiefs and the air officers to travel throughout the whole region, making it far easier to establish friendly relationships. "And if air control saves money, there will be so much more money for the making of roads, which . . . Lord Rawlinson [Henry Rawlinson, 1st Baron Rawlinson] did so successfully in Waziristan."[5]

The RAF operation in Waziristan had originally been described in a dispatch from Air Vice-Marshal Sir Edward Ellington to General Sir Claud Jacob for the period 9 March to 1 May 1925 that was characteristically upbeat. The area covered approximately fifty to sixty square miles and included about forty targets situated at altitudes between three thousand and six thousand feet, with hilltops rising to around seven thousand feet. The targets varied from good-sized villages to "purely cave dwellings and scattered huts and enclosures of various tribes." Nearly all the villages "possessed a protective cave system." The bombing was intended to continuously harass the tribes, to make them insecure, and to "prevent the pursuit of their normal activities." Ellington stated, "This is the first occasion the RAF has been used independent of the Army for dealing with a situation which has got beyond the control of the political officers." It was too early to judge how lasting the effects might be, but the RAF represented "a weapon which is more economical in men and money and more merciful in its actions than other forms of armed force for dealing with the majority of problems which arise beyond the administrative frontier." Jacob remained unconvinced, adding that "a combination of land and air action would have brought about the desired result in a shorter space of time," and only allowed it on this occasion to give the RAF their chance to prove "the effectiveness of their unsupported action."[6]

No doubt the majority of politicians, RAF officers, and their supporters preferred to dismiss these claims by senior officers of the older services, and the criticism had no discernible impact on the British government of the day. However, the work of Dr. James S. Corum, a well-known, if somewhat controversial, air historian and counterinsurgency expert, generally supports this criticism. Corum's belief that airpower should be integrated more closely with battlefield situations puts him at odds with those who firmly believe airpower operations should be fundamentally independent of army and naval control.[7] His analysis of airpower as practiced by the RAF between the wars claims that "advocating air control doctrine as the basis for US Air Force operations in the twenty-first century lies more in the realm of myth than reality."[8] As he has pointed out, "the idea of occupying and pacifying a country by airpower alone, or with the air force as the primary force employed, is especially attractive to airmen."[9] Since the mid-1990s, air force professionals and airpower theorists have considered British air control of the empire to be a good model for contemporary military-occupation missions.[10] Although both influential defense analyst and newspaper correspondent Basil Liddell Hart and RAF reports to London gave the impression that air-policing by the RAF was the primary mode of air operations in the empire, the reality was that, in most cases, large operations involved the substantial deployment of British and colonial troops. So how effective was this British model?

As mentioned earlier, air control was first applied in the deserts of British Somaliland in 1920. The undoubtedly charismatic Hassan harassed the British with a series of well-planned raids against Somaliland tribes, and between 1900 and 1904 the imperial power made a number of unsuccessful attempts to bring him to book. Despite being defeated on the battlefield in 1904 and having his forces driven back into Ethiopia, Hassan was to stage a dramatic return and in 1913 inflicted heavy losses upon a unit of the Somaliland Camel Corps. But the outbreak of World War I the following year delayed retribution until the end of the war. With a force of only eight D.H.9 bombers sent to the region in January 1920, the RAF bombarded Hassan's forts and forced him out within days. Ground forces comprising the Somaliland Camel Corps, the Indian Army, and the King's African Rifles then set off in pursuit, with the RAF maintaining a secondary role in support.[11] Hassan escaped from British territory and would undoubtedly have returned at a later date had it not been for his death from influenza in December 1920. Because of the RAF, the campaign had been conducted for the remarkably low price of £80,000, and it was this financial achievement that began to attract the interest of politicians.[12] Buoyed by the RAF's success in Somaliland, Trenchard was able to make a formal proposition at the Cairo Conference on Mideast Affairs in March 1921—that the RAF assume responsibility for military operations in Iraq, with British bomber squadrons as the main deployment.[13] In this he was supported by the legendary Arab expert T. E. Lawrence and the redoubtable Gertrude Bell, both of whom were influential with imperial policy makers. "Provided the air weapon was used with civilised restraint," Bell told Trenchard, it would work.[14] Lawrence reassured a skeptical Percy Cox, the high commissioner in Iraq, that "air control would help Britain as much as the Arabs" and that it "would safeguard the peace and enable Iraq and Jordan to grow up and prosper."

It was clear that Trenchard had now completely captured Lawrence's imagination. Both now shared a vision of aviation opening up the desert for civilization.[15] Indeed, only a year later, Captain Frederick Guest, secretary of state for air, could boast to the House of Commons that the RAF had already provided an opportunity for civil aviation to develop the nine-hundred-mile-long desert air route from Cairo to Baghdad. Official and public mails were already being carried across the desert in times of up to seven and a half hours. The desert air route also enabled aircraft and their spares to be supplied to local RAF units more quickly, citing an example of eight squadrons being sent all their "spares, new machines, and impedimenta . . . in two or three days" instead of twenty-four days by sea around the Persian Gulf. The effects of air action were also "less temporary than Army action." It was also "quicker in its action," was much cheaper, and "more humane."[16]

Colonial officers believed British control needed to be less visible, and that a force of bombers was a potential target that should be hidden from public view until required. A low profile was more difficult whenever a large garrison of British soldiers was deployed on the streets.[17] As Guest later stated, placing garrisons in "semi-civilised countries" just gave the natives something to "strike at, in the hope of eventually getting some rifles or loot."[18]

Administrators of the period looked for three "political requirements of law and order" within their territories. Broadly speaking, these were that, firstly, officials should be able to travel safely and freely within a territory; secondly, the integrity of trade routes must be maintained; and thirdly, if the natives must fight among themselves, their conflicts must not impinge upon others.[19] All of these were reasonable enough, but until now British colonial administration of these areas had been inept. During World War I the British fought a long and hard campaign against the Turks of the Ottoman Empire, imposing martial law and an Indian civil service–style administration on the newly conquered territories. This meant an unwelcome degree of official intervention and tax demands that the tribes had not previously experienced under the Ottoman Empire. Ditching promises of self-government made to the Arabs for their support against the Turks in World War I, the British engineered their nominee's accession to the throne of Iraq. Faisal bin Ali al-Hashemi, a Sunni Arab, was chosen at the Cairo Conference and became king of Iraq in August 1921. This antagonized the Shiites and Kurd majority despite Faisal's pan-Arab aspirations. By then, discontent had already exploded into open rebellion, and 60,200 troops originally stationed in the country were confronted by tribesmen armed with modern weaponry left by the Turks and led by men who had previously fought with Arab and Ottoman armies. These tribes were therefore more sophisticated in terms of contact with modern technology and aircraft than the supporters of Hassan had been in Somaliland. According to British estimates, the Iraqi rebels possessed 17,000 modern small-bore magazine rifles and 43,000 "old but serviceable rifles."[20] Approximately 4,883 British and 24,508 Indian army soldiers, and 2 RAF bomber squadrons, were sent as reinforcements, and in August 1920 a counteroffensive began to put down the rebellion. The RAF units gave good service in evacuating personnel, dropping supplies, and supporting ground forces with bombing and reconnaissance missions, but it was far from being an exclusive air war. On 13 October 1920 a large pitched battle took place at Rumaitha where some 3,000 rebels opposed a British brigade. This was a 9-hour fight involving a heavy artillery barrage, bombing, and hand-to-hand combat. The rebellion cost 1,040 killed/missing soldiers, with 1,228 wounded fighting against approximately 8,450 Iraqi insurgents killed. In cold financial terms, it had cost £40 million to retain the mandate.[21]

The RAF took over Iraq in October 1922 in the sense that all military forces in Iraq then came under Air Ministry control. This meant the British government was able to claim it had pulled all British forces out of the country and gave little emphasis to the fact that the British army units had been replaced by Indian ones. But it was still a great saving to the British taxpayer as the financial burden now fell upon the government of India. Significant ground forces remained in Iraq until full independence was granted in 1932.[22] Ten years of air control in Iraq had incurred only light casualties upon the RAF—fourteen killed in action with eighty-four wounded.[23]

Air control was also used extensively in the Aden Protectorate, an area considered strategically important because of its position on the route to India. In July and September 1933, a group of Yemeni rustlers carried out a series of raids in the Protectorate, making off with stolen cattle and hostages for ransom. The British then threatened to bomb Yemeni settlements unless all the hostages and property were returned. All the stolen property and hostages were quickly returned.[24] However, a disadvantage of this near-exclusive reliance on air control was that traditional ground-based expeditions tended to draw maps and lay tracks into remote areas in case the tribesmen had to be dealt a further lesson at a later date. The lack of adequate maps and tracks would cause the British further problems in their counterinsurgency operations that led to Aden's independence in the 1960s.[25] In fairness, nobody could reasonably have been expected to anticipate this at the time.

It is also reasonable to point out that low-intensity conflicts are not generally resolvable by military power alone. As Capt. D. W. Parsons of the U.S. Air Force pointed out in 1994, when the British employed the "overwhelming firepower" of air control, it merely suppressed "overt manifestations of some underlying socio-political conflict." However, he conceded that this was enough for British colonial needs and enabled air control to be seen as a "broad success."[26] Parsons was anxious that the British colonial experience would not be adopted by America's Clinton administration to quell the disturbances in Bosnia, asserting that the real lesson was that any application of a military power (not just airpower) that fails to take account of the "socio-political nature of the conflict" merely wastes "time, lives, and resources." Indeed, such conflicts require "patience and durability," features lacking in air control.[27]

Some of the humanitarian aspects of air control have been discussed in the previous chapter, and it is important to understand the methods of control applied by the imperial power prior to the introduction of aircraft and airpower. Hundreds, possibly thousands, of punitive military expeditions were mounted between 1840 and 1940 against inhabitants of the lesser-developed areas of the empire. The purpose was to impose discipline on rebellious tribal groups that defied imperial authority. Tribes might take an official hostage, break a treaty, or raid neighboring tribes. At great expense, an army column would march on the offending tribal area, burn villages and crops, crush any resistance, and return in the knowledge that the natives had been taught a richly deserved lesson. Unfortunately, the results were rarely permanent and within months or sometimes years the natives would again misbehave and require further chastisement. As Corum says, it was "brutal" but an "indispensable means of keeping the empire under control."[28] There can be no doubt that the use of aircraft in these smaller policing actions made for a cheaper and more effective policy since they could inflict as much damage as more traditional expeditions had done. Certainly, hardly anyone in 1920s Britain would have doubted the need for violent action against "primitive peoples" who defied imperial authority, but it was also a question of degree, and it is doubtful if it was as humane as Lawrence and Bell had hoped. Humanity was not stressed in early RAF statements on air control, most of which understandably preferred to emphasize the destructive power that aircraft could bring to bear. "The attack with bombs and machine guns must be relentless and unremitting," wrote Wing Commander John A. Chamier in a prominent defense journal in 1921. It must be carried out "day and night, on houses, inhabitants, crops, and cattle. . . . This sounds brutal, I know, but it must be made brutal to start with." He explained: "The threat alone in the future will prove efficacious if the lesson is once properly learnt."[29] Certainly, the "Notes on the Method of Employment of the Air Arm" in Iraq unashamedly pointed out that "within 45 minutes a full-sized village . . . can be practically wiped out and a third of its inhabitants killed or injured by four or five planes."[30] The attitudes reflected in these documents came under increasing attack in the press and in Parliament, especially when Ramsay MacDonald's Labour Party came to power in 1924. Unsurprisingly, the tone of RAF reports became more defensive.

A dispatch from the Indian government to the secretary of state for India in October 1925 addressed British press concerns that indiscriminate bombing of women and children had caused retaliatory atrocities against British women. The perpetrators had not used this as a justification and did not belong to any of the tribes being bombed. Neither had they any known connection to the Mahsuds and Wazirs as had been claimed. In any case, the tribes being bombed were warned by air-dropped leaflets to move their women and children in advance of the air raid, and officials rejected the accusation of indiscriminate bombing. Material damage from bombing may have been slight, but more important, raids generated fear: "As soon as the period of apprehension and the first shock are over, however, our evidence goes to show it is not the way force is applied but its effectiveness that is feared, and to that extent resented." It still remained necessary to keep in place the standing reward for the return of captured RAF airmen (see previous chapter), but the good treatment prisoners continued to receive from tribesmen "points to the same conclusion."[31]

The War Office, who instinctively resented the RAF's increasing role in colonial control, also joined in the criticism, but its criticism fell "flat" in view of the army's record of burning crops and bombarding villages with artillery during its own punitive expeditions. Also, most army officers stationed in the colonies seem to have approved of RAF methods. In fact, since the notorious Amritsar Massacre of 1919 that led to the deaths of four hundred unarmed civilians, the armed forces were instructed to act under the "doctrine of minimum necessary force," and the RAF soon learned to "report casualties of air control in vague terms."[32] Basil Liddell Hart also argued that prompt RAF action had resulted in "an immense saving of blood and treasure to the British and Iraqi governments."[33] Although the RAF adopted "minimum necessary force" as its official policy, it was unlikely to have been strictly implemented in the far-flung backwaters. According to one RAF flight commander on the North-West Frontier, there was considerable action against local tribes and the rules of engagement were very liberally interpreted. Tribes were warned that the RAF would bomb an assembly of people if the tribe became troublesome. The definition of an assembly was normally ten people, and on one occasion it happened to be nine. "That's within ten per cent and that's enough, so I blew them up."[34] However, the British were no more ruthless in their pursuit of air control than other imperial powers. According to David Omissi, the French were less likely to give advance warnings of bombing raids.[35] Against this it is argued that the Rif tribes of Morocco were more formidable than any tribes that could be found within the British Empire of the 1920s. Furthermore, the British were prepared to bomb villages for the relatively trivial motive of tax enforcement, while arguably the French operations were fighting more campaigns with features similar to large conventional wars.[36]

The use of poison gas against tribesmen was another issue in the argument over the "humanity" of RAF methods. Gas in warfare was introduced by Germany in 1915 and inevitably led to counter-use by the Allies. Outside of the armed forces, it was generally regarded with abhorrence, and the matter was much debated in the years following World War I and was referred to the League of Nations as part of the wider effort to establish international arms control. By 1920, Great Britain was bound by various international regulations, including Article 23(a) of the Hague Convention of 1907 "which states that it is particularly forbidden 'to employ poison or poisoned weapons,'" along with Article 23(c) particularly forbidding use of "arms, projectiles, or materials calculated to cause unnecessary suffering."[37] Recognizing the hostile attitudes of British civilians against gas alongside the arguments propounded by the RAF, Herbert Fisher, president of the Board of Education, claimed that "[t]he British public thought that poison gas was a low game and they think so still." However, "[i]t is argued . . . that gas is cheap, that it is humane, that it is particularly likely to be peculiarly valuable to the British Empire in its numerous conflicts with uncivilised foes." Rejecting this, he warned against being "hurried by our naval and military advisors into a precipitate acceptance of innovations which we have more than once condemned."[38]

At this time, the Cabinet possessed official correspondence recommending: (i) the official acceptance of gas as a war weapon; (ii) that the government should try to influence public opinion in favor of using gas; (iii) that future gas development be unrestricted; and (iv) during wartime, the War Office be allowed to use gas whenever it feels it appropriate. These views were also supported by the Admiralty.[39] Churchill, as secretary of state for war, included quotations from two American publications to support the pro-gas lobby. Adm. Alfred Thayer Mahan of the U.S. Navy, speaking at the Hague Conference in 1899, commented on the illogicality of being "tender about asphyxiating men with gas, when . . . it is allowable to blow the bottom out of an ironclad at midnight, throwing 400 or 500 men into the sea to be choked by the water." Another American source claimed that we should get used to gas being "a permanent and important part of war." In the event of another war "America will go in with as much reliance on gas shells as her antagonists can possibly have."[40] Ultimately, British public opinion prevailed when Great Britain signed the Geneva Protocol (Protocol for the Prohibition of the Use in War of Asphyxiating, Poisonous or Other Gases, and of Bacteriological Methods of Warfare) in 1925, and the RAF did not use it again—if it ever used it at all. Prior to this, Article XXII of *The Hague Rules of Air Warfare, 1922–23* prohibited terror-bombing, but the document remained unratified and never became part of international law.

In recent years, the question as to whether poison gas was ever actually used in Mesopotamia was posed by R. M. Douglas in 2009. How this controversial method could have been employed and simultaneously concealed both from the world press and the League of Nations has never been explained, and the evidence deployed for its use seems to have been limited to Churchill's forceful advocacy of using it against uncivilized tribesmen.[41]

Imperial air control would continue into the 1930s, but the world was gradually changing and policy makers would soon have to think about confronting more sophisticated foes. The Wall Street Crash of 1929 ended the boom enjoyed by most Western nations during the late 1920s. With hindsight this financial catastrophe can now be seen to have sparked a sequence of events that would propel Adolf Hitler to power in Germany and make another gigantic clash between technologically advanced nations inevitable. Given the apocalyptic scenarios of air warfare painted by writers since the beginning of the century, it was expected that the RAF was about to play a major role in warfare. Whether it would be able to fulfill this role was largely going to depend on how much money the politicians would be willing and able to provide.

CHAPTER 6

The Locust Years

So the Cabinet decided that the Ten Year Rule should commence
afresh each year, so that when it was revoked the three services would
always be at "ten years notice." Protest was unavailing. Gagged and
bound hand and foot, they were handed over to the Treasury Gestapo.

—Lord Chatfield on the strengthening of the
Ten Year Rule in 1928, *It Might Happen Again*

ndeed, 1929 heralded the start of a new dark age. Shortly before retiring
as chief of Air Staff that year, Trenchard warned the government that
150,000 hospital beds should be put aside for the care of civilian air raid
victims.[1] His retirement from office did nothing to modify the Air Ministry
scare-mongering, and whilst it did little to loosen the purse strings of government at the time, the constant drip of pro-air publicity continued to affect the
attitudes of press, public, and politicians. Three years later, Stanley Baldwin,
the Lord President of the Council, made his now notorious statement to the
House of Commons:

> In the next war you will find that any town within reach of an aerodrome can
> be bombed within the first five minutes of war to an extent inconceivable
> in the last war. . . . I think it is well also for the man in the street to realise
> that there is no power on earth that can protect him from being bombed.
> Whatever people may tell him, the bomber will always get through. . . .
> Imagine 100 cubic miles covered with cloud and fog, and you can calcu-
> late how many aeroplanes you would have to throw into that to have much
> chance of catching odd aeroplanes as they fly through.[2]

Of course, nothing in this statement dealt with the navigational difficulties
of finding a target in one hundred cubic miles of cloud and fog, far less the

problem of accurate bomb aiming with the equipment in use—but he was keeping it simple for the wider audience. Having authoritatively underlined the complete vulnerability of the British Isles to air attack, Baldwin then espoused a barbarous policy of indiscriminate civilian murder as the sole military option. "The only defence is in offence, which means you have got to kill more women and children more quickly than the enemy if you want to save yourselves." He continued ominously, "I mention this so that people may realise what is waiting for them when the next war comes."[3]

It was logic all too familiar to later generations living under the shadow of a worldwide nuclear Armageddon. What had become a national psychosis of bombing was the fruit grown from fears seeded fifteen years earlier by the contributors of the Smuts Report and assiduously fed and watered by an alarmist press. For his part, Baldwin had no specialized knowledge of airpower and was sincerely articulating official advice. Air Ministry advice to the Cabinet that year had been that Germany was capable of dropping seventy-five tons of bombs daily from German bases alone, at an estimated fifty casualties per ton. The casualties would double if Germany managed to occupy Holland and Belgium.[4] In the event, Germany did occupy Holland and Belgium, but it took 1.3 tons of bombs to kill one Briton during 1940–41, a "respectable" rate of return for the munitions expended but much less than had been predicted.[5] Since the German air force was dissolved in 1920 and not reincarnated as the Luftwaffe until 1933 (officially unveiled in 1935), the advice was given on the basis of what now seems extraordinary guesswork about German ability to sustain such an offensive. Baldwin's words were destined to be endlessly repeated both in Parliament and the press. Today, it remains the most well-publicized and notorious statement on airpower ever uttered by a leading politician.

Even in 1935, the Luftwaffe was still a shadow of what it was to become. On the face of it, German propaganda on the strength of their new air force seems to have convinced Lord Rothermere, who told the House of Lords in May 1935 that Germany possessed 10,000 fast long-range bombers, each capable of carrying a ton of bombs, meaning that a surprise air attack might come at any moment.[6] No wonder that, 10 years after Trenchard's retirement, the government was advised to earmark 750,000 hospital beds in anticipation of the Luftwaffe's knockout blow. The government took the advice seriously, but it was a figure it had no hope of achieving. In the event, the London Blitz of 1940–1941 required no more than 6,000 beds.[7] The air lobby had made its greatest of many gross exaggerations—this time by a factor of 125. The air lobby's record for scare-mongering now seems outrageous yet in one sense wholly understandable given the difficulties of rousing the British government and public to the dangers inherent in a weak defense policy. The reasons why these fears gained such credibility are worth a closer look.

In the years prior to 1935, Rothermere had taken a leading role in the campaign for a major expansion of the air, arguing that the large numbers of German civil airliners operated by Lufthansa represented a dangerous military threat because theoretically these could be converted into military bombers. Rothermere was to make many unsubstantiated claims of this nature; for example, that the German aircraft destroying Guernica during the Spanish Civil War included a large number of Ju.52 airliners converted for military use. The conversion argument was also used by Churchill in his strident demands for a larger RAF, and utilized to suit the purposes of both rearmers and disarmers. In reality, no such threat existed because the design requirements for airliners and military aircraft widely diverged during the 1930s, but this was not widely appreciated at the time.[8] There were to be exceptions, of course. Despite some structural limitations, the German Focke Wulf Fw200 Condor was to have notable success as a long-range maritime strike aircraft in the Battle of the Atlantic, and Britain's successful Short Sunderland flying boat was derived from the Short Empire passenger- and mail-carrying flying boat.[9] However, by the mid-1930s the focus was firmly upon the building of dedicated military aircraft for the bombing role.

Despite the difficulties of conversion, this debate was taken very seriously for much of the interwar period. The very first airliners had been converted from World War I bombers, and the Sykes memorandum, though not adopted on account of the expense, envisaged the concurrent development of civil and military aviation throughout the British Empire. Indeed, the terms of the Treaty of Versailles forbade Germany to have an air force, but in the aftermath of war, it had not escaped British attention that Germany was using its vast industries to build large numbers of civil aircraft and to establish a huge network of European routes.

Inevitably this created suspicions about German intentions even before the Nazis came to power. These suspicions had some foundation. A limited degree of secret rearmament was going on during the years of the Weimar Republic. The bans stemming from the peace treaties of 1919 meant increasing restrictions on German civil aviation, but paradoxically, this drove the few surviving aircraft firms into the hands of the German military. In the early 1920s, Junkers was building an aircraft and an aero-engine for the German army in a secret plant within the Soviet Union. Also, Ernst Brandenburg, formerly commander of the "England Squadron," was now at the helm of the Ministry of Aviation's Transport Department—his aim being to use civil aviation as a means of preserving military aviation.[10] Despite this clandestine activity, the conversion debate assumed an importance that was more rhetorical than real, and was pursued by the air lobby to raise awareness of the poor state of British military aviation.[11] None of this loosened government purse-strings until 1935. By then, the debate had subsided because the government had finally embarked on a major rearmament program.

The Road to Rearmament

All the same, one should not condemn the British interwar governments too harshly. The enormous international pressure to disarm was understandable given the heavy human cost of having to fight the 1914–18 war. Furthermore, the high level of indebtedness to the United States and American insistence on calling in their international loans from 1929 began a severe economic downturn that adversely affected all advanced industrialized nations to varying degrees, but especially those that adhered to the Gold Standard. Britain left this toward the end of 1931 and implemented a form of imperial preference, allowing a modest overall recovery over the next few years. In Germany, the economic effects were more dramatic and helped create the conditions that brought the Nazis to power in 1933, an event that soon led to Germany's abrupt departure from the League of Nations and the Geneva Disarmament Conference. Until then, the financial outlook for all services was flat. The early 1930s was the period Churchill was later to call "The Locust Years," a statement implying this was a period of irresponsible government neglect of defense matters.[12] All this was ironic given his earlier role in helping create the Ten Year Rule, and then in 1928 helping to make it self-perpetuating. Furthermore, as chancellor of the exchequer during 1924–29, Churchill held considerable responsibility for clinging to the Gold Standard, prolonging the Depression and making it harder to finance the measures he was urgently demanding only a few years after leaving office.

This constraint on defense spending led the chiefs of staff to complain in 1935 about how this had damaged the funding of air defense. Ellington explained, "It has now become necessary therefore to undertake in a period of some five years expenditure that would normally, except for the Ten Year Rule, have been spread over some fifteen years."[13]

Until 1933–34, most Western politicians remained focused on ensuring peace through the pursuance of international disarmament, and very little could be achieved in the opposite direction. The government policy of appeasement associated with Neville Chamberlain, chancellor of the exchequer between 1931 and 1937 and prime minister between May 1937 and

May 1940, has also been blamed for the British government's failure to act with sufficient energy at an earlier date. But appeasement as a process of trying to resolve international disputes by rational compromise was widely adopted throughout the 1930s. Despite all the international incidents now perceived as milestones of appeasement, very few people viewed an all-out general war as inevitable until the latter half of 1938 and the Munich Crisis.

Having reluctantly accepted the necessity for rearmament in 1934 and probably content for well-known figures such as Lord George Lloyd and Winston Churchill to erode public pacifism and agitate for rearmament against Nazi Germany, the British government began the long task of rectifying years of neglect. While the subsequent program has been much criticized by pro-Churchill historians for a lack of urgency during the early years, the government "got it right" in 1934 by having the program peak in 1939.[14] Any long-term rearmament program will run the risk of either peaking too soon or too late, and accurate forecasting requires considerable fine judgment and a measure of luck. As the official historian remarked, "Until 1935 international disarmament was still a popular hope and still the object of British foreign policy." The function of rearmament in the initial phase was to back diplomacy with a show of force in order to deter potential aggressors. Only with hindsight can the international crises over Manchuria and Abyssinia be seen as harbingers of all-out war. Acute as these events were, they subsided quickly and made small lasting impact on the considerations of the public and politicians.[15]

What British politicians had to constantly bear in mind was the fact that Great Britain was only just beginning to emerge from the Depression. A major obstacle lay in the vast 1914–18 war debt to the United States, and a major contribution to victory had been the British willingness to use their financial expertise and act as banker for the entente powers. Repayment had not been too problematic while Germany was paying reparations and remaining fairly quiescent, but Hitler's repudiation of the Versailles Treaty meant that significant rearmament was impossible if Britain was to honor its war debt. Repayments to the United States ceased during 1934 and left an outstanding balance of $4.368 billion from Britain that was never repaid.[16] It was a decision that did little to improve shaky Anglo-American relations and would make American assistance harder to obtain in 1939–40. Relations remained cool until the Anglo-American Trade Agreement of 1938 demonstrated that Britain and the United States had finally recognized the need for a broad display of solidarity against the dictators in the wake of the Munich Crisis.[17] Furthermore, the rapidly accelerating defense costs opened up an enormous balance-of-payments problem, because most raw materials for war production had to be imported by sea. This was £18 million in 1936 but an astronomical £250 million in 1939.[18] Having to accept the need to rearm was particularly unpalatable to Neville Chamberlain and his supporters, signaling, as it did, the end of his cherished plans for much-needed social reforms. As chancellor it had been Chamberlain who determined that the Defence Requirements Sub Committee of the Committee of Imperial Defence (CID) rearmament recommendations of 1934 could not be met in full and that the largest share of the funding should go to air rearmament. Under this amended scheme, the RAF was to be increased by 50 percent of its present strength, a reflection of the growing fear of air attacks.[19]

Defense spending fluctuated only slightly until the mid-1930s when the total defense supply spending jumped from £102,990,000 in 1932–33 to £254,406,000 in 1938–39, an increase of approximately 147 percent. Against this overall increase, the proportion specifically allocated to the RAF out of taxation began a modest climb from approximately 17 percent in 1932–33 to nearly 29 percent in 1938–39—nearly a third of the total supply spending.[20] This was set to increase still further given the post-Munich decision to expand Fighter Command by a further 30 percent. By then, Chamberlain was in no doubt as to the nation's precarious military position, having specifically asked for an assessment of Britain's ability to withstand Luftwaffe assault in 1938. The answer was not encouraging.[21]

In these final years of peace, the overall financial position was complicated by the government's difficulty in funding the defense budget out of each year's taxation. Chamberlain's Defence White Papers of 1936 and 1937 outlined substantial increases that were partly met by raising income tax to five shillings in the pound—a heavy increase that he successfully sold to the public through his personal appearance in a newsreel film. The Defence Loans Bill of 1937 was designed to meet the vastly increased defense costs by a program of borrowing over five years. The amounts detailed above were therefore increased from borrowings that would largely deal with non-recurrent costs such as shadow factories, barracks, and stores. In 1937–38, more was allocated from this source to the RAF than to either of the other two services.[22] Therefore the real spending position was more in the RAF's favor than a cursory examination of the figures might suggest, and was a measure of the increasing importance that the government was now placing on air defense. In the fiscal year 1938–39, the RAF spent 35 percent of the defense budget, the army 31.7 percent, and the navy 33.3 percent—meaning that the RAF was, for the first time, the biggest spender of the three armed services.[23]

The Naval Problems

The period prior to 1934 had been difficult for naval procurement because the effects of the economic downturn were devastating in the traditional ship-building heartlands of northeast England and Scotland's Clydeside. This was disastrous for armaments firms seeking defense contracts to remain in business but equally disastrous for the Royal Navy who, since 1909, had heavily relied on firms such as Vickers for their technical development.[24] Vickers, an armaments firm that did manage to stay in the ring, retained immense influence and has been described as being almost a branch of the Admiralty itself—something of a mixed blessing.[25] There had been twenty major shipyards listed in *Jane's Fighting Ships* in 1914, yet by 1939 there were only fourteen. In 1914, Royal dockyards built most major warships, but they "had largely lost this capacity by 1939."[26]

Because of the dismal economic situation and the international pressures to disarm, A. V. Alexander, First Lord of the Admiralty between 1929 and 1931 and political head of the Royal Navy, fought the Admiralty for a reduction in cruiser strength—important for imperial protection. Alexander opposed naval expansion generally and persuaded the Admiralty to accept reductions as part of the negotiations leading to the London Naval Treaty of 1930 between Britain, the United States, Japan, and Italy.[27] When Sir Frederick Field became First Sea Lord in 1930, he faced enormous problems. It was impossible to reverse the earlier decision to restrict the cruiser force to fifty ships, because the original cruiser expansion program planned by Beatty several years before had already been vetoed by Churchill and was certainly not going to be reincarnated by the incoming Labour government. However, Field did plan a workable warship building program, the first five years of which his successor, Admiral Ernle Chatfield, actually carried out.

Field is also credited with primary responsibility for ending the notorious Ten Year Rule in 1932 through his work as a member of the Committee of Imperial Defence, but his handling of fleet discontent in the Invergordon dispute has been much criticized, and colleagues have attacked him for a perceived failure to defend naval interests. The Invergordon Mutiny of 1931 was more of a "pay-strike" than a mutiny. News of the sailors' reaction to harsh pay reductions proposed as part of the national government's program to curb public spending caused panic, but the subsequent run on the London Stock Exchange finally forced Britain off the Gold Standard and by default helped correct national economic policy. The dispute was finally settled with a lower pay cut and without the mass breakdown in discipline that might have been expected, but there is no denying the fact that the Admiralty had handled the matter badly in the initial stages.[28]

The London Naval treaty placed severe limitations on the total tonnage of most categories of naval vessels. In fact, treaty restrictions had hobbled the Royal Navy since the Washington Naval Conferences of 1921–22, when it was forced to scrap new battleship plans and adjust its building program from a Two-Power Standard to a One-Power Standard. Nevertheless, for all these treaty restrictions it remained the largest battle fleet in the world until World War II, and the treaties may have prevented the development of monster British battleships similar to Japan's *Yamato* and *Musashi*. In the event, these warships had very limited utility for the vast resources used in their construction.

As a result of these factors, by 1934 most of the fleet was in need of urgent modernization. Most of the decade also witnessed the retarded development of the Fleet Air Arm (FAA), despite the Admiralty regaining a measure of control in 1924 and the international naval treaties ignoring the number (though not the tonnage) of carriers that could be built.[29] As a consequence, the FAA became short of experienced naval aviators, lacked naval airpower doctrines, and was using aircraft designed to cover too many roles. By the time the FAA was under full Admiralty control in 1939, its aircraft were obsolete. Some analysts such as Paul Kennedy have argued that this neglect led to a strategic failure to develop a fast carrier attack force for use around the globe, but information on this point is scarce.[30] One cannot blame the Air Ministry for all the FAA's problems. As Air Marshal Hugh Dowding pointed out in a public row between himself and Admiral Herbert Richmond, it was the Admiralty that had insisted on "a plurality of roles" and on hybrid types "doomed to inefficiency before pencil was laid to drawing board."[31] In reality, the most fundamental problems were the RAF's priority for strategic bombers and the Admiralty's tendency to stress the naval rather than the aerodynamic design aspects of the aircraft. Looking back, 1931 can now be seen as the nadir of the Royal Navy during the interwar period.

From 1931 up to the end of 1933, the Admiralty's plans had been made on the assumption that the only significant naval power likely to be engaged was the Japanese Empire, and fears of rising German naval power in home waters were at least partly alleviated by the Anglo-German Naval Agreement of 1935, allowing Germany to build up to 35 percent of Royal Navy tonnage. In return, Germany did not build the type of Kreuzerkrieg (cruiser war) fleet during the 1930s that advocates such as Germany's Vice Admiral Hellmuth Heye envisaged as part of a proposed *guerre de course* campaign against the Merchant Navy. While the traditional view of historians supporting the Churchillian view is that the treaty encouraged Hitler and undermined Versailles, Hitler had already declared his intention to renounce the treaty and its restrictions upon German naval rearmament, which were disappointing to the German officer corps and allowed a strategic advantage to the Royal Navy.[32] One important consequence was Hitler specifically forbidding contingency plans for naval action against Great Britain until May 1938.[33] Fears of Italian naval power in the Mediterranean also grew as Mussolini's improving relations with Hitler led toward the establishment of the "unofficial" Rome-Berlin Axis in 1936. Thus, by the mid-1930s the Royal Navy found itself in the unenviable position of having to deal with the prospect of fighting three modern fleets across the globe, all at the same time, with a single-power fleet.

By then the situation in terms of the renovation and augmentation of the fleet was improving even if, in the words of one economic historian, "compared with the Air Force, the rearmament of the Navy did not go either fast or far."[34] While equipment levels had not fallen as far as those of the RAF—meaning there was less theoretical ground to make up—it cost a great deal more to renovate warships. Some 85 percent of naval spending in the five-year program ending March 1939 went to new construction and renovation of naval vessels, but it was still not enough to satisfy the Admiralty. In part, the dissatisfaction arose because the government continued to control naval expenditure long after ceasing to control that of the RAF. Unfortunately, even in 1935, the DRC was still viewing the naval demands in the context of a One-Power Standard. The naval threat was now growing from three directions, but the DRC did not see the naval threat in home waters as immediate or very great. However, the following year the Admiralty pressed its claims with renewed vigor in the light of a rapidly expanding Kriegsmarine and succeeded in making the Two-Power Standard the ruling strategic concept for future planning. A series of ambitious expansion plans followed that, if they had been adopted, would have massively increased the size of the Royal Navy by 1942. For example, capital ships would have increased from fifteen in 1934 to twenty in 1942, with carriers increasing from nine to twenty-two and destroyer flotillas expanding from fifty to eighty-two. In reality such a vast program was beyond the financial capacity of the country and of the shipbuilding industry's capacity to provide within the timescale. The government also made it clear that expansion would still have to be governed by the financial principles underpinning the national rearmament program. What they ended up with was short of the Two-Power Standard the Admiralty wanted. In reality it was an enhanced One-Power Standard more in keeping with the DRC estimates of 1935. After much negotiation in 1938 the naval "ration" was fixed at £410 million over three years, with a further £10.5 million later that year specifically for the construction of small ships. At the end of 1938, about a quarter of the two million tons of effective naval strength was new or modernized. Another 545,000 tons of naval shipping was under construction and 125,000 tons was in the process of refitting and modernization.

Part of the modernization involved fitting RDF (radio direction finding, i.e., radar) to the larger ships for the purpose of early warning against air attack. First tested by the Royal Navy at sea in 1938, radar was not initially employed for gun laying; instead, British cruisers and battleships relied on the Admiralty Fire Control Table (AFCT), an improved version of the computerized fire-control systems used at Jutland in 1916. It should be explained here that fire-control systems had been developed to coordinate the ships' guns to achieve accurate and closely grouped falls of shot at moving targets, often at extremely long ranges. In the event, the accuracy of long-range gunfire with AFCT proved disappointing but was greatly improved when radar-assisted gunfire became more widely available. AFCT would take into account the speed at which the warship was moving and the rolling of the deck, factors that static land-based artillery would not be concerned with. Other complexities AFCT took account of included powder magazine temperature, surface wind velocity, and drift. In all, the naval program was a significant achievement but still short of what the Admiralty deemed necessary for trade protection and the defense of home waters.[35] As a consequence, the fleet remained old compared with those of Germany and Japan.

Much of the credit for the improvements belonged to Admiral Chatfield, who returned to the Admiralty in early 1933 as First Sea Lord and chief of Naval Staff. Later, succeeding Sir Thomas Inskip as minister for coordination of defense, Chatfield remained in the War Cabinet and chaired its Military Coordination Committee in the early phases of the war. The post was "ill-defined," but it replaced the prime minister as the main arbiter for settling interservice arguments over allocation of resources. As nobody else combined such a high degree of professional defense expertise with political status, Chatfield was a threat to Churchill's position when the prime minister found himself in political difficulties in 1942. A critic of Churchill's actions leading to the *Prince of Wales* debacle in 1941, Chatfield was maneuvered out of politics and into obscurity—a shabby and undeserved end to the career of a great sailor/statesman.[36]

Another problem related to the relatively fast expansion program in the late 1930s. Concerned over the recruitment of young ratings, C-in-C Home Fleet Admiral Charles Forbes worried about the tender age of recent recruits noting that in his flagship alone, 374 ratings (out of a complement of 1,360) were less than nineteen years of age. In his reply Admiral John Godfrey, director of naval intelligence, admitted that many active seamen were in this category, noting that 22,000 ordinary seamen and boy seamen had gone into the fleet over three years.[37] It was clearly regarded as an unfortunate necessity given the recent expansion.

Another consequence of the lack of resources in peacetime was the decline of the Naval Intelligence Division (NID). Under Admiral Sir William "Blinker" Reginald Hall in World War I, the NID had been highly successful in the field of cryptographical analysis, one of its more notable achievements being the decryption of the Zimmerman Telegram—a German attempt to entice Mexico into war against the United States and a major factor in the eventual entry of the United States into the conflict. The code-breaking function was later lost to the Foreign Office, forming part of the Government Code and Cypher School (GCCS) at Bletchley Park. With large numbers of naval personnel attached to GCCS, this establishment eventually made a significant contribution to the outcome of World War II. In 1939, the NID still retained responsibility for naval intelligence gathering and collation but was in a poor state, lagging behind its German counterpart B-Dienst. Being an operation of considerable complexity, it could not be quickly resurrected to full efficiency by a sudden injection of cash.[38] As will be seen, this would have deleterious consequences in the early stages of World War II.

Unfortunately, a considerable amount of classified information on British naval airpower was sent to Japan by the British aristocrat William Forbes-Sempill, from his Admiralty desk during the interwar years. Forbes-Sempill had been an early pioneer of carrier aviation and had worked in Japan as part of a military mission when Japan was still regarded as a friendly power. The original decision not to prosecute when his treachery was first discovered in the 1920s was made on the grounds that prosecution would have involved disclosing MI5's monitoring of diplomatic mail to and from the Japanese embassy in London.[39] Churchill was responsible for the later failure to prosecute Forbes-Sempill for continuing to pass information to the Japanese when caught red-handed shortly after the Pearl Harbor attack. The original failure to isolate Forbes-Sempill can only be described as nothing less than an incredible lapse of judgment on the part of the authorities.

All this aside, a navy cannot be judged solely according to what money is spent on maintaining it. As previously mentioned, the interwar Royal Navy came under attacks from the press of the 1920s and 1930s, in particular the Rothermere newspapers, for the supposed reactionary attitudes of the Admiralty that were damaging the development of airpower. Picking up on some of this criticism, a school of military historians typified by Corelli Barnett has laid into the Royal Navy for its reactionary attitudes and an "obsession" with the "lessons" of the Battle of Jutland in 1916.[40] It is claimed that consequences of this obsession included neglecting to take into account the potential of airpower at sea and the overestimation of ASDIC (Anti-Submarine Detection and Investigation Committee) in antisubmarine warfare.

A later school typified by Jon Sumida contradicted much of this criticism, preferring to stress the closeness of the competition between gun and airplane and the difficulties in deciding which of these would gain ascendancy. Here, it might be noted there would be nine battleship-to-battleship gun duels and five carrier-to-carrier engagements during World War II.[41] It was true that as First Sea Lord from 1919 to 1927 Sir David Beatty had spent too much time and energy trying to justify his controversial actions at Jutland—time and energy that could have been put to more constructive use. Furthermore, the Admiralty had been dominated by gunnery officers—for example, First Sea Lord, Admiral of the Fleet Sir Roger Backhouse and the Commander-in-Chief Home Fleet, Admiral of the Fleet Sir Charles Forbes had both been gunnery specialists. This does not mean they were blind to new developments or obsessed with Jutland. It was fully recognized in the late 1930s that developments in carrier design and torpedo bombers now threatened the line-of-battle formation—that is, the formations developed during the era of sail that would usually result in two parallel lines of warships slugging it out with guns in the hope of "crossing the T" of the opposing formation.[42] Divisional tactics, that is to say, the division of the line-ahead into smaller components of up to five ships, were first developed in the 1920s by British naval officers, including Forbes.[43] By 1935, the Tactical School was emphasizing these tactics in recognition of the threat posed by torpedoes launched from enemy destroyers. In 1937, fleet exercises involving torpedo bombing attacks against a seven-ship line-of-battle formation reported heavy damage and disruption. Similar attacks against agile two-ship battle-cruiser formations were observed to be far less effective.[44] Divisional tactics were therefore rightly seen as a partial solution to the problems of air attack.[45] But indications are that senior naval opinion had an unjustified confidence in the ships' antiaircraft system—the High-Angle Control (HAC) Mk II system for fire control. Even so, by late 1939 there was official recognition that "ideal" long- and close-range systems would not become available until 1942–43, and until then the only improvements were likely to "come from practice."[46]

Unfortunately, the *Fighting Instructions* forbade the use of high-speed maneuvering to avoid falling bombs from dive-bombers as it would throw out the HAC system—a rule that would lead to unnecessary losses from air attack in the early stage of the war at sea. By 1939 the angle of gun elevation was increased from 40 to 55 degrees, enough to deal with potential torpedo-bomber attacks but still not enough to deal with other forms of air attack. The Admiralty had become aware of the shortcomings as a result of its peace-keeping and embargo experiences during the Spanish Civil War, but installing a higher angle system on smaller vessels was complicated by the increased downward recoil of the 4.7-inch gun on weaker deck structures.[47] This was a genuine problem but one that has been over-emphasized, since later situations such as at the Battle of Crete (1941), where ships came under simultaneous air attack from several directions, indicated that no contemporary system of fire control was likely to have coped very well. As naval critics have pointed out, a tachometric system similar to that of the U.S. Navy would have been superior, but "the skills and facilities no longer existed in Britain to produce it in any case."[48]

The problems of air attack against warships were considered by a subcommittee of the Committee of Imperial Defence in 1936, chaired by Sir Thomas Inskip, a former attorney general and the first minister for coordination of defense. Inskip originally knew little about defense outside his service in World War I as an officer in naval intelligence and head of the naval law branch in 1918. His reputation has suffered, partly because of a much-quoted criticism that may have been mistakenly attributed to Winston Churchill: "The most cynical appointment since Caligula made his horse a consul."[49] Inskip still recognized humbug when he saw it. Assisted by professional experts Admiral Chatfield and Chief of Air Staff Sir Edward Ellington, he submitted the subcommittee's conclusions to the Cabinet the same year. Two of the contributors were Murray Sueter and Sir Hugh Trenchard. The terms of reference were "to consider the experiments that have taken place or are proposed in connection with the defence against aircraft and the vulnerability from the air of capital ships." All types of bombing methods, including high-level, low-level, dive-bombing, and torpedo bombing, were considered.

There were several recommendations, the first concerning the effects of instantaneously fused bombs on capital ships. These effects were considered small, but the committee called for further experiments to determine the effects on antiaircraft (AA) crews and others stationed in more exposed parts of the ship.[50] The conclusions also tentatively called for closer cooperation between the Admiralty and Air Ministry on the matter of bomb damage to ships, but recorded satisfaction that the Admiralty had taken all proper steps "to ascertain as accurately as possible the amount of damage that may be incurred by aircraft attack."[51] However, the extreme assertions of the air lobbyists with regard to naval vulnerability were dismissed. While Trenchard, Sueter, and Ellington had been careful not to make explicit assertions about navies being "doomed" or that air forces had now superseded their roles, Inskip pointedly commented that these were the logical conclusions of all their arguments.[52] Instead, the necessity for naval power was strongly asserted in the committee's statement that "the day of the capital ship is not over . . . to assume it is, and to cease to build them, would lead to grave risk of disaster."[53]

For all their confidence in the ability of the capital ship to withstand air attack, the committee had acknowledged that "cruisers and light craft" were far more vulnerable. The worst-equipped vessels to meet air attack were undoubtedly the destroyers—the "V & W" and "A to I" classes. A typical armament was four low-angle 4-inch or 4.7-inch guns and two sets of either triple, quadruple or quintuple torpedo tubes—good for engaging shipping but of little use for fending off air attacks.[54] In the event, such situations depended heavily on the skill of the individual gunner. Yet the gun mountings' inability to elevate medium-range cannon (usually 4.7-inch guns) above 55 degrees on the majority of destroyers would also prove a serious disadvantage when faced with dive-bombers attacking from steep angles. However, as part of a group, these destroyers could still make a contribution to the barrage over nearby ships. Fortunately, these vessels were extremely nimble and despite the inadequacy of the weaponry proved able to survive sustained air attacks by simply "dodging."

There was also a serious shortage of the excellent 20-mm Oerlikon and 40-mm Bofors rapid-fire cannon for close-range defense. Unfortunately, these guns had to be imported from abroad, and one disadvantage of the Admiralty's close relationship with Vickers meant having to persist too long with the development of an unsatisfactory rival gun. The Vickers gun was "slow to bear onto the target and slow in rate of fire."[55] The ships' heavy guns were used to throw up intense barrages, and these produced curtains of fire that closely packed bomber formations proved loath to fly through. As Forbes observed after the war, the Royal Navy originally assumed that Germany would rely heavily on the aerial torpedo but used the bomb instead. This meant that destroyer screens were initially spread too far out from the larger ships, but this was soon remedied by bringing the smaller ships in closer so they could shelter under the antiaircraft barrages of the others.[56]

Larger warships also had substantial passive defense characteristics, in terms of the bulged and heavily armored sides designed for protection against torpedoes but which were also useful for defense against the compression effects of near-misses from bombs.[57] All warships also had the ability to maneuver, notwithstanding the official instructions to rely on the inadequate HAC fire-control system rather than the traditional tactic of dodging—a sharp turn to port or starboard as the bomb was seen leaving the aircraft. Nevertheless, warships were encouraged to position themselves in such a manner as to force the dive-bomber to attack in a cross-wind in order to upset its aim and bring all the defending guns to bear. Ultimately, most captains ignored the instructions and continued to dodge.

More difficult to defend is the overestimation of ASDIC. This contributed to the failure of the hunter/killer experiment in the Western Approaches that led to the sinking of the carrier HMS *Courageous* by a U-boat in September 1939, though the main reason was an obsession with offensive action. The internal competition for resources led to the neglect of antisubmarine warfare, and ASDIC trials had been carried out in unrealistically ideal conditions. Nevertheless, one specialist writer has regarded this failure as the "freak application of an otherwise satisfactory system" and a tactical misconception in the early days of the war rather than the failure of pre-war development.[58] But the Admiralty's belief that the U-boat threat, which had brought Britain dangerously close to defeat in 1916–17, was now negated by the improved development of the ASDIC device fitted to antisubmarine (A/S) destroyers, corvettes, and trawlers meant the Royal Navy was only really interested in air support for detecting the surface raiders of the German battle-fleet. The Admiralty then lost interest in the further development of convoying and the use of A/S aircraft, preferring to concentrate on offensive patrols—a policy that would greatly assist the U-boats in the early phase of the war as it took the escorts away from the convoys they were meant to be protecting. ASDIC's essential weakness was an inability to locate a submarine on the surface, and this meant that many lessons from the previous conflict would need to be relearned.[59] It did not help that many of the ships intended to carry ASDIC were inadequate. Eighty-six of the larger, faster trawlers were initially taken for A/S duty, but these and those that followed would prove too slow and too small for effective operations against the U-boat. Even the fifty-six specialist "Flower Class" corvettes ordered shortly before the outbreak of war proved inadequate, required major modifications, and were never fast enough for the job. Surprisingly, the losses to be incurred in the early phase Battle of the Atlantic never revolved around the efficiency of the escort, because the great majority of ships that were sunk by submarine in late 1939 were sailing outside the convoy system. The escorts nevertheless provided a deterrent against submarine attack on convoys, and when these escorts became scarce owing to anti-invasion duties and an ill-judged resumption of the offensive in 1940, merchant ship losses rose alarmingly.[60]

Another problem likely to have had disastrous consequences was the failure to plan for a large-scale magnetic mine assault. As Churchill described in *The Gathering Storm*, German magnetic mines—a few of which were air-dropped but most of which were laid by destroyers and U-boats near harbor entrances—threatened to paralyze British seaborne trade. "Every day hundreds of ships went in and out of British harbours, and our survival depended on their movement."[61] Although an Admiralty committee examined aspects of magnetic-firing devices in 1936, very little work was done on magnetic mines. Shipping losses in September and October 1939 attributable to mines was 56,000 tons, but in November the recovery of an air-dropped magnetic mine allowed an opportunity to develop countermeasures from studying the device. In the meantime the cruiser *Belfast* and battleship *Nelson* were damaged and two destroyers lost, with other naval vessels damaged. Fortunately, effective degaussing techniques—systems of demagnetizing ships with electric cable and sweeping mines, with low-flying aircraft carrying electro-magnetic coils—were soon developed. But festooning ships with miles of cable was expensive, and a simpler system of wiping was introduced for the mass of smaller ships. By placing an electrified cable alongside the ship's hull, it was found that a few months' immunity could be given. Sweeping methods also improved, and during early 1940 Type LL sweepers began to have significant success. These small ships dragged long lengths of electrically charged cable through the water and proved able to detonate the mines at safe distances astern. By the end of 1939, Churchill could tell the prime minister that the magnetic mine threat was under control, but losses from this cause remained high up until March 1940.[62] Luckily, the Germans failed to mass produce the magnetic mine at an early stage. By deploying them in small quantities at the beginning of the war, the Germans allowed their enemy an opportunity to develop countermeasures before British ports could be overwhelmed by a mass deployment.[63]

But it was the response to the perceived technological advantages enjoyed by foreign navies that proved the Royal Navy was a tough, pragmatic outfit that could adapt to change. Apart from developing the principle of division and subdivision against air and torpedo attacks, a series of revised tactics were developed throughout the interwar period to reflect changing conditions. Believing that the Japanese navy had achieved gunnery proficiency at 30,000 yards, a range well beyond what the British could achieve in 1934, experiments were conducted with short-range actions of 10,000 to 15,000 yards.[64] These were carried out using smokescreens and fighting at night using searchlights and star shells. Night fighting became standard under the Mediterranean Fleet commanders during the 1930s and was subsequently used in victories such as at Cape Matapan in 1941.[65] The Mediterranean Fleet was recognized as the Royal Navy's premier and tactically most influential force, a place where new tactics were continuously developed and the training ground for the successful British naval commanders of World War II.

At the outbreak of war the Kriegsmarine was heavily outnumbered by the Royal Navy in almost every respect. The Plan Z expansion had barely started and was not due for completion until 1947. Plan Z was quickly abandoned and Germany concentrated on those ships close to completion.[66] Fortunately for the British, a major expansion in U-boats was not envisaged in Plan Z. Naval airpower was controlled by the Luftwaffe, and the Kriegsmarine's sole aircraft carrier, the *Graf Zeppelin*, was still under construction and never entered service. The main preoccupation of German and British naval commanders as they prepared to fight was the waging of a commerce war with German pocket battleships trying to break out into the Atlantic to intercept merchant convoys. Here, the British enjoyed a major geographical and strategic advantage in having a large North Sea base with natural defense features for the Home Fleet at Scapa Flow in the Orkneys. This was well positioned for operations against the German North Sea coast and for guarding the so-called Denmark Gate, the straits forming the entrance to the Baltic Sea. Despite having been the base for the British Grand Fleet in 1914–18, the identification of problems by a CID subcommittee in 1936, and the energetic efforts of Admiral Forbes in the late 1930s to improve the harbor defenses, deficiencies were soon brutally exposed.[67] A U-boat penetrated the harbor and successfully torpedoed the old battleship *Royal Oak* within weeks of the declaration of war. The notable interest displayed by Luftwaffe air reconnaissance and lack of air defenses had already caused Forbes to disperse the rest of the fleet to safer waters on Scotland's west coast pending essential improvements to the base. Unfortunately, the new locations were on the wrong side of the country for operations in the North Sea and a major impediment to Home Fleet operations in the first months of World War II—something that could have been avoided with a modicum of foresight and financial planning on the part of the Treasury and the government.

The Air Problems

Despite support from the press and the start of Churchill's agitation in support of a larger air force (and the other services to a much lesser extent), the pre-1934 situation had not been easy for the RAF. Its partisan support may have been the result of aviation becoming so popular by the 1930s that Britain, France, Italy, and the United States were all projecting their cultural ideals upon the aviator/aviatrix.[68] Pioneers such as Alan Cobham, Charles Lindbergh, Amelia Earhart, and Hannah Reitsch were now jostling the traditional maritime heroes of yesteryear for primacy in their respective national pantheons. Having won British hearts and minds with skillful PR and by manipulating fears of an enlarged French air force, the RAF entered the 1930s on a financial shoestring but with its existence secure. The stra-tegic bombing protégés of Trenchard were now firmly in charge at the Air Ministry—men such as Arthur "Bomber" Harris, who had learned their trade by ruthlessly bombing tribesmen and civilians in the British Empire, would become the bomber barons of World War II.

One such protégé was Trenchard's immediate successor as chief of Air Staff, Sir John Maitland Salmond, who held the post until 1933, the year Adolf Hitler became chancellor of Germany. An early prophet of military airpower, Salmond predicted, as early as 1910, the inevitability of air forces engaging in air combat to attain the conditions for unhampered air reconnaissance and that aerial bombing would become a regular military operation. Salmond gained Trenchard's respect in March 1915 following "one particularly har-rowing mission," after which he had written, "Dear Salmond: You are splen-did, but don't do it again; I can't afford to lose you. It is really a magnificent example you set." Despite sharing a belief with Trenchard that no adequate fighter defense was possible against a bomber offensive, Salmond had been air officer commanding the Air Defence of Great Britain organization in 1925, the predecessor of Dowding's Fighter Command.[69] Sharing most of Trenchard's values, but lacking the tactless abrasiveness of his predecessor, his RAF colleagues expected a great deal of him. Unfortunately, only modest progress seems to have been achieved.

As Salmond's biographer rightly pointed out, "The economic situation in 1930 was, if anything, worse than it had been a decade earlier." His view that between the wars "the RAF was always the poor stepsister to the other ser-vices" has been shared by the majority of the air lobby since the RAF came into being.[70] Few advances were made in the field of fighter defense at this time, and the fact that there was only a slim speed differential between fight-ers and bombers until the late 1930s suggested that a fighter defense of the British Isles was ultimately pointless. At this stage, the RAF's frontline fight-ers were still biplanes that would not have been far out of place in the latter stage of World War I. But the main problem faced by Salmond, Ellington, and the other chiefs of staff was the lack of money for defense as a whole. Such a situation was likely to increase competition for the limited resources available, but, the FAA controversy aside, the competition was as much over spending priorities within each service as between the services themselves.

The new political consensus over expanding the air force enabled a series of alphabetical schemes to be submitted for Cabinet approval, but one of these later schemes was so expensive, the amounts threatened to exceed those of the other services combined. In 1937, the chancellor complained, "If that scheme is approved without reservation the Air Ministry will need to expend in the five years to 1942 a sum which exceeds by nearly £350 million the amount which could be allotted to it out of the total five years expenditure of £1,650 millions for all Defence Services (including Civil Defence)."[71] The Munich Crisis of 1938 found the services still unprepared for war, and a future Air Ministry plan including the decision to expand Fighter Command by 30 percent caused the chancellor of the exchequer to warn that it was "so costly as to raise serious doubts whether it can be financed beyond 1939–40 without the greatest danger to the country's stability."[72] Schemes from A to L reflected the continuing dominance of the bomber over the fighter in Air Staff thinking. A ratio of two bombers to one fighter was deemed appropriate until Scheme M amended this to 1.7:1 in the fall of 1938, owing to political intervention. Here it should be remembered that a bomber cost around three times as much as a fighter. A Lancaster heavy bomber cost £50,000 against a Spitfire's £15,000. Therefore the capital cost favoring Bomber Command over Fighter Command was still approaching six to one without even considering the additional costs of larger airfields, larger air crews, and accommodation.[73] By 1939, the officially declared aerial objective was the creation of a balanced air force. Responding to critics, the chancellor claimed the policy of the counteroffensive had not been abandoned but tentatively admitted to a past tendency to overstate the inevitability of the bomber always getting through. Owing to recent technical developments, the strength of the offensive had diminished, but this did not mean completely abandoning the traditional policy of the counteroffensive.[74]

It was therefore the RAF that led service expansion during the second half of the 1930s; indeed, the entire British Shadow Factory Scheme was intended to boost manufacturing capacity for the supply of RAF equipment. This expansion undoubtedly weakened the hold of the RAF over the Fleet Air Arm, because the need to retain some Air Ministry control over its aircraft was no longer a factor in keeping the RAF to a viable size. Salmond's successor as CAS presided over a period of significantly increasing RAF expenditure but received little credit for his efforts. Chief of Air Staff Sir Edward Ellington held the post between 1933 and 1937. "The worst [chief of the Air Staff] we ever had, frightened of politicians," complained Air Chief Marshal Sir Wilfred Freeman.[75] Furious at the RAF's loss of the Fleet Air Arm in 1937, Trenchard told Ellington, "It's been decided over your head, which is well buried in the sand as usual."[76] Some civil servants also believed he was unable to stand up to the other chiefs of staff, and Sir Norman Warren Fisher, head of the Home Civil Service, accused the CAS of leaving Fisher's officials to defend the RAF's position.[77] A distinguished army veteran of World War I, and subsequently the holder of several senior RAF appointments, Ellington was unusually shy, a characteristic that John Terraine argued led to him being misjudged.[78] A highly intelligent man, Ellington seems to have realized that the exaggerated and overblown theories upon which the existence of an independent air arm depended were not necessarily in the national interest, and could not pursue the RAF's interests with the single-minded ferocity that characterized Trenchard's tenure. In 1934, Ellington admitted that "the RAF has to rely on 'pure guess-work' and 'arbitrary assumptions' about every detail of strategic war warfare," ascribing this to a lack of large-scale experience under "modern conditions."[79] Furthermore, it was Ellington who accurately gauged the future potential strength of the Luftwaffe in the Air Council's discussions for Scheme A in 1933, but the Air Council dismissed his findings as "unduly alarmist."[80] Ellington managed to retain the land-based aircraft of Coastal Command, but this was made easier because of the Admiralty's relative lack of interest in using aircraft for antisubmarine work and its over-confidence in the capability of ASDIC.

Ellington's alleged culpability aside, the situation would have been more satisfactory for his colleagues had it not been for Inskip. It was Inskip who made the Air Ministry relinquish its control of the FAA to the Admiralty and who modified aircraft production priority from strategic bombers to fighters—a decision that probably saved Fighter Command from complete extinction in the Battle of Britain. It is part of RAF folklore that Inskip was responsible for Bomber Command's many problems in the early phase of World War II, but the fault lay with the Air Ministry's neglect of technical development as much as the lack of money. Inskip inevitably had to work with the energetic Secretary of State for Air Philip Cunliffe Lister—Lord Swinton—but was able to win his arguments on naval aviation because Inskip had Chamberlain's support. However, criticism of the Air Ministry over British air defenses from press and Parliament mounted in the spring of 1938 as international tensions over Czechoslovakia began to grow. Swinton worked hard to overcome the neglect of nearly two decades, establishing a good relationship with the Air Ministry's scientists and firmly backing the development of RDF, but the constant carping forced Chamberlain to defend him in the Commons on a number of occasions. Unfortunately, as a member of the House of Lords, Swinton could not be held accountable to the House of Commons, and the situation led to his resignation in May 1938—a severe loss to British airpower at a time of unprecedented technological change and air expansion.[81]

By 1939, and aware there was still much ground to be made up, the chancellor announced an increased provision in the estimates, totaling £5 million, specifically for research and development, drawing attention to vast numbers of scientists outside the Air Ministry working on these subjects.[82]

This was good news but all rather late in the day. As discussed in the previous chapters, this technical neglect was rooted in the pursuance of imperial air policing and the attitudes of Lord Trenchard. Much of the available cash had gone on duplicating buildings for exclusive RAF use. Trenchard wanted separate facilities from the army and navy because of his perceived need to build an "air spirit" for the RAF. Typical of this technical neglect and indifference to the needs of the other services was the failure to build an adequate bomb. The RAF decided in the 1930s that no bomb heavier than 500 pounds would be needed, although a 1,200-lb bomb existed experimentally as early as 1918.[83] This was tragic given Bomber Command's gallant but costly raid on the German naval base at Wilhelmshaven in September 1939, where small bombs struck German warships but did little damage. It was not simply a matter of size but the construction of casings, sensitivity of fillings, and timing/reliability of fuses.

Yet it would be wrong to lay the entire blame for the defects of anti-shipping weaponry on the Air Ministry. The Admiralty had only itself to blame for specifying the ineffective 100-lb bomb as the type chiefly required for use against submarines, and it was soon realized after the commencement of hostilities that the other types available, including the 250-lb and the 500-lb, would have to explode in very close proximity to a pressure (submarine) hull to do serious damage. Unfortunately, the direct hits and near misses required for success would be hard to obtain because proper bombsights were lacking. Such an omission is hard to understand given that it had already been discovered in 1917 that the best type of bomb against submarines was the 300-lb HE (total weight 520 lbs), fitted with either an impact fuse or delay fuse timed to detonate at 40 feet below the surface—but this was forgotten or ignored. It has been said that "in no area of RAF armament was avoidable weakness so patent as in anti-submarine weaponry." Not until 1940 was there any recognition that the best weapon against submarines was the depth charge, but the air-dropped version was unsuitable for night use because it could only be dropped at heights up to 300 feet, carrying a high risk of the aircraft hitting the water.[84] The Air Ministry also shared responsibility with the War Office for the neglect of the army's close air support. Despite Wing Commander Trafford Leigh-Mallory's enthusiasm for developing tank and aircraft cooperation between the wars, very little seems to have been achieved, partly because the Air Ministry's focus remained on strategic bombing and the War Office apparently had no interest in the employment of airpower.[85]

Increased funding toward the end of the decade enabled the RAF to replace most of its biplane fighters with far superior monoplane eight-gun fighters. At the time of Munich, Chamberlain was told it would be another year before these would be ready in significant numbers—although in the case of the famous Supermarine Spitfire, it had been a close run thing as to whether enough Spitfires would become available to fight in the air campaigns of the Battle of Britain.[86] The Air Ministry was let down by the industrialist William Morris, First Viscount Nuffield, who spent £7 million on a new factory at Castle Bromwich and by March 1940 had still to produce a single aircraft.[87] In the event, the brunt of the air fighting was borne by the capable but less-exalted Hawker Hurricane. Yet, if private enterprise had let the Air Ministry down in terms of Spitfire production, the fact that there were any fast monoplane fighters at all had more to do with the efforts of aviation entrepreneurs than the dead hand of the Air Ministry. Sure enough, it was Air Marshal Sir Hugh Dowding's idea to use the British monoplane success in the Schneider Trophy races of 1931, but the concept was not energetically pursued by the Air Ministry. In fact, its design specification F.7/30 called for a biplane, and the later F.5/34 specification was only written after Vickers and Hawker had begun to develop the Spitfire and Hurricane. Given Squadron Leader Ralph Sorley's enthusiastic early support for the Spitfire, there may have been a degree of collaboration by the time F.5/34 was written. Be that as it may, there is some truth in the complaint of one writer who caustically pointed out that the object of design specifications is for the users to dictate what the manufacturers will produce, not the other way around.[88] Both aircraft went on to achieve iconic fame in the Battle of Britain campaigns, but even the historian for Vickers complained that "the Spitfire never acquired any sanctity in the eyes of the Air Staff."[89]

With this in mind it might be supposed that the Air Ministry, with its undoubted enthusiasm and energy for the bomber concept, would have given strong leadership and positive input into the design and development of the more famous British bombers of World War II. Not a bit of it. The Air Ministry specification for a "general purpose aircraft" (but intended for a new bomber series) G.4/31 was tendered for by Vickers using Barnes Wallis' robust geodetic designs for a monoplane and a biplane, hoping the Air Ministry would choose the former. Probably because of the geodetic association with the now discredited airship concept, the Air Ministry regarded both geodetic designs with suspicion and after many delays demonstrated its short-sighted attitude by choosing the inferior biplane. Disappointed, Vickers still went ahead with a monoplane prototype at its own expense. Despite the monoplane prototype being clearly demonstrated to the Air Ministry as outperforming the biplane version (in production as the Wellesley by 1935), the Air Ministry took a lot of convincing before issuing a further specification, B.9/32. The Wellington first flew in June 1936 and exceeded the B.9/32

specification in terms of bomb load and range by a factor of two—a sad indictment of the Air Ministry's underestimation of technological potential. If the
Wellington had not been accepted shortly afterward, Bomber Command
was unlikely to have had any decent medium bombers in the early phase of
World War II. Even less foresight was shown in the development of the De
Havilland Mosquito light day bomber, given that the Air Ministry had not
even issued a requirement for it. The Mosquito was ready for production at
the outbreak of war but even then was delayed by several months owing to
an ill-conceived Air Ministry attempt to impose a gun turret, something that
would have fatally undermined the whole fast bomber concept by reducing
its speed. Not until July 1941, with the shortcomings of Bomber Command
already painfully illustrated, was the Mosquito finally accepted into its now
famous role as a fast bomber without defensive armament.[90] Finally, the Avro
Lancaster heavy bomber had its roots in Vickers' 1933 concept of a super-
geodetic night bomber that on its own could maintain the destructive power
of a whole squadron of Wellingtons. It was rejected because the policy was
then for day bombers. This was changed in 1936, but the machine that finally
emerged from the Air Ministry/Ministry of Aircraft Production's tendering
process in 1941 owed its existence to the determination of A. V. Roe's designers to go it alone after the official refusal to supply the small quantity of light
alloys needed to build the Lancaster prototype.[91]

Dowding, head of Fighter Command from 1936, had been tipped as
Ellington's successor as CAS the following year. However, it has been alleged
that Trenchard's continuing influence and Dowding's unpopular pro-fighter
views caused him to be passed over in favor of Cyril Newall, another of
Trenchard's disciples.[92] Be that as it may, like his predecessor, Newall demonstrated that he could be flexible and realistic when necessary. This was
shown by his actions in the early part of World War II in favor of preserving
part of the fighter force from certain destruction in the Battle of France, and
in allowing Bomber Command to be used tactically in the event of a German
invasion of Britain.[93] His achievements did not save him from intrigue by
colleagues and a barrage of criticism for alleged weak leadership. Newall,
along with the rest of the Air Staff, has to bear some blame for the relative
neglect of fighter defense in favor of the bomber at this time. Official production priorities may have altered under Inskip, but it is clear that the subject
of bombing continued to consume the Air Staff's energy and enthusiasm.
Despite this, excessive bureaucracy and a general failure to appreciate the
importance of scientific research inhibited progress. Late in the day and with
the Battle of Britain about to commence, the supply and design of aircraft
were finally taken away from the Air Ministry in 1940 and placed in the hands

of a new Ministry of Aircraft Production. The subsequent emphasis on fighters and medium bombers at the expense of the heavy bomber program was fiercely resisted by Trenchard and the bomber school, notwithstanding the irrelevance of such a program at the time in which a Nazi invasion was imminently expected.

Fortunately, Dowding possessed powers of foresight and technical appreciation that so many of his colleagues seemed to lack. His work in developing the fast eight-gun monoplane fighter and the radar chains known as Chain Home (CH) and Chain Home Low (CHL) is well known. The adoption of radar (known as radio direction finding or RDF in 1940) as a priority had been recommended to the Air Ministry by the Aeronautical Research Committee in 1935, and Dowding deserves special credit for supporting the Bawdsey scientists during a period of test failures during 1936–37 and in recognizing the potential of an early warning system that could act as a force multiplier.[94] The point of an efficient early warning system in this sense was that it could reduce the number of fighters that would have to remain airborne at any one time. Consequently, fighters could be concentrated at a geographical point where incoming raiders were expected to arrive. Utilizing the air defense system of control rooms and communications networks bequeathed to him under the former Air Defence of Great Britain (ADGB) organization, Dowding combined RDF stations with ground observers of the Royal Observer Corps, and with improved telecommunications enabled better filtering and faster dissemination of information crucial to the defense. A system of acoustic mirrors had been tried as an experimental early warning device in the 1920s and early 1930s, but the results were disappointing and the advent of RDF put a stop to further development. Unfortunately, the systems Chain Home and Chain Home Low existed with serious limitations in 1940 and did not demonstrate their true worth until the so-called Baedeker Blitz of 1942. This was because CH and CHL stations had only been completed on the east and south coasts and all these stations faced out to sea. It meant the system had to rely on ground observers with field glasses, inclinometers, and field telephones to report the movements of enemy aircraft once they had crossed the coast, and while their assistance was valuable, they were ineffective in conditions of poor visibility. A second inland chain remedied this deficiency but did not become operational until after the air campaigns of the Battle of Britain and the Blitz. As with any new technological system there were many teething problems to be ironed out, some of which might have been resolved had Dowding gained adequate cooperation from Bomber Command to test his system. With the war nearly a year old the majority of RDF stations were still not properly calibrated (and would remain so until long after the Battle of Britain), meaning they could not read the height of attacking formations with any great accuracy, and CHL could not read height at all.[95]

The scramble to put the system into operation and the relatively low priority given to Fighter Command for resources meant that the sector control rooms, telephone lines, and most of the other equipment were in vulnerable above-ground locations rather than in underground bunkers where they should have been located—this would later prove to be an Achilles' heel.[96] Another serious problem lay in the inability of many RDF operators and mechanics to operate the equipment effectively—a consequence of poor recruitment, training, and inadequate resources within the training schools, all of which were consequences of having to compete for resources with Bomber Command.[97] Problems within the training organization also affected the training of fighter pilots. While training was reasonably thorough in the years prior to 1939, the organization proved incapable of expanding efficiently to meet the demands of war. A major problem in the years prior to the Battle of Britain was also the training syllabus, which had been subordinated to the demands of Hendon Empire Air Day—resulting in an undue focus on close-formation flying and unwieldy tactics that were not officially revised until after the Battle of Britain.

By the outbreak of war, these tactics had already been discredited by the German Condor Legion in the Spanish Civil War of 1936–39. In Spain, Luftwaffe pilots such as Adolf Galland flew loose "finger-four" formations that enabled all the pilots within the formation to scan the sky for enemy aircraft. Basic RAF formations—typically the "vic," a closely packed "v" of three or more aircraft followed by a "weaver"—only allowed the weaving rear pilot to keep watch for the enemy. All of these tactics were laid down in the *RAF Manual of Air Tactics* and included six Fighting Area Attacks, each designed for specific situations. These stately pieces of aerial choreography assumed passive postures by enemy bombers who never fired back, took evasive action or possessed fighter escorts, and were roundly condemned by fighter aces such as Johnnie Johnson, Hubert Allen, and Tom Neil.[98] Nevertheless, the Fighter Command training organization stuck with these discredited tactics up to and including the Battle of Britain.

In common with their colleagues in the RDF chain, inadequate facilities handicapped pilot training, especially in the field of gunnery. These included a shortage of towing aircraft, spare parts, and short practice ranges.[99] But as many pilots would discover the hard way, the official range at which they were supposed to open fire was far too long. An RAF officer had been to France in April 1939 for the purposes of interviewing exiled former Spanish

Republican pilots and set out conclusions for the benefit of the Air Ministry's Air Fighting Committee. They "noted" that German pilots were very skillful, that the Me.109's cannon were very destructive, and that back armor was essential. Most important, they noted the important lesson that German fighters closed in to a short range—200 meters (219 yards) for machine-gun fire, though cannon was used at longer ranges. The committee's minutes recorded that it was "unwise to base any definitive conclusions on this report, as the conditions of air warfare in Spain were unlikely to prevail in a general war."[100] How these conditions might differ from Spain was not made clear, and consequently an opportunity to benefit from the experience of others was wasted, presumably because of an unstated belief that foreigners had nothing to teach the RAF about air combat. If correct, this would have been consistent with many British upper-class attitudes that deprecated the abilities of foreigners generally. Indeed, such attitudes were not restricted to the upper classes. It was common throughout the 1930s for Westerners to regard Japanese airmen as buck-toothed, near-sighted pilots flying inferior aircraft made of rice paper and bamboo.[101] Such attitudes were quickly dispelled by the harsh reality of war.

Fighter Command's shortcomings, especially in the area of pre-war technical research, would be brutally exposed during the air campaign of the Night Blitz, where the Luftwaffe systematically devastated large tracts of London and several large British cities at the relatively low attrition rate of around 1 percent.[102] Given the problems caused to British home defenses in 1917 and 1918 by a small number of Gotha and Giant bombers described in an earlier chapter, it might be supposed that the difficulty of countering night bombing would have resulted in considerable research on the subject. The Air Ministry had begun to look at these problems in 1936, but Fighter Command would prove unable to prevent the Luftwaffe's night bombing of British cities during 1940–41, while at the same time Bomber Command would prove incapable of delivering a significant payload to targets in Germany until much later in the war.

The politicians of the 1930s inherited tremendous problems in repairing the damage to Britain's armed services incurred by their predecessors in the previous decade, but at least they had done their part in finding the money—albeit late in the day. In March 1939—the month Hitler annexed the Czechoslovakian rump and brought about the end of appeasement—the chancellor lauded the current Air Estimates to the House of Commons, declaring they were the largest in the history of the department. Acknowledging allegations that the Air Ministry has sometimes been regarded as the "Cinderella of the Defence Departments," he asserted "that statement cannot be made today." The £74 million increase in that year, "which has come upon a succession of previous increases, is equal to all of the Defence Estimates for 1913," noting that on the imminent twenty-first anniversary of the RAF, the figures reflected "the country's recognition of the importance of this new arm of the Services, and its determination to make adequate provision for air defence."[103]

Despite having much ground to make up, the RAF's contribution to the balance of power in 1939 was considerable, consisting of 1,750 aircraft added to France's 1,234 and Poland's 500, making 3,484. Against this, Germany could field around 4,210 aircraft, a significant though not overwhelming numerical advantage over the Allies.[104] But the RAF's strength was more impressive on paper than in reality. Greatly increased spending from 1938–39 could not transform it into a highly efficient fighting force in time for the air battles of 1940.

For its part, the Royal Navy entered the war in 1939 as a force to be reckoned with, despite having much ground to make up in terms of new equipment. At the outbreak of war in 1939, most German heavy ships could outrun their British equivalents, but their technical advantages were by no means sufficient to risk engaging the Royal Navy in a large set-piece battle such as had occurred at Jutland in 1916. Now the Royal Navy possessed fifteen capital ships plus six aircraft carriers against Germany's numerically paltry (but newer) five capital ships and no aircraft carrier.[105]

But even the limited picture provided by these basic statistics demonstrates a powerful British air and sea contribution to the forthcoming struggle. The remainder of this book will look at some of these early struggles, in particular those relating to the defense of the United Kingdom in the early phase of World War II.

CHAPTER 7

The Air War: The Battle of Britain

The Battle of Britain was the lot of us, not just the RAF.
> —Group Captain Sir Douglas Bader, CBE, DSO and Bar, DFC
> and Bar, *Heroes of the Skies*

*So whoever won the Battle of Britain, surely the Luftwaffe did not
lose it.*
> —Wing Commander H. R. Allen, DFC, *Who Won the Battle of Britain?*

*[T]his war, from Great Britain's point of view, is being conducted from
now on with their eyes only on one place, and that is the United States.*
> —Ambassador Joseph Kennedy to President Franklin D. Roosevelt,
> 31 July 1940

It is held that before the U.S. Army Air Forces began to make their presence felt in World War II, the "Royal Air Force suffered four resounding defeats—the air campaigns in Norway, France, Greece, and Malaysia—and achieved one decisive victory—the Battle of Britain." The same authors regard the RAF's fighter sweeps over France in 1941–42 as an expensive draw.[1] There is just one problem with this statement. The Battle of Britain air campaigns may have represented a victory of sorts, but in isolation from the Battle *for* Britain—the crucial wider conflict—*it was by no means decisive.* In my opinion, it had more in common with the later fighter sweeps and with only slightly more operational relevance. As three academic historians stated in 2006, "the idea that a small number of young pilots had alone prevented a German invasion is something that historians have long disputed."[2] Despite this, it seems that many Britons, Americans, and Germans continue to accept this aspect of the Battle of Britain. Who can blame them? Even the Luftwaffe ace Heinz Knocke would write in 1941, "In the final analysis it was they [the British fighter pilots] who made the German attack on the British Isles impossible."[3]

For most people, the story usually begins sometime around the end of the Battle of France—or around the evacuation of the British Expeditionary Force from Dunkirk. Dowding, still at the head of Fighter Command, wrote in his dispatch that for him the Battle of Britain began in September 1939, but ultimately settled for 10 July 1940.[4] In reality, the main air fighting campaigns commenced at the *beginning* of the Battle of France on 10 May 1940 and raged more or less continuously until Hitler's invasion of Russia in June 1941. Tactical surprise on the ground was achieved by striking through the weakly guarded Ardennes forest, and the subsequent Wehrmacht success in Belgium, Holland, and France was as surprising to the German High Command as it was to the Allies. The air fighting was largely determined by the ground situation but was savage enough, and both sides suffered heavily. Despite gallant RAF efforts to support the Allied drive to the River Dyle—an ill-fated move that actually played into German hands—the British Expeditionary Force was soon reeling back to the port of Dunkirk, and by 26 May, Operation Dynamo (the Dunkirk Evacuation) was under way. With their airfields quickly overrun or destroyed, flying with little rest, and encountering fierce air opposition from the Luftwaffe, RAF aircrew casualties escalated alarmingly. Bomber Command was pressed to give direct support to the beleaguered ground forces but chose to stick to its pre-war plans of bombing Germany until it became clear that the BEF would have to be evacuated. Concerned about the diversion of fighter aircraft from home defense to assist the continental commitment, Dowding went to see the prime minister on 15 May 1940. Winston Churchill had only succeeded Neville Chamberlain as prime minister a few days earlier and was determined to keep the tottering French in the fight. Dowding's carefully prepared statistical analysis was disregarded, causing him to send his now famous letter warning of "complete and irredeemable defeat" if further resources were sent from home defense to bolster the forces already in France.[5] However, six more squadrons were sent into the fray, but these now had to operate from British bases and only land in France for the purposes of refueling and rearming.

As long lines of weary British and French soldiers waited on the Dunkirk beaches, the Luftwaffe tried unsuccessfully to prevent evacuation. That they failed to do so had as much to do with naval determination as the protection afforded by British and French aircraft. The weather handicapped air operations, and the sand contained the worst effects of the bomb explosions.[6] All the same, losses would undoubtedly have been higher without determined RAF efforts to help. The British air strategy was to use large formations of fighters to provide an air umbrella. Theoretically, smaller units would have provided more or less constant air cover, but it was decided that sending larger formations of two squadrons for just some of the time would be better. This was not what the Admiralty wanted, but the decisions were made by the air officer commanding (AOC) of 11 Group, Sir Keith Park, after consultation with his pilots.[7] There were many desperate air battles, but the Luftwaffe soon learned to wait until the British formations ran low on fuel and turned home before swooping onto the embarkation area. There is still much disagreement about the precise air losses for each side, and in all probability the German losses were higher, but without doubt both air forces suffered heavy losses. Low cloud prevented accurate high-level bombing and also limited the opportunities of the Ju.87 Stuka dive-bombers. Unfortunately, the weather also hid the RAF fighters from the soldiers, who naturally assumed there had been little or no RAF presence. However, there was enough German air activity to cause resentment among the soldiery, leading to some unpleasant scenes between army and RAF personnel later.[8] It therefore seems that Churchill played down the success of the naval evacuation in order to lavish praise upon the pilots and heal the sense of betrayal felt by the soldiery.

Valuable lessons were learned by some pilots; and Adolph "Sailor" Malan's squadron reharmonized its guns at a range of 250 yards. According to one writer, in the fighting over Dunkirk, "more than one squadron learnt to harmonize their guns at 250 yards instead of 400 yards and to forget about textbook tactics."[9] This was important because the official ranges were far too long, especially when engaging German bombers with self-sealing fuel tanks and ever-increasing levels of armored protection. Unfortunately, the change was not widely adopted because no official order to reharmonize the guns was given during the Battle of Britain.[10] "We couldn't shoot for toffee," claimed fighter ace Tom Neil, although his own record of fourteen kills proves he was one of those who could. Neil's later association with operational research led him to understand that "of every hundred bullets fired by us," he said, "ninety-seven missed."[11] Dunkirk marked the end of the RAF's campaign in the Battle of France. It had not achieved "its admittedly vague objectives" during the Battle of France because "it was intended to support a more or less static front, [and] it was totally out of its depth, given the mobile nature of the campaign that developed, for which it was not designed, equipped or organized."[12] At the same time, with an air force that *was* designed, equipped, and organized for this type of campaign, and having ironed out some its teething problems in Poland a few months before, the Germans had achieved an outstanding success.

With the last British soldiers withdrawn from the Continent and the French request for an armistice, Churchill prepared the British for the storm to come by making what is now known as "The Finest Hour" speech. Though now almost exclusively identified with the air campaign, Churchill's spirited review of Britain's defenses made ample reference to all three services.[13] At about the same time, he reviewed the pilot situation with Archibald Sinclair, secretary of state for air. Almost certainly regretting his generosity in putting so many air defense resources into the lost cause of France, the prime minister demanded an explanation for the lack of pilot reserves.[14] Between 10 May and 24 May, nearly two hundred fighter pilots were lost, "a fifth of our most highly trained fighter pilots."[15] A shortage of highly trained and experienced pilots would eventually become the main limiting factor in the air campaigns to come.

Some of the shortages in trained pilots were made up by the Royal Navy. In June, Churchill demanded they supply "fifty trained and half-trained" pilots from their resources.[16] This resulted in a useful supplement of fifty-six naval pilots, who took part in the air battles after they had completed a short period of conversion training. Seven of these were to be killed and two wounded during the battles. Four naval pilots would become Battle of Britain aces, and Richard J. Cork, DSO, DFC, would become the wingman of legendary Douglas Bader, facts rarely acknowledged in anniversary celebrations.[17]

The first (or contact) stage was the so-called Kanalkampf—a series of air fights between Fighter Command and Field Marshal Albert Kesselring's aircraft from Air Fleet II over the English Channel, commencing with air attacks on Dover in late June. The RAF's objective was to protect merchant shipping in the English Channel, but the outcome of the combats was inconclusive. Because of the limitations of the British internal transport infrastructure, it was absolutely necessary for the British to keep coastal shipping moving. As James Holland points out, the coal ships were vital to fuel the power stations and to keep the aircraft factories working. While the Luftwaffe air attacks, in concert with those of the Kriegsmarine's E-boat arm, caused some disruption, and the large ocean-going convoys sailing to and from London were eventually forced to take the long route around Scotland, the Germans failed to bring Channel traffic to a permanent halt. That the colliers and trampers kept moving in the teeth of these ferocious attacks was testament to the heroism of their crews.[18] Yet only a fraction of the shipping lost around the coast between July and 8 August was attributable to air attack. Most of the sixty-seven ships lost at this time were sunk by mines.[19]

The main Luftwaffe offensive had to wait until its squadrons relocated from their operations against the French army into their new bases along the Channel and North Sea coasts. According to Dowding's aide, Robert Wright, Bomber Command was asked to raid these bases but refused to do so.[20] Air attacks on their airfields was, according to Luftwaffe ace Adolf Galland, precisely what his colleagues expected, and they were surprised and relieved when this did not occur.[21] This was because these airfields still had very few air defense and warning systems in place. As Wing Commander Hubert Allen later wrote, Bomber Command's refusal to help him did not mean Dowding could not have gone ahead with the aircraft under his command.[22] Aircraft are relatively fragile machines, and their vulnerability to damage from machine-gun fire strongly suggests that Dowding missed a golden opportunity to damage the Luftwaffe's efforts before the main phase of the Battle of Britain had begun. Whilst such a preemptive strike could not have been without attendant risks, given the fact that RAF intelligence had overestimated the Luftwaffe's strength at nearly twice its real frontline strength (and would go on exaggerating this), it seems remarkable such a blow was not attempted out of sheer desperation.[23]

The Luftwaffe was ready for its main effort (Adlerangriff) by early August, but bad weather delayed this assault until the thirteenth. It got off to a bad start, but the air fighting soon got hotter and reached its peak on the eighteenth, a day usually described as "the hardest day" because of the fierce intensity of the air combats. The Luftwaffe did not specifically target civilians and went for a variety of military targets that did not always directly relate to its declared objective of beating down the Royal Air Force in preparation for an invasion. A major German aim was to draw British fighters into the air where they could be engaged and destroyed by German fighter sweeps. It failed because, wherever possible, the RAF declined to go up after the German fighters, only attempting to engage if the incoming raiders included bombers. Although much damage was incurred, none of it seriously endangered aircraft production, and most writers have accused the Luftwaffe of haphazard targeting and failing to follow up on partially damaged targets. It has thus been represented as a failure to comply with Clausewitz's principle of concentration of force. This was largely down to poor Luftwaffe air intelligence. Whilst the Luftwaffe's air intelligence branch was undeniably poor (British military intelligence was not much better at this time), it is hard to imagine how the Germans might have assessed the damage with much accuracy. Lacking a network of reliable agents (the Abwehr network had quickly been rounded up and induced to return misinformation) on the ground, they were only left with photo reconnaissance from high-flying aircraft, with all the limitations that implied. The Luftwaffe fighter pilots were also frustrated by having to fly close escort to the bombers when they clearly preferred a "free hunt" to clear the sky of British fighters. Understandably, this was difficult for the bomber crews, who preferred to see the reassuring presence of their fighter aircraft. The Luftwaffe commander, Hermann Goering, who had been a successful fighter pilot in 1917–18, backed the bomber crews and unwisely accused his fighter pilots of "cowardice." This was unfair, but having a glittering record of twenty-two confirmed aerial victories and a *Pour le Mérite*, and having once been the commander of the elite Richthofen Jagdgeschwader Nr. I, he clearly considered himself entitled to make such an allegation.

By the next stage—sometimes known as "the critical time"—from 24 August, the Luftwaffe started to get its strategy right, and even experienced RAF pilots such as Malan, Al Deere, Peter Townsend, and Hubert Allen were clearly feeling the strain.[24] As an expedient, Dowding devised a system of rotating squadrons in and out of the main combat area to spread the strain more evenly upon Fighter Command as a whole, but it was found that fresh squadrons rotated into 11 Group suffered more than tired but experienced ones.[25] By contrast, German fighter pilots had little opportunity for relief, and despite their fatigue may have been the better for it. Though sometimes diluted by raids on aircraft factories, the main German objective was now Fighter Command's airfields, but lacking reliable intelligence the Germans often hit airfields of other commands. No matter—it was all grist to the mill as the attacks soon took their toll. Even a successful attack on airfields belonging to the RAF's Training Command must have impacted upon the quality of pilot training, given the shortage of suitable aircraft and facilities available to it. Between 24 August and 11 September, Fighter Command lost 103 pilots killed/missing, with 128 seriously wounded.[26] Out of an establishment of just under 1,000 pilots, Dowding was losing 120 pilots a week—a situation that could not be sustained indefinitely. On the other hand, the RAF's training organization was filling the gaps faster than the Luftwaffe fighter training schools could fill theirs. In the middle of this period, Fighter Command had 1,492 pilots against approximately 735 German fighter pilots, and the RAF mostly maintained a numerical superiority throughout the battles. Contrary to myth, it was "the few versus the very few."[27] However, this numbers game had only limited significance as it was pilot *quality* that counted, and German training was very thorough. In 1940–41, German trainee pilots logged 250 hours total flying time, including approximately 100 hours in the aircraft they would fight in. During the same period, RAF pilots would have approximately 200 hours of training, including perhaps 60 to 75 hours in their operational aircraft.[28] The operational training period—the time allowed for the pilot to familiarize himself with his fighter—had been a month, but during the Battle of Britain the high losses forced it down to a fortnight. Before the war, it had been a year. As Churchill admitted, many pilots trained during the Battle of Britain had their programs cut short, and according to the official narrator, in operational terms a new pilot could enter combat with only 10 hours' solo flying experience and without ever having fired his guns.[29] A contributory factor seems to have been a training bottleneck. An understandable but undue haste in pushing trainees out from basic flight training in Service Flying Training Schools (SFTS) into Fighter Command Operational Training Units (OTUs) meant that at one stage OTUs were receiving four-fifths of SFTS output, causing 80 to 90 pupils to be turned out at the end of a fortnight "as best they can."[30] As Air Commodore Peter Brothers remarked, "The new boys were the poor chaps who got the chop."[31] Indeed, it is horrifying to think that anyone at the Air Ministry saw any point in sending men so unprepared into battle.

Bombers, though not a major factor in the battle's outcome, sometimes inflicted significant casualties so long as strict formation and disciplined cross-fire was maintained. This happened when a crack unit of nine Heinkel IIIs shot down three Hurricanes on 29 September 1940.[32] Experience would have taught the Hurricanes' flight leader to attack from several directions at once to confuse the enemy gunner's aim. It might also be remembered that even capable pilots fell victim to German air gunners. The gunner of a "vulnerable" Ju.87 Stuka once unwittingly ruined British propaganda plans to promote the heroic image of American pilots in the RAF to British and American audiences by mortally wounding American volunteer William "Billy" Fiske III during the Adlerangriff.[33] Most German bomber casualties occurred as a result of falling behind their formations with damage or mechanical problems, allowing several British fighters to fall upon them. If the bomber went down, then the system of half-scoring meant that each could claim a half, even if, say, six fighters had engaged. A very persistent myth originating from over-hyped official accounts holds that German bomber formations were often broken up, sometimes by head-on attacks, but more recent research has thrown considerable doubt upon this. Indeed, for a German pilot to break formation when under attack would have been "foolhardy in the extreme."[34]

As more fighter aircraft became available from Hugo Sperrle's Air Fleet III, Luftwaffe fighters began machine-gun strafing attacks on Fighter Command's forward airfields, forcing them to be abandoned. Stacked formations of aircraft with layers of escort fighters barged through the defenses by sheer weight of numbers and reached their targets.[35] High-flying Me.109 fighters performed better at higher altitudes than the Spitfires and Hurricanes struggling up from below, and with the sun at their backs, the Germans held the advantage.[36] Dive-bombing attacks on the RDF stations had occasionally put these establishments out of action for short periods—notably at Ventnor—but the main weak point turned out to be the sector station control rooms located at the sector airfields. As Luftwaffe air intelligence lacked a full appreciation of Dowding's system, including the importance of these control rooms, it was success by default. According to Park, *"Contrary to general belief and official reports* [my emphasis], the enemy's bombing attacks by day did extensive damage to five of our forward aerodromes and also to six of our seven Sector stations." The functions of Kenley and Biggin Hill were transferred to emergency facilities, which could not handle the normal operation of three squadrons per sector. Park wrote that the damage incurred between 28 August and 5 September was seriously felt for a week in the handling of squadrons by day to meet the enemy's massed attacks.[37] Less damage may have been inflicted if the squadrons assigned to protect these bases had been patrolling overhead at the right time—Douglas Bader's Duxford Wing was asked to cover Biggin Hill on 30 August but failed to intercept a Luftwaffe raid that did heavy damage, killed thirty-nine, and injured twenty-six. Tactical dissension within Fighter Command over the so-called "Big Wing" had now become a serious issue and caused two of Dowding's key commanders to be at each other's throats.[38] The tactics developed by Bader of using two or more squadrons operating together had originally been pioneered in the Battle of France with a degree of success. Bader, undoubtedly frustrated with being based in an area of limited combat activity, sought a way of getting into the main fighting and concentrating more fighter resources to assist the struggling 11 Group. His ideas were sold to his AOC, Trafford Leigh-Mallory of 12 Group, who then tried to push them onto Park. Keith Park was unconvinced, but Leigh-Mallory allowed Bader to continue with his experiments at the cost of undermining an agreement that Leigh-Mallory's fighters would guard Park's airfields while 11 Group's fighters did battle with the Luftwaffe. Because of the time taken for Bader's formations to form up, the Luftwaffe bombers had usually reached their targets, meaning important airfields were hit with heavy casualties and damage. Bader blamed the shortcomings of the Chain Home system for not giving enough warning for his fighters to organize, and there was indeed some justification in his complaints.[39]

It needs to be recognized that it only took a very short time for bombers to cross the Channel. It then took approximately twenty minutes for a bomber to reach Croydon, South London, after crossing the coast.[40] The time taken to filter out friendly aircraft from hostiles took anything between one to four minutes. Depending on the state of "readiness," a further six and a half minutes to sixteen and a half minutes was required to get airborne.[41] A Hurricane might then take about seventeen minutes to reach 20,000 feet, all of which strongly underlines the importance of response times.[42] According to Allen's logbook, only on 50 percent of occasions did his squadron fire its guns after the order to scramble was given. This was probably a conservative estimate as another source gives the rate of failed interceptions as 69 percent, hardly surprising given the personnel and calibration problems outlined earlier.[43] Nevertheless, the "Big Wing" notched up the occasional success—the best known being the Duxford Wing's well-known interception of bombers over London on 15 September 1940—now celebrated as Battle of Britain Day. The ensuing dog-fight was visible to watching London crowds, and witnesses recalled fighters getting in each other's way in their eagerness to get at the bombers. However, it was not the most intense day of air fighting, and its real significance is connected with Hitler's need for a face-saving excuse to postpone the invasion because of the naval threats in the English Channel and North Sea—something to be discussed further in the next chapter.

Data sources slightly disagree, but the Luftwaffe lost fifty-six aircraft to the RAF's twenty-six on this day, causing Park to criticize the performance of 11 Group, stating that with so many available targets the actual numbers shot down ought to have matched the inflated figures published in the newspapers.[44] The reasons are not hard to find. Later experience in using large formations over France in 1941 indicated that pilots got in each other's way during a fight, and the number of available radio channels was inadequate for the flight leaders to control their sections. The attrition of experienced fighter pilots by mid-September was another factor. That the Duxford Wing managed to intercept at all had almost everything to do with an unusually high headwind that impeded incoming bomber formations, while driving the British aircraft down from East Anglia.[45] The headwind also reduced the already brief time that Me.109 escort fighters could remain with the bombers. However, the shock of seeing so many British aircraft airborne simultaneously temporarily shook the German bomber crews, who had been told there were only one hundred British fighters left.

From this point the main German bombing effort was at night, though daylight fighter versus fighter combat remained intense for some time to come. While bombers devastated British cities by night, Londoners were kept under pressure by day with fighter-bomber "gadfly" attacks. German fighters would climb to high altitudes above the French coast for a fast diving attack on the capital before the defense could react—though such attacks did little damage and were of negligible military value. The German focus on London had taken place on 7 September before the climactic raid of the fifteenth and is generally portrayed as revenge for the earlier "successful" bombing of Berlin. However, the limited damage inflicted on the German capital suggests there were other reasons for this, in particular a growing realization that the problems surrounding an invasion were insurmountable. The daylight bombing of London marked a new phase in the battle, caused by Luftwaffe air intelligence's erroneous belief that Fighter Command had been virtually wiped out—though it had certainly been severely mauled. The respite enabled a much-needed reorganization of the system that allowed Fighter Command to partially recover from the ordeal of the previous weeks. The new focus also allowed for more effective early warning now that most raids were heading for the capital or other large cities.

Unfortunately, the final phase known as the Blitz revealed the major shortcoming of Fighter Command, and writers have tended to separate this from the Battle of Britain because it is easier to project the "successful" daylight battles in splendid isolation. The case for the daylight victory rests solely on whether or not it prevented invasion, and part of this argument relates to the relative damage inflicted upon each side. Statistically, the period from 10 July to 31 October 1940 shows that the Luftwaffe sustained around 1,765 aircraft losses in exchange for 957 British fighters, giving a ratio favoring the RAF of 1.84:1. But if all commands are included in the calculation, the exchange rate becomes a less impressive 1.46:1, given all the advantages of defense.[46] The picture becomes even less inspiring when it is realized that in addition to these figures, many British aircraft were destroyed on the ground. If British and German personnel losses are compared, the ratio is 4.96:1, a heavy blow to the Luftwaffe given its heavier investment in training. However, if all RAF commands are included—as I believe they should be—the rate drops significantly to 1.78:1, favoring the British.[47]

But it was the shortage of *experienced* pilots that became the true limiting factor. As Dowding recognized, "It was one thing to be a trained pilot, and quite another to be a *combat-ready* fighter pilot."[48] Efforts were naturally made to bring the trainees up to standard by finishing off their training with squadrons in backstop areas, but this was a poor substitute for actual combat experience. Most German fighter pilots had significant combat experience, in some cases from serving in the Spanish Civil War. Fighter Command was saved from extinction by the reluctant inclusion of pilots trained in foreign air forces, who already had some combat experience.

The comparative success of these foreign-born and -trained airmen certainly throws doubt upon the efficiency of RAF training, despite the difficulty in obtaining definitive data. The leading Battle of Britain ace was Sergeant Joseph Frantisek of Czechoslovakia at seventeen victories, and the second-highest scorer was Flying Officer W. Urbanowicz of Poland at fifteen. Incredibly, the Polish 303 Squadron had shot down three times the average RAF score but only sustained one-third of its casualty rate, suggesting the results were achieved by something other than bull-headed recklessness.[49] All of this is remarkable considering European-born airmen only made up 275 out of 2,936 RAF participants.[50]

At this point it is worth reflecting a little on what makes a good fighter pilot. It has been alleged that there is no such thing as an "average pilot" in terms of victory scoring. In World War II, only 5 percent of pilots shot down five or more aircraft, the remaining 95 percent mostly serving to provide victims for the talented elite.[51] The exact qualities required to be an ace (a pilot with five or more kills) seem to defy analysis, and the air fighting in the Battle of Britain tends to bear this out. Only seventeen RAF pilots notched up more than ten kills during this period. Most pilots in the Battle of Britain never shot down a whole aircraft—only 15 percent claimed to do so—contrasting with around 50 percent of all pilots throughout the war as a whole.[52] What marked out the foreign-trained airmen was, firstly, their exceptionally strong motivation. Many had undergone great hardships to leave their homelands and fight with the British. Secondly, having for the most part trained and fought in poorly armed biplanes, they already had some experience and were used to boring in at point-blank ranges—a great advantage when engaging heavily defended bombers with the increasingly ineffective Browning 0.303-inch machine-gun configurations of the Spitfire and Hurricane. A third possibility was their indifference to RAF discipline and general disregard for inappropriate RAF tactics. Dashing at the enemy without pausing to think about the consequences strongly indicated that the "Boelcke Dicta" of World War I was as relevant to the fighter pilot of 1940 as his predecessor of 1916. Of course, the RAF pilot training would greatly improve by 1943 as the Luftwaffe went into terminal decline, but there was little sign of this in 1940. After it was all over, Dowding summed up the RAF situation neatly. Contradicting an Air Ministry assertion that Fighter Command was stronger at the end of the fighting than the beginning—which numerically it was—he wrote that whatever the paper return showed, the situation toward the end was "extremely critical" and most squadrons were "fit only for operations against unescorted bombers."[53] This was a devastating indictment. For its part, the Luftwaffe had lost a large number of aircrew trained to a more exacting pre-war standard, but it still managed to achieve further victories in Greece, Yugoslavia, and Russia, with the RAF enduring further setbacks across the globe before the tide of war turned in 1942–43.

With or without the foreign participants in the RAF and irrespective of aircraft statistics, it might still be argued that the mere continuing existence of Fighter Command represented a formidable obstacle to German invasion. Yet it is hard to imagine how rifle-caliber 0.303 bullets from Hurricanes and Spitfires might sink troop barges weighing anything between two hundred and six hundred tons with steel or thick wooden hulls. They were, after all, originally constructed to hold heavy cargo.[54] In fact, these bullets were becoming progressively more ineffective against relatively fragile bombers, never mind shipping. The argument might then progress to Fighter Command's essential protection for British bombers, which could then destroy the barges at sea. However, even slow-moving barges provide small and difficult to hit targets for high-level bombers, and because the German invasion plans meant the invasion barges would cross the Channel in darkness, the difficulties of navigation, identification, and bomb aiming became much greater. Furthermore, the melee of British and German vessels that would have ensued, either during the crossing or off the beaches during the morning, would have posed considerable friendly-fire problems for the attacking aircraft of both sides. In fact, Bomber Command had only limited success against static shipping in harbor, and moving targets would have been even more difficult for the bomb-aimers.[55]Another problem was the lack of suitable bombs for use against heavy warships, and this will be discussed in more detail in the next chapter. It therefore becomes clear that whatever the importance of the Battle of Britain daylight air campaign to future British participation in the war, it had very little operational relevance to preventing an invasion.

In some respects the Adlerangriff phase had been almost a private war waged between two combative air forces. Furthermore, the Night Blitz had nothing to do with invasion. The Luftwaffe itself had seen no conclusive evidence from the Spanish Civil War experience that the terror-bombing aspects of Douhet's theory worked, especially if the population had received adequate civil defense training and shelters.[56] This didn't mean that Goering's thinking was necessarily in line with his own service, and the Blitz was an attempt to put this aspect of Douhet's theory into practice. Neither did it mean that "terror-bombing" was deployed for its own sake with British civilians as the principal targets of the bomb-aimers. Indeed, until the British attempts to bomb Berlin in September, Hitler had expressly forbidden the targeting of British civilians. The idea was to destroy morale with the bombing of ports and food stocks, but inevitably the dense concentrations of working-class housing around these areas and the limitations of bombing accuracy meant that areas such as London's East End would be hit disproportionally hard.[57]

With the invasion now unlikely to go ahead, there was little option anyway but to make the attempt in order to force Britain into negotiation. Almost by default, the Luftwaffe had become a tactical air force but with a strategic capacity. It lacked the heavier bomb loads that could have been provided by four-engine bombers, and though heavier bombardments would have increased the misery for city-dwellers, there is no reason to think civilian morale would have broken under heavier bombardment. German morale did not crack during their ordeals over the next few years, despite enduring far heavier bombardment than the British. That British morale endured might be put down to a number of factors. Firstly, bad as it was, the bombing was nowhere near as devastating as the interwar prophets of airpower had forecast. Secondly, even when the victims had lost their houses and possessions, the continuing need to earn a living meant workers still turned up for work in the morning and kept society functioning. Thirdly, with censorship in place and legislation designed to stifle dissent, it was difficult for those who wished to stop the war to be heard or take any other action that would have brought down the government. The Emergency Powers (Defence) Act of 1939 gave the government extensive powers to regulate the life of the British people, and on the eve of the Battle of Britain the scope was further extended so as to "permit Regulations to be made by the Government giving them complete control over persons and property." This was, according to the Lord Chancellor, "to call from our people the last ounce of effort of which they are capable."[58] In other words, anyone expressing open criticism of the government or demanding that the war be stopped could find him- or herself imprisoned.

That the German objective of breaking morale was not achieved had little to do with Fighter Command. The main night defense was a barrage from antiaircraft guns, which was probably as dangerous to civilians as to the German airmen, but it gave some positive reassurance to the city-dwellers. This barrage pushed the attacking formations to altitudes above 25,000 feet, beyond which RDF height estimates became wildly inaccurate. But though it made the accurate bombing of "military targets" more difficult, it also made it harder for defending fighters, as shorter response times were needed to allow enough time for the longer climbs required for interception. Dowding came under intense pressure from critics to streamline the filtering procedure, and he was obdurate in resisting this. He correctly recognized that the main problem was bringing night fighters to within visual range of the bombers. Even in daylight, the Chain Home system struggled to provide enough information for the interception to be made, because even experienced pilots have difficulty in distinguishing a dead fly on the windscreen from an aircraft at more than two miles.[59] This becomes even more problematic in the dark and at higher operational altitudes, where there is no frame of reference. The ultimate solution was the use of airborne radar (AI) in night fighters, but in the fall of 1940, AI was still not ready. Sadly, Dowding proved reluctant to implement interim measures to mitigate the effects of the bombing, and he exhibited signs of paranoia over being made to explain aspects of his system. Under pressure, he sent a few black-painted Hurricanes to stumble around in the dark, and this half-hearted response compares unfavorably with the Luftwaffe's reaction to the blinding of their own radar later in the war. In this later campaign, large numbers of patrolling day fighters were sent over German cities at night to intercept RAF bombers. Luftwaffe fighters utilized the glow from burning cities, star shells, flares, and searchlights to light up the skies—a system known as "Wild Boar." While far from a complete solution, it nevertheless continued to impose fairly significant casualties on Bomber Command until a better solution could be worked out.

In marked contrast to the RAF, the Luftwaffe had paid attention to the problems of night bombing. It developed an efficient system of airborne navigation known as Knickebein, using signals from ground transmitters. This made bombing more accurate than would otherwise have been the case. This advantage was soon compromised as British scientists mitigated the worst effects of the bombing by jamming the signals and employing camouflage experts to divert the bomb aimers from their targets. However, considerable damage was still inflicted. Coventry, an industrial center producing some 25 percent of British aircraft, was destroyed on 14 November 1940 using the more advanced X-Gerait, with airborne pathfinders, for the loss of one bomber, which represented a singular demonstration of successful German night-bombing techniques.[60] In fact, given the circumstances of the 1940 air war over England, the Luftwaffe performed as well as might reasonably have been expected. Admittedly vague German aims and objectives prior to 24 August do point to some deficiencies in German air-war doctrine, but a degree of experimentation in this largely unprecedented campaign was to be expected. After all, military doctrines can only be established in the crucible of battle, and whilst there were clear lessons to learn from 1917–18 about the effects of bombing, the air campaigns of 1940 were larger and more complex affairs. James Corum is also one who believes the Luftwaffe's "failure" in these air campaigns "was largely rooted in a deficient air-war doctrine," and convincingly argues the German failure to develop naval airpower.[61] In my view, this failure to develop naval airpower was the only significant failure (doctrinally or otherwise) that the Luftwaffe could have avoided in 1940. Given that Germany was a continental nation and did not seriously regard maritime Britain as a potential enemy until 1938, this failure was far more justifiable than the British neglect of this aspect between the wars.

Coventry also meant the end of Dowding's tenure as C-in-C Fighter Command. Dowding has attracted considerable sympathy among the wider public because of the circumstances of his dismissal and his sympathetic portrayal in the popular feature film *The Battle of Britain* (1969). Whilst he barely put a foot wrong before the Kanalkampf, there were grounds for complaint about his conduct of the air battles. Here, it must be emphasized that his retirement had been deferred several times at the request of the Air Ministry, and at fifty-eight he was old for a field appointment. His careful, methodical, and scientific approach to problems was a great advantage during the period of rapid technological expansion in the last years of peace, but he lacked the tact, imagination, communication skills, and decisiveness that tend to mark the great commander. Indeed, he may have recognized this himself, thus providing some explanation for having left the brunt of the day-to-day fighting to the able Keith Park instead of instigating a more proactive campaign. Furthermore, he was slow to intervene in the dispute between Park and Leigh-Mallory. Even Churchill, once his most ardent supporter, seems to have modified his attitude after a barrage of complaints about Dowding's attitude from the Air Staff and after personally observing Dowding's relationship problems with colleagues through the prime minister's chairmanship of the Night Air Defence Committee.[62] As might be expected, Dowding got on well with the Bawdsey scientists who pioneered RDF, but was contemptuous of government weapons experts and other senior colleagues and made little effort to hide it. Finally, both he and Park were replaced at the end of the main daylight battles by two of his critics—W. Sholto Douglas and Trafford Leigh-Mallory. While Dowding's reputation as a field commander rides sky-high in the public estimation, he was not well regarded by many of his senior colleagues. This cannot be held solely to jealousy or to his unpopular stance on fighter defense. Why the Air Ministry did not allow him to retire as C-in-C in 1939 but retained his services for the next two years as a technical consultant is a mystery. Nevertheless, it would be unfair to place the burden of blame on this brave and honorable man forced to remain in his post at the wrong place and at the wrong time. He deserves his statue at the RAF Chapel, St. Clement Dane, London, if only for his contribution in the years before the Battle of Britain.

Had Hitler been serious about launching such an invasion, he could have gone ahead in September but for the inability of the Luftwaffe (with or without British air opposition) to support a landing, in the sense of sinking significant numbers of British warships while simultaneously degrading coastal defenses. Dowding's objective of keeping Fighter Command intact for a possible invasion has also been criticized by some of his own pilots—notably Bader, P. B. Lucas, and Allen—who clearly preferred the more aggressive strategy of inflicting as much damage upon the Luftwaffe as possible, something that would at least have mitigated the effects of the bombing upon civilians. Given the relative ineffectiveness of British and German naval airpower in the particular circumstances of Operation Sea Lion, there was a lot more to be said for this as a defensive strategy than the one actually adopted. If all of this relegates airpower to the sidelines of the invasion scenario, then it follows that, in operational terms, the importance of sea power in 1940 was absolutely paramount. However, there was one dimension in which airpower was of great significance in the crucial battle for maintaining American logistical support.

Propaganda

Whatever one might be inclined to believe about the operational effectiveness of the Royal Air Force against the Luftwaffe, there can be little doubt that the actions of pilots and aircrew were closely scrutinized in Britain and America because of a belief that the outcome of the air battles would determine whether or not there would be an invasion. After all, this was what Churchill had said the Battle of Britain was going to be about weeks before the Luftwaffe assault began in earnest. His opening sentence in the Battle of Britain chapter of *Their Finest Hour* was: "Our fate now depended upon victory in the air."[63] Nine years earlier and with the air battles at a crescendo he had broadcast to the nation that "this effort of the Germans to secure daylight mastery of the air over England is of course the crux of the whole war . . . we must regard the next week or so as a very important period in our history." Drawing upon past glories, he continued: "It ranks with the days when the Spanish Armada was approaching the Channel."[64] American ambassador Joseph Kennedy was clearly suspicious of British motives, but what the British and American public was unaware of at the time was Churchill's skepticism that an invasion was imminent.[65] He later admitted this in his published memoirs in 1949 when he described the war tensions of September 1940. "[T]he Chiefs of Staff were on the whole of an opinion that invasion was imminent, while I was skeptical and expressed a contrary view." He also told Admiral Forbes during a 1947 naval club function that he "never believed an invasion was possible." This belief is also supported in a diary entry made by Churchill's private secretary, Sir John Colville, during July 1940. Responding to First Sea Lord Admiral Dudley Pound's fear that the enemy might commandeer fast fishing boats from Norway for a surprise invasion, Churchill stated that he did not believe this likely and doubted if "invasion was a serious menace," but thought maintaining fears was useful for keeping everyone "tuned to a high pitch of readiness."[66] About this time, the prime minister sent a memorandum to the commander-in-chief Home Forces, arguing for the release of military resources for the Middle East and justifying the request by stating, "I find it difficult to believe that the South coast is in serious danger at the present time."[67]

Churchill's famous June 1940 speech was influenced by William Philip Simms, foreign editor of the American Scripps-Howard newspaper chain, and reflected concerns that the United States intended to keep out of the war. Simms' suggestions, subsequently adopted, were that Churchill should state that Britain would fight to the end and nothing less than the whole future of civilization was at stake. There is little evidence that the speech made a decisive difference to what the British people thought at the time, but it was a diplomatic intervention that had repercussions well beyond that of trying to influence Churchill's British listeners.[68] Equally keen on obtaining help for the British, American newspaper correspondent Walter Lippmann initially ignored the impending air battles, emphasizing instead the importance of the forthcoming battles at sea. But as the likelihood of the British fleet surrendering to the Axis diminished and air battles intensified, it was only natural that press attention should focus heavily on the action in the skies.[69] This "intense interest" in the exploits of RAF pilots was confirmed by Sir John Slessor, then air attaché to the British Embassy in Washington in December 1940, who worried that Dowding, then due to visit the United States and unused to the American press culture, would find the questions of American reporters intrusive and irritating.[70]

As scientific opinion polling was still a relatively new phenomenon, it is impossible to arrive at any definitive conclusions regarding the effect of the Battle of Britain air campaigns on American opinions, but a small rise in sentiment favoring U.S. entry into the war can be noted from 15 percent, following the reorganization of British strength entering the war on 19 July 1940, to 17 percent in October, following what Dr. George Gallup described as the "aerial blitzkrieg." More significant, on the question as to whether "it was more important to keep out of war ourselves or to help England win even at the risk of war," the pollsters were more enthusiastic, as this had risen fairly steeply from a modest 35 percent choosing "to help England" in May to a more comfortable 60 percent in November. On the more general question of giving more aid for Britain without consideration of attendant risks, support had always been high—88 percent in July and about the same in November.[71] The most that can be claimed from these data is that most

Americans wanted the British to win but were wary of the United States becoming directly involved in the conflict. They were still very interested in the British war effort as a whole. For American newspaper correspondents, the best place to see the action was looking upwards from British towns and cities, especially London and Dover. From the ground they could observe aircraft vapor trails from German bomber formations that sometimes filled the entire sky, see the intercepting British fighters climb from below, and watch the stricken victims fall to Earth. American correspondents, accustomed to higher levels of cooperation from American officials, began complaining to the Ministry of Information (MoI) about a lack of facilities and the constraints of official censorship. The MoI did its best to oblige and sent liaison officers to help the newsmen get their copy. One of these, Barry Cornwell, south-eastern regional press and liaison officer of the MoI, recalled driving Gottfried Keller of the American Press Association around the countryside so that Keller could personally check the victory claims of British airmen by physically counting the German wrecks. After an exhausting day of fence climbing and trudging around fields, Keller conceded defeat.[72] After this, American correspondents seemed content to publish British victory claims without reservation. To British officials, a favorable ratio of Luftwaffe losses to the losses of the RAF came to be seen as the best way to express British prospects "in a simple statistic."[73]

The Foreign Office urged the Air Ministry to help the correspondents because they were believed "to have the most important influence on the help we get from the United States in the near future."[74] Another Foreign Office memorandum written during the height of the air battles was brutally frank in wishing to manipulate American audiences. "Publicity of exploits of individual American pilots in our service, even if exaggerated, would have an excellent effect, and would give the hero-worshipping public of the United States a feeling of identity with the conflict." Unfortunately, the man they chose for the campaign, Pilot Officer William Fiske III from New York, was promptly killed in action, restricting the propaganda opportunities to a trans-Atlantic radio broadcast of his funeral.[75] One of the best known pro-British correspondents was Quentin Reynolds, who narrated the Ministry of Information Crown Film Unit's documentary film *Britain Can Take It* (1940). Reynolds was chosen for the narration because his well-known American voice might conceal the fact that it was an official British production, making the film appear more credible.[76] As the main focus turned to night bombing, correspondents began stalking the burning streets for compelling human-interest stories. *New York Times* reporter Raymond Daniel was undoubtedly typical of many correspondents who ignored the pleas of air raid wardens to take shelter, writing that he "gambled on his luck" rather than trying to seek shelter during raids. There were plenty of stories to be had. These covered a wide range of human interest, from supernatural warnings of dogs howling twenty minutes before the air raid sirens to a gruesome spectacle of human bones strewn around the streets following the devastation of a church graveyard. Most enduring have been inspirational tales of cheery cockneys singing their way through air raids in underground tube stations.[77]

None of this suggests that correspondents falsified or exaggerated the effects of the bombing on civilians. The suffering was real, as was the spirit of defiance. Casualties may have been worsened by a general contempt amongst the population for the falling bombs, with the result that many had become casualties because they ignored the warden's warnings to take cover. But air raid shelter provision was poor, taking shelter in a raid was not compulsory, and many decided it was not worth the discomfort of trying to sleep in a cold, wet shelter in exchange for what seemed a negligibly increased chance of survival. Yet the casualties, though far less than the numbers predicted by airpower theorists, were still high. Between September 1940 and May 1941, deaths amounted to 41,480 people killed, more than half of whom were women and children.[78] Despite a British distaste for "an exhibition of our sufferings from air raids," facilities were given to American broadcasters such as Edward R. Murrow, London chief of the Columbia Radio Network.[79] Murrow was an influential journalist who knew both Franklin D. Roosevelt and his envoys to Churchill, "Wild Bill" Donovan and Harry Hopkins.[80]

More than anyone else, the American film director Frank Capra was responsible for the wider dissemination of the idea that the Battle of Britain was an exclusive air campaign, fought to prevent invasion. Capra had originally been recruited by U.S. Chief of Staff George C. Marshall to make documentary films explaining why the war was being fought and to explain the principles to the wider public.[81] Capra's *Battle of Britain* (1942) film was initially shown to audiences of U.S. servicemen, but at Churchill's instigation was also shown to British cinema audiences. For the British, the film assumed a special significance because it paid them generous compliments and was supported by Churchill's personal introduction, in which he assured the cinemagoer that the film represented "the facts."[82] What the *Battle of Britain* showed clearly was a "Disney-style" animated map showing warships being sunk by bombers over which a narration intoned, "The British knew it would be suicide to use the fleet in the English Channel without control of the air." The narrator went on to describe a German fleet of high-speed barges, when the reality was an improvised armada of towed river-barges expected to make up to three knots in speed. The climactic daylight battle of 15 September

1940 was shown using dramatic newsreel footage of swooping British fighters and an exaggerated claim that 185 enemy aircraft had been shot down. The film acknowledged that when bombs started to fall at night, "the RAF wasn't much help," but used the opportunity to show heroic images of cheerily defiant British cockneys who demonstrated they knew how to "take it." Class unity was projected with a statement that bombs would "fall alike on the East End and Mayfair rich," when in reality bombs fell far more heavily on the East End docks and adjoining areas. Failing to acknowledge the importance of Coventry as a leading munitions and aircraft production center, the film also portrayed the Coventry Blitz as vindictive revenge for the "successful" bombing of Bremen's submarine yards.[83] Capra was naturally assisted by the MoI and his influences included the Air Ministry's official pamphlet *The Battle of Britain* (1941), officially described as "how a thousand anonymous young men had fought one of the decisive battles of the world." Official files also recorded satisfaction that the publishers, His Majesty's Stationery Office, were predicting sales exceeding a million, what would have amounted to "an all time record for such a pamphlet. A similar response was believed to have awaited it in the United States."[84]

The propaganda campaign had evolved into an Anglo-American media construct, a largely uncoordinated effort involving British officials, politicians, media representatives, and American correspondents. Thanks to their efforts, the message reached America that Britain was worth supporting and the country would survive the storm. It can hardly be said the Battle of Britain brought America closer to war, but the air battles made it easier for Roosevelt to push legislation that would keep Britain going with greater logistical help. Determined ongoing efforts to convince Americans that the British were worthy of support were absolutely essential, and what some British figures perceived as an American susceptibility to "hero worship" was clearly exploited. Hero worship also had a place in the British culture but was less evident in Britain, because of a feeling prevalent among the leadership that too much attention on the individual tended to detract from the efforts of the many. Consequently, it was left to the press to celebrate the achievements of the individual without official encouragement, an attitude that contrasted strongly with other countries where men such as Manfred von Richthofen received considerable official PR support and something akin to "pop-star" status. This is not to say that the war at sea had no propaganda value. As we shall see, there were moments when British naval successes would have an important impact at home and abroad, but the American "man in the street" was more likely to readily identify with the airmen than with the sailors. As the British, Germans, and Italians had also done, Americans projected their cultural ideals upon the aviator during the interwar period, and I believe the association of the Royal Navy with British imperial history made it harder for naval heroes to inspire them in the same way.[85] Aviation was still young enough for its participants to be seen as pioneers, and a better figure than the heroic pilot daily battling impossible odds is hard to imagine.

These perceptions aside, the air campaigns cannot be viewed in isolation from events occurring at sea during the same period. The invasion never came, and despite the retention of too many naval units in home waters, the summer of 1940 was to provide plenty of action for the Royal Navy.

CHAPTER 8

The Naval War: The Battle *for* Britain

He told me . . . he, himself [Churchill], had never believed that
invasion was possible! To which I replied to the effect that he had
camouflaged it very well. He then had a go at me. . . . However, we
made it up (he had perhaps had one over the odds).

—Admiral Charles Forbes to
Godfrey Style, 6 February 1947

T he story of the Battle *for* Britain started before the air campaigns over
Britain and before the Battle of France. Hitler's Operation Weser-
Exercise (Weserübung)—the attacks on Denmark and Norway—
commenced in April 1940, and though not planned as any kind of preliminary
to the invasion of Great Britain, the consequences greatly impacted on
Germany's ability to implement the future Operation Sea Lion. The seeds of
Hitler's Scandinavian adventure owed much to his perception that controlling these countries must damage Britain's ability to wage war rather than as
a purely reactive measure to protect the vital supply of iron ore to German
factories. Indeed, the opportunity to erode British war-making potential was
the essence of Grand Admiral Erich Raeder's lobbying in favor of such an
operation. A series of other operations and campaigns followed, all of which
had important consequences for a potential invasion of the British Isles.

The Bombing of Ships in 1940

To properly understand these early campaigns, some appreciation of the
bombing techniques deployed against warships is needed. Originally developed by RFC/RNAS pilots during 1914–18 as an ad hoc improvisation to
improve the poor levels of bombing accuracy, the dive-bombing technique
was neglected by the RAF but further developed by the Fleet Air Arm and

Luftwaffe during the 1930s.[1] The Air Ministry had been advised of the German dive-bomber's potential by Archibald A. Jamieson, chairman of Vickers Ltd. Jamieson passed on the observations of his chief test pilot, who was impressed by flying a German dive-bomber. Jamieson was then told, "Kindly tell your pilots to mind their own bloody business."[2] The effectiveness of dive-bombing was later demonstrated by the Fleet Air Arm when its dive-bombers sank the light cruiser *Königsberg* in harbor on 9 April 1940, a feat the RAF would have been incapable of because it lacked the necessary equipment and training.

Without doubt, the Luftwaffe's most effective ship-destroyer in the spring and summer of 1940 was the Ju.87 Bertha (more commonly known as the Stuka), followed by small numbers of Ju.88 twin-engine level bombers used in a dive-bombing role. However, the Ju.87 used at Norway was the Ju.87R—a sub-type with extended range but with a reduced bomb load.[3] One reason for the relative success of the Ju.87 Stuka against the smaller ships was the inability of their gun mountings to elevate medium guns above 55 degrees, while the Ju.87 could dive vertically. However, the Ju.87 was slow in the dive, and unless attacking an isolated target the aircraft would have to dive a straight course through the intense barrages put up by the larger ships. It was also vulnerable to AA fire during the pull-out at the end of the dive. A high cloud ceiling was also required, preferably between 10,000 feet and 15,000 feet, not something that can be relied upon for very long in the English Channel and North Sea.[4]

Admiralty analysis of successful anti-ship attacks between September 1939 and February 1941 showed that it was the smaller ships that suffered most from dive-bombing attacks, but high-level bombing against ships at 6,000 to 19,000 feet was generally ineffective, with low-level bombing in the region of 1,000 feet only slightly better. Even a near-miss could cause extensive damage as compression exacerbated the explosive effects, especially against the smaller ships where brittle cast-iron machinery was particularly vulnerable.[5] Another factor was the lack of a suitable bomb for use against capital ships—a point made by Grand Admiral Karl Dönitz to the British Naval Intelligence Division after the war.[6] This is not to say that a well-placed Luftwaffe bomb was incapable of sinking such a ship. HMS *Rodney* suffered a close shave during the Norway campaign when an SD 500 (1,102-lb) semi-armor-piercing bomb cracked an armored deck, almost penetrating a cordite handling room. Had the detonator not parted company from the explosive, a disaster would have ensued.[7] Nevertheless, the majority of Luftwaffe bombs were much smaller and of the general purpose high-explosive type. The majority of these were approximately 250 lbs—and hitting a vital spot was difficult. The Ju.87 B2 gradually introduced from mid-1940 could carry a bomb of approximately 2,200 lbs, but the more numerous B1 usually carried a 551-lb bomb, the SC 250/SD 250, plus a few small bombs.[8] A full armor-piercing bomb known as the PC 1000 "Hermann" later became available, but the first use of armor-piercing bombs of this size was not made until January 1941 against the aircraft carrier *Illustrious*. Even then, the Ju.87 pilots were disappointed because despite inflicting heavy damage they still failed to sink her.[9] Admiralty reports also suggest that large bombs in excess of six hundred kilograms (1,323 lbs) were rarely encountered before March 1941 and the majority of German bombs were fused for delay—essential for damaging heavily armored ships.[10] The RAF was even worse equipped. As already noted, the Air Ministry had not previously seen fit to develop bombs above 500 lbs for anti-ship use, and Dowding's correspondence with the Air Ministry in the light of the failed attempt to sink the German fleet at Wilhelmshaven in September 1939 indicated that the Ordnance Board had not fully appreciated the importance of a timed delay fuse—usually one-tenth of a second. Instead, the Board favored an "expert" presumption that bomb blast effects could significantly damage a capital ship and consequently, Dowding wrote, "[W]e now have no means by which we can sink a German battleship."[11] In fact, little was achieved by Bomber and Coastal Command against capital ships until 1944 when very large bombs had been developed. Torpedo bombing did not figure in the Admiralty analysis because the Germans had no decent torpedo bombers, and the only aerial torpedo available to the Luftwaffe was fragile, necessitating long, slow, and straight attacks that even the HAC system could cope with.[12] These, then, were the bombing techniques available to the combatant air forces when Hitler invaded Scandinavia.

Norway

The roots of Weserübung were sown in the minds of Hitler, Raeder, and their naval planners by the retired vice-admiral Wolfgang Wegener in his book *Seestrategie des Weltkrieges* (*The Naval Strategy of the World War*, 1929) described by the British naval attaché as Hitler's "sea gospel." Wegener stressed the importance of a German navy operating from Norway, the Kattegat, and the Atlantic coast of France—crucial for the success of U-boat operations and for breaking the British naval blockade.[13] However, now at war with Britain and having got wind of British plans to mine Norwegian waters (Operation Wilfred), Hitler gambled on using the Kriegsmarine to land forces along the coast of Norway in order to secure the coastal transport routes that took the vital Swedish iron ore to Germany. Disguised as coal ships, the first transports sailed from German ports between 3 April and 7 April, and by 8 April almost the entire Kriegsmarine was off the Norwegian coast.

Despite a number of indications that an invasion was under way, British intelligence misled Commander-in-Chief Home Fleet Sir Charles Forbes about the situation. At this point in the war, British intelligence was in a woeful state. There was no such thing as a German naval Ultra in home waters until August 1941, although a limited amount of information could be gleaned through the use of RDF and the decryption of low-grade keys. A major failing was the inability to collate the available information, which often went to different Whitehall departments.[14] The state of the British Naval Intelligence Division relative to its German counterpart has already been commented upon in previous chapters, and Germans' expertise at code-breaking meant they were reading British naval signals until August 1940, when the code was changed. This and their ability to read the strength and direction of Allied signals meant the Kriegsmarine was well placed to evade Forbes' ships and land its forces on the Norwegian coast. Having received a report from Bomber Command on 7 April about unusual German naval activity, Forbes immediately set sail from Rosyth. Along with Churchill and Pound, Forbes feared a German breakout of surface raiders into the Atlantic and sent his warships scrambling hither and thither in a vain bid to intercept the raiders. Finally realizing a full-scale invasion of Norway was under way, Forbes sent ships to Narvik to prevent a German landing there. Unfortunately, Forbes' dispositions and a successful German diversionary feint to the west gave the Kriegsmarine an almost clear run to its objectives at Narvik, Trondheim, Bergen, Kristiansand, and Oslo. By the time the British 2nd Destroyer Flotilla reached Narvik, the town had already been captured and garrisoned by German troops and the harbor occupied by German destroyers. Fortunately for the British, German airpower had yet to extend this far north. On 10 April, Captain Bernard Warburton-Lee led five destroyers against ten larger and better equipped German vessels, sinking two destroyers and damaging three as well as sinking seven ore-carriers and a supply ship. Two British destroyers were lost, along with Warburton-Lee, who was awarded a posthumous Victorian Cross. A further eight German destroyers and a U-boat were sunk on 13 April at the second Battle of Narvik, meaning that the German destroyer force had now suffered 50 percent losses. This setback alone was going to make it extremely difficult for the Germans to provide a reasonable degree of surface protection for future Sea Lion convoys.[15]

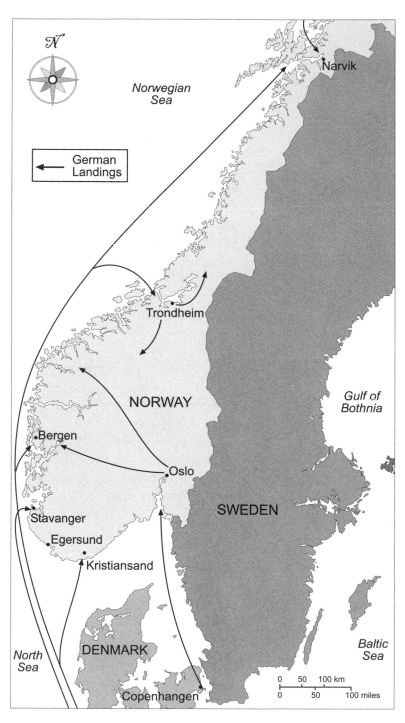

Operation Weserübung, 1940

A Supermarine Spitfire on board the USS *Wasp* in 1942. The version shown is a later variant of the Spitfires used in the Battle of Britain.

A Junkers Ju.87 Stuka in flight. A Blitzkrieg icon, this Luftwaffe dive-bomber could do considerable damage to warships. However, in 1940 Stuka crews lacked the training and bombs necessary to sink naval forces on a large enough scale.

HMS *Hood* was Admiral Sir James Somerville's flagship at the controversial Battle of Mers-el-Kébir in 1940. She was sunk by the *Bismarck* in 1941.

A Fairey Swordfish torpedo bomber on the flight deck. Despite an antiquated appearance, the "Stringbag" was an effective aircraft, playing key roles in the naval battles of 1940–41.

A Fairey Swordfish torpedo bomber, with its wings folded for storage, on board USS *Wasp* in 1942.

Despite the heavy loss of life and graphic scenes of devastation in Coventry (above), and elsewhere, the blitz failed to knock Britain out of the war.

HMS *Dreadnought* was launched in 1906. The *Dreadnought*-class battleships represented cutting-edge naval technology of the pre–World War I era, including steam turbines and a uniform main battery.

A rooftop observer scans the sky for enemy raiders during the Battle of Britain. (*National Archives and Records Administration*)

HMS *Ark Royal* saw service in the Norway campaign and the Mediterranean before falling victim to a U-boat in late 1941.

Commissioned toward the end of World War I, HMS *Argus* had a full-length flight deck that allowed aircraft to take off and land. She later served in a variety of roles throughout World War II. *Argus* is accompanied here by a *Revenge*-class battleship.

Air Chief Marshal Lord Dowding talking with Group Captain D. R. S. Bader and other veteran pilots before a Battle of Britain anniversary fly-past over London, June 1945. *(Imperial War Museum, London)*

Herbert Asquith, prime minister of the Coalition Government until 1916, watches a squadron of airplanes returning to RFC Headquarters at Frévillers. With him (center) is General Hugh Trenchard, later considered the "Father of the RAF" by colleagues. *(Imperial War Museum, London)*

Meanwhile, Forbes prepared to attack the German landing at Bergen with four cruisers and eleven destroyers, an operation that might have resulted in the destruction of the cruiser *Köln* and all of the shipping for the German 69th Division. This, according to James Levy, was the last chance to check the German advance in central Norway.[16] Sadly, the operation was canceled by Churchill and Pound at the last moment in the mistaken belief that the Germans controlled the Bergen shore batteries. The Admiralty then ordered a direct assault on Trondheim (Operation Hammer), an operation that Forbes declared "not feasible" on various grounds. He lacked high-explosive shells, and the plan would involve taking the fleet up a long and narrow fjord to attack entrenched German troops, where air attacks including mines dropped at the entrance could trap the fleet and lead to its destruction.[17] Churchill was furious but finally backed down when the other chiefs of staff supported Forbes' decision, opting instead for pincer movements from the north and south of Trondheim.[18]

Here it should be understood that on 9 April Forbes' ships had been bombed by aircraft from Fliegerkorps X (Air Corps X), a Luftwaffe unit that had received some anti-shipping training. In the space of three hours, a naval force that included three cruisers and the tribal class destroyer HMS *Gurkha* underwent a series of attacks that resulted in the first British destroyer to be sunk by air attack in the war. With hindsight, the sinking was almost certainly avoidable, since *Gurkha* had detached herself from the main formation of ships to improve her arc of fire and deliberately chose to maintain a steady course without weaving.[19] Had she remained under the cruisers' protective barrage the story might well have been different. Despite the shooting down of four aircraft, the incident demonstrated the inadequacy of the HAC system and led to Forbes' decision not to operate the Home Fleet within range of enemy land-based aircraft whenever possible. Nevertheless, there would still be many occasions when warships were forced to accept the risk. The destroyer *Somali* was attacked on 14 April while supporting the Allied landing at Namsos but emerged unscathed. Two liners were bombed at anchor in the same operation but escaped undamaged. But the following day, while bombarding Stavanger airfield, the heavy cruiser *Suffolk* came under Ju.88 dive-bombing attacks for seven hours, sustaining such heavy damage she had to be withdrawn from the fighting. To the horror of Admiral Pound, *Suffolk* returned to Scapa Flow with her quarterdeck awash—an incident that clearly contributed to the sudden amendment of Operation Hammer.[20]

Sixteen Blackburn Skuas from *Ark Royal* and *Glorious* did much better than anyone expected when they attacked *Königsberg* in Bergen Fjord on 10 April 1940. The dive-bombers attacked at 7:20 a.m., taking the ship's crew by surprise and inflicting at least five hits with 100-lb bombs. After three hours, *Königsberg* finally capsized and sank, becoming the first major warship to be sunk by dive-bombers.[21] Lieutenant W. P. "Bill" Lucy, commanding No. 803 NAS (Naval Air Squadron), received the Distinguished Service Order (DSO) for his part in the operation and later had the distinction of becoming the first FAA ace of the war. Lucy would achieve most of his victories flying from carriers off Norway.[22] Given the relatively poor performance of the Skua in the fighter role, Lucy's tally of seven shared victories was a remarkable achievement.[23]

On 27 April, the Allies decided to abandon central Norway, and the evacuations were carried out under intensive air attack. The sloop *Bittern* was sunk by a combination of bombing and torpedo attack, and during the main evacuation on 2–3 May a French destroyer was badly damaged. Shortly afterward, the destroyer *Afridi* was sunk by two bombs. Nevertheless, the troops were rescued despite air attacks by more than fifty aircraft. Operations that had commenced in the Narvik area on 14 April continued for several weeks, and the Allied withdrawal from central Norway meant the Luftwaffe and Royal Navy could now concentrate their efforts in the north. Naval forces successfully landed two Foreign Legion battalions and bombarded Bjerkvik on 13 May, but as the month wore on naval resources were gradually taken away from the Home Fleet.[24] The process escalated after the German attack in the west on 10 May, and by 23 May the decision to abandon Norway was finally taken.

The evacuation from Norway was successfully completed but for a tragic incident on 8 June 1940 that embarrassed the Royal Navy and illustrated the shortcomings of RAF Coastal Command. Forbes' signal to the Admiralty on 15 June 1940 complained bitterly of "[t]he quite unexpected appearance of enemy forces . . . in the far north on 8th June which led to the sinking of the *Glorious*, two destroyers and a liner. . . . The enemy reconnoiter Scapa daily if they consider it necessary." Forbes demanded an improvement in air reconnaissance.[25] The *Glorious*, an aircraft carrier carrying the remainder of the RAF's fighter contingent from Norway and escorted by two destroyers, had raced ahead of the main convoy. This was because the captain was eager to have his air commander court-martialed at Scapa Flow, and it was a mistake by the vice admiral, aircraft carriers, to have approved the request, given the *Glorious'* vulnerability. Unfortunately, the ships ran into the *Scharnhorst* and *Gneisenau*, and despite the destroyers scoring hits on the *Scharnhorst* all the British ships were sunk with heavy loss of life. This was certainly a failure by RAF Coastal Command to sweep the Norwegian Sea for German surface warships. The official historian who was working in the Admiralty at this time blamed an atmosphere of obsessive secrecy covering the final phase of the Norwegian campaign, and while the air officer C-in-C was unofficially told about the evacuation, the information was not communicated downward.[26] On the other hand, with resources amounting to approximately 170 largely obsolete aircraft in home waters operating at the limit of their endurance and in adverse weather conditions, there were clear limits to what could have been expected of Coastal Command.[27] In theory, *Glorious* should have mounted her own air reconnaissance but probably failed to do this on account of a lack of deck space, owing to the number of RAF aircraft on board. A number of tactical and avoidable communication errors also contributed to the disaster.[28]

The land campaign was a humiliating debacle characterized by confusion, inadequate preparation, and feuding between the military commanders. However, it had underlined the need for more efficient combined operations—despite the creation of the chiefs of staff committee between the wars.[29] Sadly, combined operations had been neglected owing to the desire of each service to go its own way. There had also been too much meddling from the Admiralty and by Churchill himself. Churchill later admitted that, with hindsight, the Admiralty controlled Admiral Forbes too closely and should have let him force the passage to Bergen.[30] But a suggestion in the official historian's draft history that Churchill himself tended to take control too often spawned an internal investigation.[31] Churchill was exonerated, but there can be no doubt that Churchill liked to meddle in military affairs and not always to good effect.[32] However, there is plenty of evidence indicating that Pound was a compulsive micromanager and "worrier."[33] This was naturally resented by Forbes, who blamed the constant stream of instructions from Admiralty "warlords" for giving away the positions of his warships at the "slightest provocation."[34] Technically, Pound had the right to intervene, and before the war he had clashed with Forbes over the right of a C-in-C to run his own operation. Unlike the War Office or the Air Ministry, the Admiralty was an operational center as well as a department of state. But it was clearly a matter of degree. Pound has sustained considerable criticism for his conduct of the war—by Field Marshal Alan Brooke for falling asleep at meetings, by others for his tragic decision to disperse convoy PQ-17 later in the war.[35] But Pound was seriously ill, finally dying in 1943 from a brain tumor that had been growing for a long time, and there is no way of telling to what extent this illness compromised his decision-making ability. For all his shortcomings it must be remembered that Pound presided over the Battle of the Atlantic when the advantage permanently turned in favor of the Allies in the spring of 1943.

But the most fundamental question relating to the interaction of air-power and sea power during the Norway campaign was whether warships could now operate effectively against land-based aircraft. Here it must be appreciated that Forbes was one of the last British admirals of the war to go to sea and direct operations from the bridge of his flagship. Having person-ally experienced the effects of German airpower, Forbes initially thought the fleet could not endure these air attacks, but despite his decision not to oper-ate naval forces within range of the Luftwaffe, the continuing need to move troops along the coastline meant having to suffer these attacks anyway. As the HAC system had now proved ineffective, much now depended on the war-ships' passive defense characteristics, the morale of sailors enduring murder-ous fire, and the determination of divisional commanders to keep their forces together for mutual covering fire. Despite official disapproval, warships of all sizes had to "dodge" to survive. At the end of the campaign, Admiral Louis "Turtle" Hamilton wrote to Forbes from the cruiser *Aurora*, reporting that "provided one has sea room and independence of maneuver in a ship of this size, one is most unlikely to be hit." *Aurora* had been subjected to a com-bination of dive-bombing and high-level bombing for thirty-six consecutive hours, and had completed fifty-one days with no leave or let up to the men. He conceded there had been a moment when the men got "a little jumpy over the bombing," particularly those working below deck, but even they reached a point where exhaustion enabled them to sleep through a raid.[36] The captain of the AA cruiser *Curacoa* reported on 5 May 1940 that his Royal Navy Volunteer Reserve ratings manning the guns "were very much shaken after the first bomb salvo of near misses, but after a few encouraging remarks, their behavior was all that could be desired." One problem around the fjords was the mountainous terrain shielding the approach of enemy aircraft, nul-lifying the RDF, and minimizing the available warning time. "In the fjords, everything is to the bomb-aimers' advantage." Despite the problems of short- and medium-range AA fire mentioned, the ship's long-range gunnery proved effective against closely packed formations of high-level bombers, with wit-nesses describing the unnerving effect of shells exploding in front of the for-mations and causing the bombers to accelerate from 200 to 250 knots as soon as they burst.[37] On the flagship *Rodney*, engine room artificer Ron Babb recalled the wail of the Stukas through the engine-room ventilation system, but occupied with a great many jobs he did not feel concerned about it. Some ratings working deep inside the ship were worried about escaping from the ship in an emergency, but he did not recall anyone breaking down over it.[38] In fact, there had been many occasions when the sailors had been subjected to murderous fire, but the Royal Navy had carried out its work without the mass psychological breakdown that might have been expected. This was symptomatic of good morale among the ships' crews, something usually considered the responsibility of each individual captain.

However, despite all the limitations described above, the traditional conclusion drawn from the Norwegian campaign is that it demonstrated the undermining of sea power by airpower. A similar view was promulgated by Group Captain F. W. Winterbotham of the Secret Intelligence Service (SIS) Air Section after the later Battle of Crete.[39] Even some naval officers agreed. Vice-Admiral Sir Arthur Hezlet stressed the reluctance of the Home Fleet to engage Fliegerkorps X off Norway, suggesting that it would have needed to cope with approximately four times the number of aircraft encountered off Crete in a "suicide operation" without air support in the English Channel—an argument that wrongly assumed the Luftwaffe would have four times as many capable ship-destroyers available to them.[40] However, international security expert Olav Riste argued in 1975 that the real lesson of the Norwegian campaign "was not so much the effectiveness of air power against warships, but the speed and mobility which it imposed on and contributed to land warfare." Basil Liddell Hart was not convinced that sea power had been undermined either, but he did accept that the Luftwaffe was the decisive factor in the campaign. Geoff Hewitt points out that "the German view of the campaign was that the Luftwaffe was less effective against naval targets than had been expected." In fact, Hewitt sums it up perfectly by stating, "[T]he Norwegian campaign seems not to have demonstrated that air power had superseded sea power, but rather that air power could influence the outcome of a land campaign in a manner that naval operations could not."[41] It should be remembered that the RAF was only there at all because the Royal Navy had transported its aircraft to Norway. Once operational, they were heavily constrained because they lacked the level of local support provided to FAA aircraft by their carriers. Forced to fly off a frozen lake, one squadron was quickly put out of action by frozen engines and a devastating German attack that destroyed many of its aircraft on the ice. From then on, the only RAF air support in central Norway was from inadequate Blenheim fighter bombers operating at long range from British bases.[42]

The naval balance sheet at the end of the campaign showed that the Kriegsmarine had been decimated, having lost three cruisers, a gunnery training ship, eight U-boats, an E-boat, and ten destroyers, plus a number of support craft. U-boats had proved a great disappointment owing to numerous torpedo failures (caused in part by the strong magnetic fields present in northern waters adversely affecting the magnetic pistol detonators), though they did manage to sink two Allied submarines. By contrast, British submarines had done well, accounting for one cruiser and a gunnery training ship, as well as damaging a battle-cruiser and a pocket battleship.[43] British losses were also heavy but far more sustainable. These were two cruisers, nine destroyers, six submarines, an aircraft carrier, plus various support craft. Bombing represented the main single cause of Allied naval losses, and this method accounted for approximately one-third of the total Allied naval losses.[44]

In the end it all boiled down to attrition. The German naval C-in-C Admiral Raeder later wrote: "The losses it [the Kriegsmarine] suffered in doing its part weighed heavily upon us for the rest of the war."[45] Indeed, Raeder was now down to a small handful of destroyers, and the damage inflicted upon German capital ships was so severe that none would be available for operations in the English Channel that summer. Even Churchill later admitted that after Norway "the German Navy was no factor in the supreme issue of the invasion of Great Britain."[46]

Dunkirk

It was fortunate that the Admiralty had made contingency plans for the emergency evacuation of the BEF from the Continent as far back as October 1939. It was equally fortunate that the officer in charge of Operation Dynamo was a very capable officer who would later be the naval C-in-C of the Allied Naval Expeditionary Force for the D-day landings in 1944. Vice-Admiral Bertram Ramsay was C-in-C Dover in 1940, and for Dynamo, Ramsay would command staff from all three services. Serious planning for the imminent evacuations began on 19 May, and by this time a large number of pleasure craft owners with boats of between thirty and one hundred feet long had already registered with the Admiralty. By the time the evacuations began on 26 May the main harbor at Dunkirk had already sustained heavy damage from the Luftwaffe, but the dispositions of the land forces meant that Dunkirk would have to be the main point of evacuation. By then, only a jetty west of the harbor and a wooden mole five feet wide and 1,400 yards long were usable as embarkation points, and the mole had not been designed for use by large ships. Neither was Dunkirk a good natural harbor as strong tidal currents made it difficult to enter. However, there were approximately sixteen miles of gently sloping beaches that were one mile wide and included numerous sand dunes at the rear that could provide a degree of cover for the troops. The beaches could certainly accommodate large numbers of soldiers, but getting them off the beaches and onto the transports may have proved impossible without the help of "the little ships." These would play an invaluable role shuttling men to the larger ships.

Desperate evacuations had already taken place at Boulogne and Calais, during which a number of British destroyers—including the *Keith*, *Whitshed*, and *Vimy*—supported nine French destroyers in a bombardment of German positions on 23 May. With the order given to evacuate Boulogne, the destroyers, reinforced by *Vimiera*, *Venomous*, *Wild Swan*, and *Venetia*, entered the harbor to embark troops, some of these sustaining heavy attacks from approximately sixty Ju.87s but without effect. Nevertheless, with the ships operating in close proximity to the 2nd Panzer Division, damage from small arms and tanks resulted in ship-board casualties that took the lives of two captains. *Venetia* was also badly damaged by a German-held shore battery. The operation continued in the face of constant air attack into the afternoon of 24 May with the loss of one French destroyer and one damaged by air attack, with another lost to coastal artillery.[47] No further British ships were sunk, but the focus then turned to Calais where intense naval operations continued in the face of heavy air attack until 27 May. One of the German participants was the highly decorated Major Oskar Dinort, commanding Stukageschwader 2 (Immelmann). Leading an attack on shipping off Calais on 25 May, he found the sun's reflection off the sea made visibility difficult but led 3 Stukas into a dive from 12,000 feet onto a destroyer. During this dive, the destroyer made two violent changes of course, causing Dinort to lose sight of his intended victim. His bomb exploded uselessly approximately 300 feet away. The other Stukas also failed to hit the target. From this Dinort concluded that his men needed to acquire more expertise for attacks on warships than had been needed for other types of operations.[48]

By this time the main evacuation from Dunkirk was under way. Ramsay set down three routes to Dover, Z at 39 miles long, Y at 87 miles, and finally X at 55 miles. Z was quickly closed down by German artillery fire, forcing all shipping onto the long and winding Y until X was opened on 30 May following the sweeping of an obstructing French mine field. The loss of route Z inevitably slowed down the evacuation and increased the pressure on everyone involved. The exhausted destroyer crews previously engaged in the demanding Boulogne and Calais actions were then flung back in to the fight, with other destroyers forming the backbone of the main operation. Luftwaffe attacks on British shipping were at their most intense on 29 May and 1 June, placing massive psychological pressure on the sailors. The main German effort was now being made by the Luftwaffe because of Colonel General Gerd von Rundstedt's "stop" order to German land forces on 24 May, a controversial decision resulting from several factors, including the breakneck speed of his panzers outstripping the logistical supply train, a desire to preserve the tanks for a new thrust against the French, the unsuitable waterlogged terrain now being encountered, and the fear induced by Anglo-French spoiling attacks.[49] The order was confirmed by Hitler the same day, probably because Hermann Goering had given assurances that the Luftwaffe alone could finish the job. Goering was prone to the same kind of institutional hubris surrounding many senior commanders in the RAF, and this seems to have clouded his judgment. His subordinate commanders disagreed. The capable Kesselring of Air Fleet II and Wolfram von Richthofen of Fliegerkorps VIII both expressed opinions that the Luftwaffe could not stop the evacuation but were ignored.[50] So it was to prove, and realizing the British were escaping, the panzers resumed the attack on 27 May.

Loading troops from the beaches to the bigger ships was to prove time consuming, and to load a destroyer from the beaches could take 6 hours, even in good weather. To speed up the embarkation, the ferry *Queen of the Channel* successfully berthed at the mole late on 27 May and by doing so demonstrated the practicality of using this facility despite it being subject to a tidal range of up to 16 feet. Soon, up to 16 ships at a time were being moored at both sides of the mole. This helped considerably; for example, between the night of 28–29 May and the end of 29 May, 47,310 troops were embarked, 33,000 of which were taken from the mole. In fact, some 200,000 Anglo-French troops, from a total of 338,000, were embarked from the mole during the operation. Unfortunately, stationary or very slow moving ships waiting around the mole area, some of which were heavily laden, made for relatively easy targets. Fearful of losing the newer destroyers, Pound ordered their withdrawal on 29 May, a decision that threatened to seriously hamper the evacuation, but Ramsay persuaded him to reverse the order on the afternoon of 30 May. That day was very successful, since not only did the newer destroyers return, but the first of the little ships arrived, Route X opened up for the first time, and, most important, the Luftwaffe was grounded by bad weather. The following day was the high point of the operation despite damage from several collisions and groundings, but the navy's efforts resulted in 23,000 men lifted from the beaches and 45,000 from the mole. The Luftwaffe's last major fling took place on 1 June, and despite the RAF carrying out 8 squadron patrols, there were 5 periods when there was no air cover for the fleet or the men at the mole or on the beach. Low antiaircraft ammunition stocks further handicapped the defense as the need for a fast turnaround overrode the time required for replenishment. Thirty-one vessels were sunk and 11 damaged—the hardest day for the naval forces during the whole operation. Operation Dynamo terminated on 4 June, and despite heavy losses, the Royal Navy had pulled off a spectacular feat. From an original Admiralty estimate of evacuating approximately 45,000 men over 2 or 3 days, more than 338,000 had finally been extricated in 10 days—an achievement that also owed a great deal to the fierce resistance of the Anglo-French troops holding the Dunkirk perimeter. More than half had been transported in warships and most of the remainder in ships manned by personnel from the Royal Navy and Merchant Navy. Some 6,000 were brought home by the little ships, including Royal Naval Lifeboat Institution lifeboats, naval motorboats, and war department launches.[51]

One of the little ships was skippered by David Divine, later to become a war correspondent and the well-known defense correspondent for the *Sunday Times*. Divine crossed the English Channel three times to rescue British soldiers but on the final trip was shot in the stomach. He survived and for his exploit received the Distinguished Service Medal. It was Divine who first exposed the myth that the evacuation had been carried out as a mass spontaneous action by the small-boat owners on the south coast. He would also go on to write the screen play for the feature film *Dunkirk* (1958) and may have been the inspiration for the skipper of the motorboat *Vanity*, played by the British film star Bernard Lee.[52]

Sadly, what nobody could do was bring back the BEF's modern heavy equipment—meaning that the British Army was left with ancient and antiquated transport for its subsequent campaigns in the Western Desert.[53] Some 243 Allied vessels of all types had been sunk out of approximately 860 involved. British shipping losses were approximately 56 sunk including 6 destroyers, 2 of which resulted from air attack, with 19 destroyers damaged.[54] Despite the fact that like Norway, much had been to the bomb aimers' advantage, the Luftwaffe had demonstrated its failures to prevent naval operations and inflict crippling losses. Nevertheless, the naval losses sustained at Norway and Dunkirk by air attack caused the Admiralty to urgently investigate the installation of high-angle antiaircraft guns in destroyers. Unfortunately, it would not be until 1942 that substantive improvements to the smaller ships' antiaircraft capability would be carried out.[55]

Other Evacuations

Dunkirk was not the end of difficult naval operations in the face of Luftwaffe air attack during 1940. Churchill had still not given up on providing support for France. On 4 June, there were still around 100,000 troops at various locations in France, and the prime minister was intent on sending further reinforcements. On 7 June, British troops began to arrive in the port of Cherbourg. However, two days later it became necessary to evacuate Le Havre—Operation Cycle—where 11,059 troops were rescued. The evacuation at St. Valery-en-Caux failed because of thick fog, but more than 3,300

Anglo-French troops were lifted from nearby beaches at Veules.[56] On 14 June, the day the German army entered Paris, the remnants of the BEF were instructed to evacuate and the following day the Royal Navy commenced Operation Aerial. Evacuations from Cherbourg and St. Malo were organized by Portsmouth Command, and those from Brest, La Pallice, and St. Nazaire by Plymouth Command.[57] Operation Aerial was complicated by the distances involved—Portsmouth to Cherbourg alone was 73 nautical miles (84 ordinary miles), with the other ports even farther away. This meant having to use large ships, and the worst disaster in British maritime history occurred with the sinking of the troopship RMS *Lancastria* in the Loire estuary, with at least 3,000 lives lost. While air attacks during Aerial had not generally been as intense as those experienced in Dynamo, *Lancastria* had been sunk at anchor by Ju.88 dive-bombers. News of the disaster was suppressed on Churchill's orders, possibly one reason why the incident is still relatively little known. The operation continued until 25 June and rescued nearly 292,000 servicemen and much equipment, including 310 guns, 2,292 vehicles, and 1,800 tons of stores. Altogether, some 550,000 troops, including 365,000 British, had been lifted from all of these operations. One destroyer was lost as the result of a collision with an antiaircraft cruiser.

One final example of unsung operations conducted under air attack was the demolition of enemy harbor installations between May and June 1940 known as Operation XD. Often under intense air attacks, Royal Navy destroyers transported teams of army and navy sappers, including the army's Kent Fortress Royal Engineers (KFRE), to destroy port facilities that might be used for an invasion of the British Isles and to burn their oil stocks.[58] Some two million tons of oil were successfully denied to the Germans, and harbors including Zeebrugge were put out of action until November, with Calais and Boulogne unusable until September. As the operations were hastily improvised and made at short notice, many demolitions took place in the vicinity of advancing German troops, resulting in several exchanges of fire. As a result of these operations, the KFRE became one of the most highly decorated units of the British Army, and the naval personnel alone received two Distinguished Service Orders, two Distinguished Service Crosses, six Distinguished Service Medals, and eleven others mentioned in dispatches.[59] The German Naval Staff was later to report that the extensive damage to these harbors, installations, and adjacent waterways meant they could not be immediately used as invasion ports.[60]

Battle of Mers-el-Kébir

By contrast to the secrecy surrounding XD, Operation Catapult (the Battle of Mers-el-Kébir) was internationally reported, but because of the controversial moral issues surrounding the operation it plays no part in popular mythology. Yet it was one of the most pivotal actions of the war and had considerable ramifications for the potential success of Operation Sea Lion and the wider war. Churchill was convinced that he could not rely on French assurances about keeping the French fleet out of German hands, and that the ships needed to come under British control or be permanently removed from the equation. In a 2005 radio interview featuring naval historians, naval veterans, and a distinguished Battle of Britain air ace, it was rightly stated that German and Italian assurances that French ships would not be used on the side of the Axis could not be relied upon, meaning that decisive action had to be taken. Admiral Pound wrote as early as 7 June that the French fleet had to be sunk. The War Cabinet considered the possibility of giving the French an ultimatum or of sinking the fleet around the 20 June onwards, with Churchill insisting that the ships had to be sunk. This French fleet was "one of the most formidable naval forces around at the time," and it would be extremely alarming if it fell into German hands. Despite Churchill's anguish over the prospect of taking this action, he and Pound were "absolutely resolute" and there was no Cabinet dissent over this at the key meetings. The French fleet was mainly gathered at Alexandria and at the Algerian town of Oran—at Mers-el-Kébir. On 3 July 1940, Admiral James Somerville and Admiral Andrew B. Cunningham gave an ultimatum to the French admirals to join the British, sail to the French West Indies, demilitarize in place, or suffer an attack. The French admiral at Alexandria chose to disarm, but there was no compromise at Mers-el-Kébir. Negotiations failed and Admiral Somerville was under pressure from the Admiralty to resolve the situation. In the harbor "were some of France's most modern warships; tarpaulins covered their decks and their boilers were cold." Captain Val Bailey, watching from the destroyer *Active*, saw two ships explode and admitted to having "an exciting time, [but was] far too busy to bother about what the moral issue was, which wasn't an issue to me." Naval historian Andrew Lambert stated that even in 1940 it was a contentious action. Churchill was attacked over the conduct of the action in the House of Commons but said history would have to judge. Churchill's actions were necessary even if implementing them was "unpleasant," and he was prepared to break the rules. Mers-el-Kébir has been forgotten because "we can explain our success in resisting invasion in 1940 much more conveniently by stressing the things we did face to face with the Germans." Therefore the Battle of Britain is "perfect." But if the only way the Germans could invade Britain was across the Channel by sea, then removing the French fleet makes the task simpler for the Royal Navy, since it allows more ships to be released from the Mediterranean for the defense of the United Kingdom. This played a critical part. Predictably, none of this impressed Air Commodore Brothers, who doggedly asserted that in the event of an attempted invasion of Great Britain the Royal Navy could have done little. Dive-bombers would have sunk the fleet in the Channel, the enemy had overwhelming numbers, and the fact that the fleet was kept out of the way at Scapa Flow, plus the later sinking of the *Prince of Wales* by Japanese aircraft in 1941, clinched the argument.[61]

Gentlemanly forbearance, the iconic status of "The Few," and Air Commodore Brothers' age and distinguished war record seem to have prevented the naval historians from directly attacking his views. However, the severe limitations of dive-bombing as explained earlier should have been vigorously pointed out. Neither was it true that the navy had been kept out of the way at Scapa Flow, and as will be made clear, very substantial and active naval forces were operating in and near the English Channel during the invasion crisis. The sinking off Malaya of the battleship *Prince of Wales* and the battle-cruiser *Repulse* in 1941 also raises a common misconception of airpower, because the Japanese airmen responsible for sinking these ships had—unlike their German counterparts—received proper training in anti-shipping techniques and possessed both effective torpedoes and torpedo bombers. Furthermore, the British ships were swamped with attacks by a swarm of eighty-five aircraft, fifty-one of these armed with torpedoes. Both ships suffered some bomb damage, but they were sunk by torpedoes.[62]

The agreement at Alexandria put a battleship, four light cruisers, and some smaller ships beyond German reach without bloodshed. However, the Battle of Mers-el-Kébir was short, bloody, and one-sided. The engagement commenced with a ten-minute bombardment upon the French ships followed by attacks from FAA aircraft. The battleship *Bretagne* exploded, the battle-cruiser *Dunkerque* ran aground, and the *Provence* was beached. FAA aircraft torpedoed the battle-cruiser *Strasbourg*, but it eventually escaped to Toulon, where the deaths of 1,297 French seamen during the bombardment are still recorded on a memorial plaque. Actions elsewhere also degraded the fighting potential of the French fleet. The battleship *Richelieu* was seriously damaged by an FAA torpedo bomber at Dakar, and an aircraft carrier and two light cruisers were immobilized in the French West Indies. French ships at Portsmouth and Plymouth were seized without incident, except in the case of the submarine *Surcouf* where a British and a French seaman were killed in a violent scuffle. Nevertheless, the ease with which some of these ships were impounded supported Churchill's contention that the operation showed how easily the Germans could have seized warships in any ports they controlled.[63] The British actions in 1940 may not have completely destroyed the French fleet, but they certainly crippled it. For now, the operation at Mers-el-Kébir dashed a real possibility of the Kriegsmarine recovering its naval strength at the expense of the French.

Val Bailey's relative disregard for the moral aspects of Catapult were undoubtedly shared by many colleagues at the scene, but Somerville, with the burden of operational responsibility falling on his shoulders, was deeply affected by this assault on a former ally.[64] Germany ruthlessly exploited this attack in its widely distributed wartime picture magazine *Signal*, using dramatic photographs of blazing ships and tragic rows of coffins, further describing the affair as "this unparalleled, monstrous British crime against an ally of yesterday."[65] The battle and subsequent Nazi exploitation soured Anglo-French relations, but in the longer term the political aspects turned out to be as crucial for survival as the maintenance of naval superiority. Churchill's Conservative party colleagues had behaved coolly to him since the ousting of Chamberlain, but they were now cheering, and the battle may have prevented his ousting by one of his many rivals. It also helped convince America that Britain was determined to fight on.[66] This was essential because American newspapers had been questioning whether it was worth sending war material to Britain if this was going to be surrendered to the Axis along with the British fleet.[67] Sadly, the difficult circumstances surrounding Catapult have made the operation as awkward for the Royal Navy as the later bombing of Dresden would become for the RAF, and in my view, this has led to an underestimation of its real significance.

Battle of the Atlantic

Another manifestation of the British determination demonstrated by the Mers-el-Kébir affair was increased collaboration between the Royal Navy and the United States Navy, essential for the future prosecution of the Battle of the Atlantic. Within months, negotiations resulted in the controversial destroyers-for-bases agreement providing fifty old American destroyers in exchange for Caribbean bases, something the Germans clearly recognized as an event increasing future Anglo-American collaboration.[68] They were right. Shortly afterward, President Franklin D. Roosevelt extended the Pan-American Security Zone, providing escorts for shipping within this area and broadcasting U-boat sightings. Such actions, though contrary to U.S. neutrality, considerably eased the passage of British-bound merchant shipping. These events paved the way for further aid, including the Lend-Lease Bill of March 1941, and provided some relief for the hard-pressed British maritime forces.[69]

Indeed, the Battle of the Atlantic would become the longest running and most important campaign for the British in the entire war since virtually everything required for continuing participation had to come by sea. This campaign naturally assumed a greater importance to Hitler and the German naval staff as Operation Sea Lion's prospects receded with the approach of winter. In the longer term, it was essential for the British to gain a decisive ascendancy over the U-boat, for this was the only way that conditions essential for the liberation of Europe in 1944 could ever be achieved. This decisive ascendancy was not achieved until the summer of 1943, and while the U-boats never came close to knocking Britain out of the war, the second half of 1940 saw the handful of operational U-boats achieving results out of all proportion to their numbers.

The successful conclusion of Weserübung in June and the acquisition of new bases in the captured territories meant that Dönitz's U-boat arm could now concentrate on attacking British trade and, with the advantage of B-Dienst decrypts revealing convoy routing, began to develop wolf-pack tactics. This involved up to six U-boats fanning out in a wide skirmish line in front of the convoy's path. Sightings would be relayed to U-boat HQ and the convoy shadowed until a sufficiently large pack could be assembled for a night attack. The pack would then attack simultaneously, some evading the escorts and attacking from the middle of the convoy. These wolf-pack tactics sometimes proved very effective against heavily escorted convoys. This occurred when HX-79, sailing from Halifax (Canada) to Liverpool, was ambushed off Rockall in late 1940, losing a quarter of its ships.[70]

U-boat captains such as Gunther Prien (U-47), Otto Kretschmer (U-99), and Joachim Schepke (U-100) sank 270 Allied ships during the period they called "The Happy Time." Shipping losses escalated from 273,219 gross tons in May 1940 to 442,634 in September 1940, and it is reasonable to assume these would have been much higher had the U-boats been more numerous and in possession of reliable torpedoes.[71] I have calculated that approximately 1,730 merchant seamen were lost during the period of the Battle of Britain, a figure that might reasonably be compared with Fighter Command's 537 lost between 10 July and 31 October 1940.[72] One reason for the German success was Dönitz's efficient centralized command and control system, with similarities to Fighter Command's system of aircraft control. However, where the British relied on RDF and visual observation from the Royal Observer Corps for their eyes, the Germans utilized long-range aircraft and the U-boat's own visual/audio observation. The problem with periscopes was their narrow field of vision and inability to operate in rough conditions, but even when surfaced the lookout in the conning tower was close to the water, meaning that enemy shipping was likely to see them first in daylight. Aircraft were easily the best means of locating convoys at longer distances. There were no German aircraft designed specifically for this role and those used were mainly Focke Wulf Fw200 Condor civilian airliner conversions. Yet despite structural problems and the small number of Condors, they were to prove alarmingly effective both in the reconnaissance role and for direct attacks on shipping. The Condor's main advantage was a standard range of two thousand miles. This proved enough to fly from Brittany, skirt around the British Isles, and land in Norway. But inadequate numbers of Condors and Germany's own interservice rivalries meant their aerial reconnaissance was less effective than it might have been.[73]

This phase ended in the spring of 1941 as Western Approaches Command moved from Plymouth to Liverpool and closer to the center of operations. Airborne radar became more widespread and more effective tactics had evolved. Post-war analysis showed that convoying was the crucial factor in the Battle of the Atlantic. A nine-knot convoy suffered half the loss rate of one traveling at seven knots, and once air cover became more widespread it was noticed that aircraft cover for eight hours in twenty-four further reduced losses by two-thirds.[74] But by November 1940, the increasing recognition of maintaining adequate air cover for convoys led to an attempt to seize Coastal Command from the RAF, whose leaders remained fixated on the bombing of Germany. As previously discussed, both the Admiralty and Air Ministry shared much of the responsibility for the deficiencies of the maritime air forces between the wars. Now the demands of the Battle of Britain and the Blitz meant that priority for the latest electronic aids was going to Fighter and Bomber Commands, and dissatisfaction with Coastal Command's performance led to Minister for Aircraft Production Max Aitken, 1st Baron Beaverbrook, pushing for immediate change. Surprisingly, Churchill supported this proposal, noting that the RAF had now grown to such an extent it was now less likely that it would suffer "serious consequences" if this reorganization took place. In the end, and after meetings by the service departments at which the matter was thoroughly discussed, the Defence Committee decided to keep the status quo because of the dislocation it would cause in wartime.[75]

Nevertheless, although the Air Ministry retained the means of production, operational control of Coastal Command's land-based aircraft would pass to the Royal Navy in April 1941. Ultimately, many improvements in Coastal Command's performance later in the war can be traced back to the appointment of Patrick Blackett, who led notable academics in the power-ful and successful Operational Research Section (ORS) to scrutinize every scientific aspect of Coastal Command's work. Among its many achievements, the Operational Research Section discovered that the spacing of depth charges at 36 feet when dropped from aircraft was relatively ineffective, and a stick spacing of 100 feet was widely adopted.[76] Sadly, the main benefit of ORS research would not be fully realized until 1943. What finally decided the Battle of the Atlantic in 1943 were the improved convoying techniques; the enormous American effort to produce more merchant ships than the U-boats could sink; the closing of the Mid-Atlantic Air Gap between Nova Scotia and Iceland by land- and carrier-based aircraft; and convergence in new technologies enabling the use of more effective tactics.

The Battle of the Barges and the Fateful Decision

No summary of naval operations during 1940 can really be complete without acknowledging the role played by British warships operating from Plymouth, Portsmouth, the Nore, and Harwich against German invasion harbors. To the chagrin of its commander, the Home Fleet had been forced by the Admiralty to adopt a passive role hanging around in northern bases at Rosyth and Scapa Flow—"the fleet in being."[77] It might therefore be thought that British naval forces took absolutely no action against these targets during the summer of 1940. One comparatively recent Battle of Britain author has written: "In the absence of any Royal Navy offensive operations, it was left to Bomber Command to frustrate German invasion plans in what the bomber boys had christened the 'Battle of the Barges.'"[78] Yet, naval anti-invasion missions were regularly conducted from local bases. These warships were not part of the Home Fleet as such, though Forbes was forced to lend a great many destroy-ers to the Channel flotillas during the summer of 1940. Offensive opera-tions were conducted at night and in a variety of weather conditions, when aircraft could play no significant role. These naval raids also demonstrated that the British were not content to keep their ships in harbor as a mere passive deterrent. Night after night, the Royal Navy broke into ports such as Dunkirk, Boulogne, Calais, and Ostend, raking lines of invasion barges with point-blank gunfire. Anti-invasion patrols were mounted throughout the summer but were particularly evident during September, the month an invasion was most likely to have been mounted. For example, on the night of 8–9 September, three motor torpedo boats broke into Ostend and torpedoed two vessels. That night, another force of cruisers and destroyers entered Calais and escaped recognition, while another group bombarded Boulogne's inner harbor. On the night of 10–11 September, three Harwich destroyers engaged barges and tugs off Ostend and were fired upon by shore batteries, but no British ship suffered damage. On the night of 13–14 September, three destroyers damaged several German trawlers.[79] In fact, the nights of 12–13 and 13–14 September witnessed "almost a tour of inspection" covering virtually the entire enemy coast of Holland, Belgium, and northern France, shelling or torpedoing shipping and port installations with impunity. "It was an awesome demonstration that, at night at least, the Germans did not yet have command of the Channel, for all the attackers got back to England unharmed."[80] As already mentioned, the German plan was to cross at night, so their failure to control the Channel at night by airpower or any other means automatically doomed the operation to failure.

The attrition of barges amounted to the equivalent of the German reserves, and Hitler's decisions to partly disperse the fleet on 19 September 1940 and then to postpone operations on 12 October 1940 was partly determined by the fact that these losses could not be allowed to deteriorate beyond this point.[81] Whether Bomber Command or the Royal Navy were responsible for the majority of these losses has proved hard to determine. In an attempt to show that the Luftwaffe had not gained air superiority, Raeder stressed the raids of English bombers upon the barges in his reports to Hitler but, having always been lukewarm in his support for Sea Lion, was inclined to overemphasize the importance of the air dimension.[82] Churchill for one was unconvinced by the evidence presented to him of a successful bombing raid upon an invasion port. Commenting on one aerial photograph, he wrote, "What struck me about these photographs was the apparent inability of the bombers to hit these very large masses of barges." He continued, "I should have thought that sticks of explosive bombs thrown along these oblongs would have wrought havoc, and it is very disappointing to see that they have all remained intact and in order with just a few damaged at the entrance."[83]

At the conference on 14 September, Hitler ostensibly postponed the decision to launch Sea Lion, because air supremacy had not been obtained. It was reviewed again on 17 September, and now the bomber losses of 15 September were enough to provide him with an excuse to postpone the decision until 19 September. Finally, a limited dispersal of the invasion barges was ordered, a clear admission that for now an invasion of the British Isles was off the agenda. But even before these events, the Naval War Staff had already noted Hitler's hesitations and lack of enthusiasm for Sea Lion, and was concerned that the Luftwaffe was doing nothing to focus its attacks upon the British naval forces and their installations in the crossing area. Their report of 10 September stated: "[T]he Fuehrer looks upon a large-scale attack upon London as possibly being decisive, and because a systematic and long drawn-out bombardment of London might produce an attitude in the enemy which will make the Sea Lion operation completely unnecessary." It concluded, "The Naval War Staff therefore does not consider it necessary to make such a demand."[84] But according to Admiral Kurt Assmann, the German Naval Staff was skeptical that the operation could succeed, even with a Luftwaffe victory in the air, and hoped it would not have to go through with it. "Not one of the responsible persons was inclined to take a clear-cut stand against the operation . . . ," he wrote. "Yet all felt relieved when, failing to gain air supremacy, they had a valid reason which justified calling off the operation."[85] Having worked to establish the prerequisite of air superiority into the operation, Raeder and his colleagues clung to this as a "get-out clause" and, in my opinion, were predisposed to overemphasize the effect of these raids upon the barge concentrations or indeed any other evidence of failure to gain control of the air.

The Combatant Fleets

Hitler's decision not to go ahead with the resources at his disposal was well founded, as British naval superiority in and near the Channel alone was overwhelming anyway. On 14 September 1940, the force at Plymouth comprised one battleship, two cruisers, and four destroyers. Portsmouth retained one cruiser and twelve destroyers. Two cruisers, sixteen destroyers, and four corvettes lay at Harwich, along with three cruisers and four destroyers in the River Humber. The larger part of the Home Fleet was based at Rosyth, with the remainder at Scapa Flow in order to deal with any breakout by the Kriegsmarine's heavy ships, then still under repair in Norway. All of these reinforcements were capable of arriving in the Channel within forty-eight hours, but the twelve destroyers at Rosyth might have arrived in just twenty-four hours. To these forces should be added the Royal Navy's thirty-five submarines reinforcing the miscellaneous flotilla of small craft, posted to give warning of German coastal movements.[86] The available German warships then amounted to two obsolete battleships, one heavy cruiser (to be used in a diversionary operation), two light cruisers, one training cruiser, eight destroyers, and nine E-boats.[87] Theoretically, a handful of U-boats were available for operations, but they barely figured in the plans for Sea Lion.[88] To compensate for this inferiority in numbers, Admiral Raeder suggested flanking mine barriers, but there were not enough mines to maintain a continuous barrier, and as his colleague, Vice Admiral Friedrich Ruge, later acknowledged, "Mines are not an absolute barrier."[89] Inadequate mine stocks and a pathetically small mine-laying force meant the plan to lay and maintain protective mine barriers at either end of the channel was hopelessly optimistic. Even with stronger mine barriers there was nothing preventing attacking British naval units from forming line-astern and forging through. Even if the leading warship was hit, the way would still be clear for the remaining warships.[90] As mentioned in a previous chapter, it was fortunate for the British that the Germans shot their magnetic mine bolt in 1939, because by the summer of 1940 the British had developed effective countermeasures to this potentially devastating threat.

The brunt of the naval defense was placed upon the destroyer flotillas based at Plymouth, Portsmouth, and the Nore, but if these were overcome it would have been necessary to call upon the heavy ships of the Home Fleet at Rosyth and Scapa Flow. Those who doubt the ability of British capital ships to survive the relatively constricted waters of the English Channel in daylight should perhaps consider the success of a German heavy cruiser and 2 *Scharnhorst*-class battle-cruisers sailing from Brest to Germany later in the war. When these powerful ships ran the Channel gauntlet in daylight during February 1942, attacks were made by British destroyers, bombers, and Fleet Air Arm torpedo-bombers, together with bombardments from coastal artillery. Bomber Command had launched 242 aircraft but owing to a variety of circumstances only 39 were able to engage. All the German ships successfully made the journey back to Germany.[91]

In fact, naval strength in home waters during the summer of 1940 was, if anything, too strong. Churchill and the Admiralty had over-insured in the Channel, the likely reasons being a desire to impress foreign newspaper correspondents with a visible military presence and Admiral Pound's propensity toward caution. Even Admiral Forbes, ironically a man once considered by Admiral Chatfield as being a little over-cautious, was highly critical of this policy, arguing that many resources, especially the antisubmarine trawlers and destroyers, should be redeployed to the deteriorating Battle of the Atlantic, where the U-boats were enjoying their first "Happy Time."[92] It was on 31 October, a date when the immediate invasion threat had already passed, that Churchill asked Forbes for his opinion at a meeting of the War Cabinet. In terms reminiscent of an earlier invasion crisis, Forbes stated, "While we are predominant at sea and until Germany has defeated our fighter forces, invasion by sea is not a practical operation of war."[93] Forbes' reference to the fighter force was doubtless rhetorical as there could be no doubt about British naval dominance in the Channel during the fall of 1940.

So much for the situation in home waters close to and around the British Isles. Yet there was one other area to be fought over during 1940 where longer-term British survival was at stake. Forbes had already told the prime minister back in June and before the commencement of the air battles over England that a German invasion of the British Isles was not a practical operation of war, and therefore "first line troops" should not be withheld for home defense if they were needed elsewhere.[94] No heed of this good advice was taken at the time but judging by his later actions, Churchill was more convinced than he was prepared to let on. The Mediterranean Sea was a theater where land-based airpower was expected to make a decisive difference to naval operations should Benito Mussolini decide to go to war. We must now turn to the actions of the British Fleet Air Arm and the Italian Regia Aeronautica to complete our understanding of how air forces influenced both naval operations and the strategy essential for British survival.

CHAPTER 9

The Vital Mediterranean

*Don't forget, Mr. Churchill, if there is a war, we will have the Italians
on our side this time.*
—Joachim von Ribbentrop, German ambassador

*My dear Ambassador, [in response] it's only fair. We had them
last time.*
—Winston S. Churchill, 1937, *Churchill by Himself*

For many Britons, the idea that the wartime Italian armed services were ever a force to be reckoned with evokes scorn. Newsreel films show-ing long lines of Italian prisoners of war being marched off to prison camps by small numbers of smiling British "Tommies," together with images of antiquated tanks and biplane fighters, have all given the unavoidable impression that Italy's participation in World War II was simply a handicap to the German war effort. The Regia Aeronautica's unsuccessful participa-tion in the Battle of Britain air campaigns has reinforced this view, providing as it did propaganda opportunities for showing bullet-ridden Italian aircraft wrecks to British cinema audiences. The picture is further embellished by images of uniformed Italian dictator Benito Mussolini's comic-opera postur-ing from the balustrade overlooking the Piazza Venezia. All this has invited widespread ridicule. In truth, the Italian armed forces had many problems, including a traditional Italian "disdain" for military affairs, lack of war pre-paredness, and Mussolini's emasculation of service chiefs by dealing directly with field commanders.[1] The key problem bedeviling the entire Italian war machine was Italy's weak economy, which could not sustain a large military apparatus over an extended period.

Many would be surprised to learn that Italy was one of the most air-minded nations in the world during the interwar years. Indeed, between 1920 and 1926 Italy won three out of six Schneider Trophy seaplane races, costing the lives of five Italian pilots preparing for the races.[2] These competitions would provide inspiration for some of the famous fighter aircraft of World War II, including the American P-51 Mustang, British Spitfire, and Italian Macchi C.202 Folgore. In 1933 and 1934, Italian pilot Francesco Agello twice broke the world speed record over water, the second time achieving an average speed of 440.678 mph, a record that remains unbroken for a piston-engine seaplane.[3] During the 1930s, it was common for any large formation of aircraft to be referred to by RAF pilots as a "Balbo," after Italian air pioneer and architect of the Regia Aeronautica Italo Balbo—a reflection of the international regard in which he was held. Along with Trenchard and Billy Mitchell, the Italian general Giulio Douhet was one of the three principal airpower theorists of the interwar period and certainly the most influential.[4] Douhet's book, *The Command of the Air*, first published in 1921, still remains one of the most cited works on the subject.[5] In 1922, Douhet was head of aviation in Mussolini's government, and the link between aviation and politics both in Italy and Germany would become extremely well developed in the years to come. By 1940, Italy was as air-minded as any other Western nation. But Douhet's influence in favor of developing the strategic bomber with Italy's limited resources was responsible for several failures, including air force leaders refusing cooperation with other services, the failure to develop suitable anti-maritime bombs, and the neglect of torpedo bombing.[6] However, these negative aspects of Italian airpower were not widely appreciated at the time.

It must be conceded that Italy had the least effective armed services of all the major combatant nations during World War II, but it would be wrong to think that all Italian soldiers, sailors, and airmen lacked fighting spirit and were without military skills. Neither would it be correct to assume that a fear of what Mussolini and the Italians might do never seriously impinged upon British planners. Even American newspaper correspondents viewed Mussolini's declaration of war in June 1940 with alarm, and a slump in the American Gallup opinion polls registered a low point in perceptions of British survival prospects.[7] During the early stages of the Battle of Britain air campaigns, influential American columnists were viewing the real Battle of Britain as a forthcoming war at sea around Great Britain and Gibraltar, rather than an exclusive air battle determining the prospects of a Nazi invasion.[8] As we have seen in the previous chapter, the German surface fleet was seriously weakened by mid-1940, but the Regia Marina was still a force to be reckoned with.

Both British and American economic survival was at stake because of the danger to Britain's influence in an area containing so much of the world's crucial oil reserves. If British supremacy at sea was lost, then the last free market outside the Americas would disappear, leaving the United States struggling to compete economically with the totalitarian powers. This would become critical if Axis naval power spread to the Cape Verde Islands and the Caribbean—or so the popular theory went. These American newspaper interpretations were probably exaggerated to support President Roosevelt's pro-British stance.[9] Indeed, Walter Lippmann, an influential correspondent, had several key British contacts, including Philip Kerr, 11th Marquess of Lothian and British ambassador to the United States, and British economist John Maynard Keynes, and was a strong supporter of Roosevelt's policies of helping the British. Subsequent perceptions of the Middle East as a sideshow, footnote, or irrelevance have been bolstered by historians cynical of Churchill's "obsession" with the Mediterranean. This attitude contrasts strongly with a more recent view seeing the Middle East as a pivotal theater in which the Allies could have lost the war even if Hitler could not win there.[10] In fact, this newer school of thought disregards the simplistic "brute force" argument that as more Allied resources were often tied down here, the campaign must have been a net drag on the Allied war effort. There is much to be said for an argument emphasizing the diversion of German resources away from Russia at key moments, the training and preparation given to raw American units for D-day, and the political advantages to the Allied cause of Americans engaging the Germans in battle at the earliest possible moment (Morocco and Algeria, 1942). Possession of the Middle East assumed a new importance when Japan entered the war in December 1941, because it provided a vital communications link between the battlefronts. If Churchill was right to press the continuing importance of the Mediterranean even into 1944, then being driven out of the area four years earlier would have had serious consequences for the continuation of the war. From this, the prospect of engaging the Italian armed forces at such a crucial moment can now be seen as a great opportunity for the British.

The "vital importance" of the Middle East was asserted by the chiefs of staff and the War Cabinet within weeks of war with Germany, and the potential requirement for sending "considerable forces" was recognized should the situation require. No additional forces were then required, but administrative arrangements for the rapid dispatch of further land and air forces were being put in hand should the strategic situation require—in other words, a declaration of war by Italy.[11] In practice, the requirements of the strategic situation meant priority for the European theater, and, later, the anti-invasion requirement for strong land, sea, and air forces to be retained at home meant that few British resources would be spared for the Mediterranean until it became known that Mussolini's declaration of war was imminent. Churchill's decision to send most of Britain's tank force to the Middle East at a time when the Battle of Britain air campaigns were still raging also testifies to the relative importance of the Mediterranean and the fear of losing influence there.[12] With possession of the Gibraltar naval base controlling traffic in and out of the Western Mediterranean and the port of Alexandria adjacent to the Suez Canal in the Eastern Mediterranean, the depleted British fleet could still cling on. In the Central Mediterranean lay the Royal Navy's base at Malta, giving the Royal Navy and British Western Desert Force (the precursor of the British 8th Army) a key geographical advantage for the forthcoming battles in North Africa. Unfortunately, Malta's close proximity to Sicily and the Italian mainland meant it was exceptionally exposed to land-based airpower, thereby forcing the fleet to move to Alexandria.

Furthermore, the Royal Navy had previously shared control of the Mediterranean with the previously powerful French fleet, and the British could not be sure whether the French would eventually side with the Axis. Even after the seizures of French shipping and the Battle of Mers-el-Kébir in July, the remnants of the French fleet existed in sufficient strength to cause the Admiralty to exercise considerable caution in its future dealings with French warships. The potential of Vichy naval units to influence operations was demonstrated when a French naval squadron bluffed its way through the Straits of Gibraltar in September and "sealed the fate" of the expedition to Dakar, a British-sponsored effort to rally the French African Empire to the cause of the Free French. The successful defense of Dakar went a long way in restoring the morale and prestige of the Vichy fleet since the disasters of July.

Neither could the British be sure about the future intentions of Spain's General Francisco Franco, who was in Hitler's and Mussolini's debt for their support during the Spanish Civil War. A hostile Spain could be a real threat to the security of Gibraltar as the countries shared a land frontier. In the event, Franco recognized that his country's weak economic infrastructure, heavily damaged during the civil war, meant direct involvement in a major war would be too risky. Spain therefore remained aligned with the Axis powers but as a non-belligerent. However, the possibility that Franco might allow German troops through Spanish territory to attack Gibraltar was taken seriously well into 1941.[13]

The immediate response of the Admiralty to the Italian declaration of war on 10 June 1940 was to go on the defensive and contemplate withdrawing the fleet to Gibraltar. Commercial traffic though the Mediterranean was suspended, and the decision was made to route future military convoys bound for Egypt around the Cape and use overland supply routes from West Africa and the Red Sea rather than run the sea gauntlet from the west. The effect of this closure became apparent when a small reinforcement of seven thousand troops, ready to leave Britain in May, took until August to arrive in Egypt.[14] It had long been recognized in Britain that war with Italy would mean the closure of the Suez Canal and the addition of 3,500 miles to the route supplying India, a grim prospect should Japan decide to go to war within the foreseeable future.[15] The closure of the Suez Canal did not, in itself, mean British forces in the Middle East were in any immediate danger of running short of fuel, thanks to an oil pipeline from Iraqi oilfields to a new refinery at the Palestinian city of Haifa. From there it was tankered to fuel bunkers at Alexandria, but abandoning the Eastern Mediterranean would obviously have nullified this important advantage owing to the difficulties of protecting the oil convoys without a local base. Unlike the Axis forces, fuel would never be a constraining factor for the Allies in this region.[16]

A defensive stance was not unreasonable given the current problems in home waters, but this did not suit Churchill's aggressive temperament and would not have impressed Britain's continuing determination to fight upon the Americans. He therefore vetoed the withdrawal to Gibraltar and urged the Royal Navy to go on the offensive as soon as it was able. Fortunately, this was also the instinct of Admiral Sir Andrew Cunningham, C-in-C Mediterranean Fleet, who took the opportunity to go on the attack. His leadership in the forthcoming war at sea would make Cunningham Britain's most successful sailor of the war and, even against Churchill's wishes, propel him to the First Sea Lord's chair when Pound died in 1943. These aggressive instincts proved correct. If the Italians proved unable to hold their own against the Royal Navy, then a long and undefended coastline would make Italy vulnerable to naval bombardment and amphibious assault.

The Regia Marina, however, possessed 6 battleships, including 2 modern Littorios mounting 15-inch guns. The Littorios were faster than British heavy ships but more lightly armored because of the Italian emphasis on speed and maneuverability. It also possessed 19 modern cruisers, 59 destroyers, and 67 torpedo-boats, together with 116 submarines.[17] Key drawbacks were a shortage of officers and chronic fuel supply problems, the latter being a constant factor in operational planning. This was particularly ironic given the vast Libyan oil reserves the Italians would have controlled had they been aware of their existence. Italian gunnery, though good, was behind that of the Royal Navy, which was now introducing radar-assisted range finding in its *King George V*–class battleships. Radar also enhanced the Royal Navy's already well-developed night fighting capability. Sadly for the Italians, night-fighting techniques had not been developed, and "this was surely a serious gap in our preparations for war," wrote Vice Admiral Angelo Iachino.[18] Another major problem was the lack of an aircraft carrier. The causes for this have been much debated and are usually laid at Mussolini's door. Indeed, it was Mussolini who decreed that the Regia Aeronautica should hold the monopoly of Italian airpower.[19] This was a major misjudgment, given the effective use made of carriers against Italy in all the major sea battles, but the idea that mainland Italy itself was an aircraft carrier seemed reasonable enough until the Regia Marina suffered a string of embarrassing defeats. Neither did the Regia Aeronautica possess effective torpedo bomber units in 1940, despite having a better aerial torpedo than the Luftwaffe. Only when the complete failure of high-level bombing against warships was finally exposed did it begin to form effective torpedo-bombing units. The Italian armed services were backed by a surprisingly efficient intelligence organization, Servizio Informazioni Militari (SIM), which was reading many British ciphers. This gave Mussolini "priceless" information on the state of the British forces in the Mediterranean, especially the Royal Navy.[20] SIM successfully monitored the Gibraltar through-traffic but also had a tendency to overestimate British strength, leading to planning errors. However, British military intelligence in the area was efficient, quickly rounding up Italian espionage agents in Egypt and breaking Italian naval codes. In fact, the Regia Aeronautica code had been broken by the British in May 1940, but the advantage was lost when the codes were changed at the outbreak of war. In the long term, British Ultra decrypts would prove decisive in the Mediterranean intelligence war, and the Italian use of German Enigma machines made their security extremely vulnerable.

However, of immediate concern to the British was the potential of the Regia Aeronautica to disrupt naval operations. With a total of approximately 3,707 aircraft distributed throughout the mainland and overseas empire, it was the fourth largest European air force, and there is no dispute that it heavily outnumbered the RAF and FAA in the Mediterranean. The main bomber was the tri-motor S.79, a capable level-bomber that would later give good service as a torpedo bomber. But the Italian aircraft industry suffered from short production runs of too many types and failed both to move onto all-metal airframes and to fully embrace mass-production techniques. It also failed to develop aero-engines of sufficient power, and the Italians relied heavily on their German ally for engines capable of fully developing their better designs.[21] For these reasons, in qualitative terms the aircraft were comparable to those of the French but were generally below German and British standards.

The RAF could field 75 fighters, including several Gloster Gladiator biplanes, plus 96 bombers based in Egypt and Palestine.[22] Fortunately, the RAF officer in charge of No. 204 Group (forerunner of the Desert Air Force) was the redoubtable former RNAS ace Air Commodore Raymond Collishaw. All the leadership skills Collishaw displayed in 1917 in fighting the German Jastas under adverse conditions were about to be tested again. The FAA started the war with 232 aircraft in 1939, but only small numbers were available for the Mediterranean during 1940 and were limited by the number of carriers that could be brought to bear in any single operation. For example, 20 aircraft flew from the sole carrier *Eagle* at the Battle of Punta Stilo (Calabria to the British) to provide fighter cover, reconnaissance, and a torpedo strike force. The mainstay of the FAA was the Fairey Swordfish torpedo bomber, an undeniably dated-looking biplane with short range but extremely robust, reliable, easy to service, and stable—the latter a particularly important quality in a torpedo bomber. Fighter cover for the fleet was provided by the equally dated Sea Gladiator, the maritime version of the Gloster Gladiator, but it could fight on roughly equal terms with Italy's Fiat CR.42 biplane fighter. Later in the year the more modern Fairey Fulmar monoplane saw action with the FAA. Though inferior to the Messerschmitt Me.109 and other land-based fighters, in the hands of skilled FAA pilots it had notable successes against the Italians. Furthermore, its long range meant it excelled in the reconnaissance role. Aircraft carriers performed an invaluable role in most clashes that occurred during 1940 and also at Matapan the following year. Unlike American carriers, the British flight decks from *Illustrious* onwards were armored, but there were a number of operational disadvantages with British carriers when compared with American and Japanese counterparts. Aircraft engines could not be warmed up below deck in enclosed hangars; the practice of stowing an aircraft before allowing the next onto the flight deck and the relatively slow speed of British carrier aircraft also militated against rapid deployment for defense and attack.[23] More positively, the enclosed hangars gave better protection against bombing and could be sealed against chemical attack.[24] Furthermore, the ability to provide fighter cover and launch air attacks against the Regia Marina would allow the British a crucial advantage in 1940.

The action with the Italian fleet off Calabria on 9 July 1940 was described by Admiral Cunningham as the first occasion serious attention from the Italian air force was given to the British fleet, and the "first time serious contact was made" with the larger surface units of the Regia Marina. Both sides were engaged in covering important convoys, the British sweeping the sea to cover two convoys from Malta to Alexandria and the Italians needing to protect a convoy of supplies to Marshal Rodolfo Graziani's army in Libya, where he was preparing his ill-fated attempt to invade Egypt. The Italian naval plan was correctly anticipated by Cunningham as an attempt to lure the British close to Italian air bases and to a concentration of submarines, after the submarine *Phoenix* sighted the enemy forces. Cunningham then moved to cut the Italians off from their base at Taranto. The action developed into a long-range slugging match, with the modernized *Warspite* as the only capital ship to get within range of the heavy Italian ships. *Warspite* managed to achieve a single hit at 26,000 yards on the *Giulio Cesare*, damaging the boilers and slowing its speed. Cunningham acknowledged this was a possible lucky shot at extreme range, but it caused the Italians to promptly break away. Unfortunately, in terms of scoring hits on enemy ships the FAA aircraft from the obsolete *Eagle* disappointed him by only reporting a single torpedo hit on a cruiser. But he acknowledged the crews were inexperienced in making high-speed attacks, since *Eagle* had recently been transferred from duties in the Indian Ocean. Cunningham also praised her aircrews for finding and maintaining contact with the enemy and carrying out constant daylight A/S patrols throughout the five-day period. All this was achieved in difficult circumstances and often in the "fleeting intervals" between and during bombing attacks. The FAA reconnaissance role was also assisted by RAF flying boats patrolling Malta–Cape Spartevento and Cape Colonne–Corfu, Malta-Zante-Malta and Malta-Zante-Alexandria. Cunningham reported that enemy gunfire was initially accurate with several straddles but deteriorated when the Italians came under fire themselves. Italian smoke tactics from the destroyers were also "impressive," successfully screening the "high-speed retirement" of the enemy fleet.[25]

It is worth examining the Regia Aeronautica's bombing attacks during this action in some detail. On 8 July, *Warspite* sustained seven attacks between 1205 and 1812 of approximately fifty bombs but no hits were made. Some eighty bombs were dropped on Force C (two battleships, a carrier, and eleven destroyers) between 0951 and 1749 in the course of six attacks but without achieving any hits. Most ships experienced near-misses, but the only casualties were incurred in Force A. The light cruiser *Gloucester* was hit on the compass platform, killing eighteen (including the captain) and wounding nine. The bridge was so damaged that gun control and steering had to be relocated to an emergency position aft. Between 1640 and 1925 on 9 July the Regia Aeronautica delivered a series of intense air strikes that focused mainly on *Warspite* and *Eagle*. However, the 7th Cruiser Squadron received many attacks, with bombs falling close to the destroyers. No hits were obtained and only a few minor casualties were sustained from splinters. Unfortunately for the Italians, the Regia Aeronautica demonstrated its inability to recognize ships by bombing its own fleet at 1705 and at 1857 but with no more effect on its own ships than those of the Royal Navy. On 11 July, the fleet was again subjected to heavy air attack. Between 1248 and 1815 *Warspite* and her accompanying destroyers received 5 heavy air attacks, with a total of 66 bombs dropped. Twelve attacks were also carried out with 120 bombs on the 1st Battle Squadron accompanied by the *Eagle* and battleships *Royal Sovereign* and *Malaya*. No damage or casualties were reported. More bombing attacks were reported the following day between 0850 and 1150, when 300 bombs fell on *Warspite* during 17 attacks. Three attacks were made on the 1st Battle Squadron and *Eagle* between 1110 and 1804 with 25 bombs, but again without result. As a result of these attacks the fleet changed course toward the Egyptian coast in order to obtain cover from land-based RAF fighters. After this, the air attacks ceased for the day. The Regia Aeronautica's final effort was made on 13 July as the convoy approached Alexandria. The 1st Battle Squadron endured further attacks between 1056 and 1623 but without loss. The *Eagle*'s Gladiators claimed to have shot down a shadowing aircraft plus two bombers with another damaged. Land-based Blenheims also provided protection during the afternoon.[26]

The tangible results of these engagements were summed up by Cunningham as "meager," but there was clearly some value in demonstrating to the Italians that their air force and submarines could not prevent the British fleet from penetrating the central Mediterranean, with only the Italian main fleet seriously interfering with operations. As he said, it showed even heavy and accurate high-level bombing will achieve few hits and was "more alarming than dangerous," and the claims of the airpower theorists and Admiralty pessimists regarding the overwhelming superiority of land-based aircraft over warships had been greatly exaggerated. In one day, 126 bombers dropped 514 bombs without hitting a single ship. They deserved better success, for the bombs had been well aimed with explosions all around the ships. But even if more hits had been obtained one wonders if serious damage would have been achieved against anything larger than a destroyer, given that only 8 bombs were of 500 kg, 236 were of 250 kg, and 270 were of 100 kg.[27] Cunningham himself experienced "a most virulent attack on 12 July," when "24 heavy bombs fell on the port side of the ship simultaneously, with another dozen on our starboard bow, all within two hundred yards, but slightly out of line."[28]

Had the Italians been able to deploy the battleships *Littorio* and *Vittorio Veneto*, the outcome off Calabria may have been different, but at this point they were still working up. Cunningham was also correct to emphasize the inadequacy of long-range gunfire. There had been a prevalent idea before the war that long-range gunfire could bring decisive results, but it had mostly resulted in an enormous expenditure of ammunition in exchange for a small return. Only with the widespread adoption of efficient gunnery radar later in the war would good results be achieved at long range against moving targets.[29] In the meantime, it was necessary to close in for "decisive results." The Regia Aeronautica might have achieved more if it had coordinated more closely the actions of its aircraft with those of its naval commanders. Italian fleet commanders could only request air support from their local maritime command, but this was subject to further referral to Air Sector Command and even to Superaero—the air force headquarters. Therefore hours could pass between the original request and take-off. This over-centralization of command, and control was a feature of the Fascist regime and contrasted poorly with Cunningham's more relaxed management style, allowing subordinate officers to use their initiative.[30] As British warships were outnumbered in terms of cruisers and destroyers and endured constant bombing attacks, Cunningham could claim a "moral ascendancy" had been established, and in at least one respect this was correct. There seems little doubt that the battle boosted fleet morale, but there was ample justification for the Italian decision to break off when the balance had tipped against them.

A more decisive victory was unattainable in the circumstances given the superior speed of the Italian fleet, its effective smokescreen, and spoiling destroyer attacks. Plain language signals had also been intercepted indicating the British were approaching the Italian submarine line, and there seems little doubt that the British decision to abandon pursuit at a point within twenty-five miles of the Italian mainland was the correct one. Enthusiastic claims by Italian bomber crews, the fact that the British had broken off the pursuit, and the safe arrival of the supply convoy all enabled Mussolini to claim a victory of sorts, but hardly anyone, least of all his German ally, was convinced. Count Gian Ciano, Italy's foreign minister, recorded in his diary on 13 July the antagonism that existed between the air force and the navy's chief of staff. Admiral Domenico Cavagnari complained that air action was lacking in the first stage of the encounter and that when it came, the Italian ships came under their bombardment for six hours. "Other information also gives the lie to the glowing reports of our Air Force," Ciano recorded.[31] No blame should be attributed to Admiral Inigo Campioni for breaking off the engagement. Campioni knew his two battleships, with their smaller caliber guns, were unlikely to best three British battleships better manned and equipped for this type of action. His intention had been to utilize the massive bomber and submarine strength theoretically at his disposal. However, the Regia Aeronautica had let him down, and the submarines were given no opportunity to play their part because of the British decision not to pursue his fleeing ships any further.[32]

Had events turned Campioni's way, then an Italian victory would have forced the British to choose between diverting substantial naval resources from the defense of Great Britain and the possibility of losing their position in the Mediterranean. As it was, Cunningham's success had persuaded the Admiralty that the Mediterranean Fleet should now be given a higher priority for warships than previously given. It might be argued that this diversion of warships should have boosted the chances for Sea Lion's success, but as we have seen, Great Britain remained a powerful "fortress," with plenty of resources in and around the English Channel throughout the summer of 1940.

There were further naval operations in the wake of Calabria, including bombarding the Italian lines of communication in Libya and coastal targets in Sardinia, Sicily, and the Italian mainland. But after Calabria the Regia Marina tended to avoid fleet actions, preferring to use its naval strength in guerilla fashion by trying to disrupt British convoys.[33] It did not mean an end to naval confrontations, and shortly afterward a further clash of warships occurred at the Battle of Cape Spada where the light cruiser *Sydney* sunk the Italian light cruiser *Bartolomeo Colleoni*. The Italians had been engaged in an operation to intercept British merchant shipping plying between Greece and Turkey, but were unsuccessful largely because of the lack of air reconnaissance. Four Italian float planes were standing by for action, but the sea conditions meant their engines had to taxi at full power for long periods. When the engines finally overheated the float planes were no longer able to take off and could play no part.[34]

But it was the Battle of Taranto on the night of 11–12 November 1940 that showed what aircraft might achieve against warships, providing there was at least one aircraft carrier available. An operation with aerial torpedoes against the heavily defended home of the Italian First Squadron, situated inside the heel of the Italian mainland at Taranto, had been contemplated back in 1938 as a contingency operation should Italy go to war as a result of the Munich Crisis. However, the war with Italy was several months old before a serious attempt could be made, and the attack on Taranto, known as Operation Judgment, would now be part of the overarching Operation MB8, involving the running of four convoys in various directions across the Mediterranean.

One problem to be addressed was the need to avoid "bottoming out"—in other words, to prevent the torpedo plunging into the harbor floor. A conventional torpedo might plunge nearly one hundred feet before continuing horizontally to the target, but Taranto Harbor averaged forty-nine feet in depth. The solution was to attach a wire lanyard to the Mk XII 18-inch torpedo that held up the nose on release. This produced a flat "belly-flop" rather than the normal nose-down water entry technique. Auxiliary wooden fins were also fitted to maintain the horizontal position, and these extemporizations limited the running depth to around thirty-five feet. To achieve success, the Swordfish had to launch their missiles at least three hundred yards from their targets so that the detonators could arm. They also had to be dropped from an altitude not exceeding 150 feet. As the torpedoes had to run underneath torpedo netting before detonation, Duplex magnetic detonators allowed them to explode under the hulls without direct contact. This was a gamble given the unreliability of the Duplex system but in the event it worked well.[35] Torpedo attacks could only be carried out in the outer harbor because the inner harbor was too shallow. It was therefore decided that attacks would be made on the inner harbor, with bombs dropped from the flare-droppers after the flares had been lit. Many of these techniques were copied by the Japanese and used for their attack on Pearl Harbor; they had not previously believed that air-dropped torpedoes could work in a shallow harbor.

But according to Cunningham, the first and most important planning requirement was "good and timely photographic reconnaissance" in order to ascertain the precise position of each warship in the harbor. This was only possible when long-range American Martin Maryland bombers operating from Malta became available. The flying boats previously available were too slow and vulnerable to fighters during the approach to a heavily defended port. It was also necessary to extend the somewhat limited range of the Swordfish torpedo bomber by fitting long-range fuel tanks, which did not become available until September. Time was also required for the crews to acclimatize to night-flying conditions, and the necessary training was not completed until mid-October. The operation was originally intended for 21 October, but a fire in the hangar of *Illustrious* destroyed several aircraft and caused it to be postponed until 30–31 October. This was postponed a second time because there was no moon and the crews lacked adequate training with flares. It was then discovered that the defenses in the outer harbor had been bolstered with the addition of balloons and torpedo nets necessitating further reconsideration of the method of attack. Another setback occurred when one of the two carriers to be deployed, the *Eagle*, developed technical problems that meant she could no longer be used for the operation. Nevertheless, six of her aircraft with crews were transferred from the *Eagle* to the *Illustrious*. The striking force was therefore made up of twenty-four aircraft to be flown from *Illustrious*, but three Swordfish were lost shortly before the operation because of contaminated petrol, thus reducing the strike force to twenty-one.

RAF reconnaissance aircraft obtained some "extremely good" photographs of Taranto Harbor on 10 November, confirming that no major movements had taken place.[36]

The first force of twelve aircraft took off for their 170-mile flight to Taranto between 2035 and 2040 hours on 11 November, under a "three-quarters moon" and with a light and variable surface wind. The second force took off between 2128 and 2134, but one damaged Swordfish was left behind. Nevertheless, this aircraft was later flown off at 2158 in time for the attack. The first problem occurred when the first force was separated by cloud, meaning that all the aircraft did not arrive simultaneously at the target area. Shortly before 2300 hours, the squadron commander led an attack of eight aircraft comprising five torpedo bombers, two flare-droppers, and one dive-bomber. The others went into the attack as they arrived. All these aircraft are identified below with the surnames of their aircrew.[*]

The Sparke/Neale torpedo bomber could not identify the planned *Littorio* target but instead aimed at a *Cavour*-class battleship directly ahead. Dropping the torpedo at seven hundred yards, the pilot turned 180 degrees back through the intense antiaircraft fire he had experienced at the harbor entrance. An explosion was observed approximately one minute later. Another torpedo was dropped at the same target by the Macaulay/Wray Swordfish at six hundred yards. The Kemp/Bailey Swordfish attacked from the west at four thousand feet and dropped its torpedo one thousand yards from the *Littorio*. The crew did not report an explosion but observed the torpedo was running accurately. Swayne/Buscall, one of the detached aircraft, also arrived from the west but at the lower altitude of one thousand feet. At the Taranto shoal breakwater the pilot turned the Swordfish in order to approach the *Littorio* from the east. The torpedo was launched at four hundred yards and the aircraft passed directly over the ship, where a sudden column of smoke was seen to rise abaft the funnels. The other more southerly *Littorio* was attacked by the Maund/Bull Swordfish, which managed to dive under the antiaircraft fire, flatten out, and drop the torpedo at approximately 1,300 yards from the target. Other aircraft made bombing attacks on an oil storage depot and a line of cruisers and destroyers, but no definite results were observed except for a large fire near a seaplane hangar.[37]

The second force went into the attack but with only seven aircraft, as Morford/Green had already turned back owing to a fuel tank problem. Flares were dropped to illuminate the target and heavy AA fire opened up on the

---

[*] More complete details of the aircrew involved can be found at "FAA and the Strike on Taranto," Fleet Air Arm Archive, http://www.fleetairarmarchive.net/RollofHonour/Battle honour_crewlists/FAATaranto_1940.html (accessed 24 September 2014).

attackers. Hale/Carline dropped its torpedo at seven hundred yards toward the same *Littorio* previously attacked by Swayne/Buscall and Kemp/Bailey. Lea/ Jones gave its attention to the most northerly Cavour, dropping its torpedo at eight hundred yards and turning sharply to starboard in order to escape between two cruisers. Torrens-Spence/Sutton endured AA fire from three positions, having been silhouetted against the flares. Nevertheless, it dropped a torpedo at seven hundred yards against the *Littorio* previously mentioned. Welham/Humphreys approached over the town and dodged an AA balloon before diving into the attack. Several machine-gun bullets hit the Swordfish, damaging an outer aileron rod and causing the pilot to temporarily lose control. On regaining control the pilot dropped his torpedo at five hundred yards on the port quarter of the *Littorio* previously attacked by Maund/Bull. The flare-droppers also bombed an oil storage depot, and a small fire was observed. Clifford/Going, the aircraft originally left behind from the first strike force, arrived half an hour late but successfully bombed the cruiser line. An intention to repeat the operation the following night was abandoned owing to an unfavorable weather report. The RAF bombed Taranto shortly afterward with Wellington bombers but did little damage. The controversial decision to use Duplex pistols had been amply justified owing to the fact that some nine to eleven 18-inch torpedoes had sunk or crippled three battleships.[38] Without doubt, the attack had been carried out in very difficult circumstances and without prior rehearsal. Some of the crews were not experienced in landing on *Illustrious'* flight deck, or very familiar with the landing procedures and use of the barrier. As Captain Denis Boyd, captain of the *Illustrious,* wrote at the time: "In spite of this the zeal and enthusiasm of everyone to carry out this great enterprise was unabated and it is impossible to praise too highly those who in these comparatively slow machines made studied and accurate attacks in the midst of intense antiaircraft fire."[39]

Churchill was understandably jubilant when he told the House of Commons on 13 November: "I felt it my duty to bring this glorious episode to the immediate notice of the House. As the result of a determined and highly successful attack, which reflects the greatest honour on the Fleet Air Arm, only three Italian battleships now remain effective. This result, while it affects decisively the balance of naval power in the Mediterranean, also carries with it reactions upon the naval situation in every quarter of the globe."[40]

All this had been achieved for the loss of only two aircraft. Sadly, it did not affect the balance of power in the Mediterranean for very long and the result was not decisive. But the losses, along with those sustained at the Battle of Matapan in March 1941, may well have deterred the Regia Marina from intervening in the later evacuations from Greece and Crete. Just as important, it ruled out an immediate invasion of Malta, the loss of which would have interfered significantly with future British ability to disrupt the Afrika Korps' lines of communication. It had, for the time being at least, crippled three out of Italy's six available battleships and altered the "odds more in Britain's favor than at any time since the fall of France."[41] The *Caio Duilio*, new *Littorio*, and *Conte di Cavour* were later raised from the harbor floor, but the latter never reentered service. The remaining three Italian battleships were removed to Naples, and the British remained on the offensive, greatly diminishing the threat to British convoys bound for Greece and Crete and harassing Italian convoys to Libya. Perhaps more might have been achieved if the Air Ministry had not been in charge of the FAA for so long. As a result, the FAA had no modern dive-bombers or torpedo bombers, but it is difficult to prove exactly how the use of more modern equipment would have resulted in significantly greater damage. Arguably a diversionary raid with Wellingtons on the night of the attack may have distracted Italian AA gunners, but as Robert Farley states, "information on that decision remains scarce."[42] One unfortunate effect was the unwitting assistance it gave to Japanese planners for their operation at Pearl Harbor just over a year later. As a result of the Japanese naval attaché's visit to Taranto, the Japanese realized that modifications to the aerial torpedo could permit a viable attack in the shallow waters of Pearl Harbor, home of the American Pacific Fleet.[43] As previously described, the Japanese were also receiving technical information from a spy at the Admiralty right up to Pearl Harbor.

In December, the fleet was free to support General Archibald Wavell's Operation Compass in the Western Desert, bombarding Bardia and Tobruk, moving three thousand tons of supplies, and maintaining a ferry service for the troops through the newly captured ports.[44] Collishaw's antiquated aircraft also gave useful support, preventing enemy reconnaissance and thereby contributing to the surprise of the attack. By sending out single aircraft on offensive patrols he also managed to convince the Regia Aeronautica that the RAF was stronger than it was, forcing the Italians to adopt wasteful standing patrols over their widely dispersed desert forts. But there were limits to what could be achieved with very limited resources against an apparently overwhelming numerical superiority in the air. As his biographer states, "Nevertheless, under Collishaw's direction the RAF showed plenty of tactical ingenuity, forged excellent relations with the army commander (Lieutenant-General Sir Richard O'Connor), and concluded a triumphant campaign." Collishaw's contribution to the combined operations earned him the Companion of the Order of the Bath. The award was given at the same time as Cunningham received the Knight Grand Cross of the Order of the

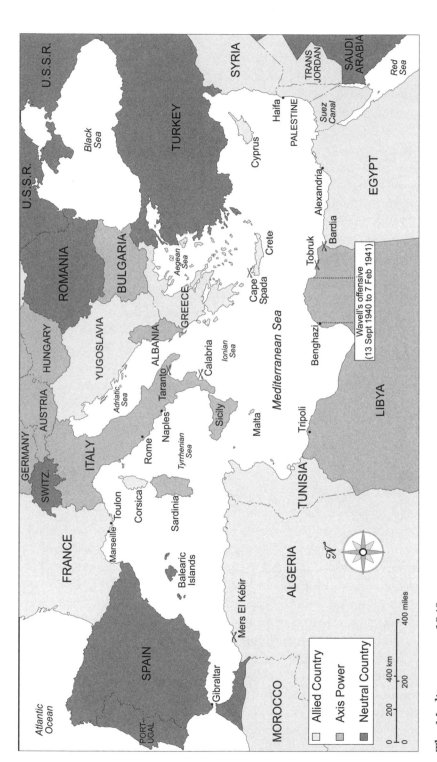

The Mediterranean, 1940

Bath for his contribution to this highly successful campaign. None of this saved Collishaw from being replaced in 1941 for an alleged unwillingness to delegate and for "foolish optimism" as to what could be achieved with small numbers of aircraft and personnel.[45] The real reason for his dismissal is unknown, but it appears that his superiors considered he subordinated his forces too closely to the commanders of the other services. Although he subsequently received promotion to air vice-marshal, his talents were wasted in backwater commands. He "voluntarily" retired from the RAF in 1943 at only fifty-three years of age.

Operation Compass had been a great success and might not have occurred had Admiral Forbes, C-in-C Home Fleet, not urged Churchill to release troops and resources from home defense if they were required elsewhere.[46] In the event, the opportunity to fully capitalize on these successes was squandered by Churchill's meddling. Just as O'Connor was preparing to seize a virtually undefended Tripoli and finally drive Graziani's shattered forces out of North Africa, the prime minister ordered that British resources in the Western Desert be transferred to Greece to bolster the defense of that country.[47] This meant that in early 1941 the German invasion of Greece forced the Royal Navy to make yet another humiliating evacuation of British forces. In February 1941, Erwin Rommel's Africa Korps began to arrive in Tripoli, with the result that the North African campaign dragged on for a further two years at great human and material cost. In his defense, Churchill believed he needed to support crumbling Greek resistance, continue to demonstrate British willingness to fight to the Americans, and confront the possibility of a German drive upon the Middle East from the Balkans.[48] Even so, such an intervention was already too late, and risking near certain victory in Africa for a negligible chance of success in Greece was a wild gamble.

German intervention also marked the end of the Royal Navy's ascendancy in the Mediterranean—at least for the time being. This was markedly demonstrated when German dive-bombers caused such damage to *Illustrious* in January 1941 the carrier had to be withdrawn from the fighting, finally having to undergo permanent repairs in North America. *Illustrious* then took no further part in Mediterranean operations until 1943. None of this meant the Royal Navy was unable to undertake operations during 1941, and it successfully ran further convoy operations to Malta and North Africa, as well as evacuating 17,000 troops from Crete following the successful German airborne invasion in May. But the Regia Marina began to gain the upper hand, even gaining revenge for Taranto by penetrating Alexandria harbor with underwater frogmen and sinking the battleships *Queen Elizabeth* and *Valiant* with limpet mines. Land-based German aircraft also imposed heavy losses on the Royal Navy, but the Luftwaffe was never able to negate all the advantages of mobility and logistics that a powerful navy conferred on the land forces. Intense Axis efforts to bomb Malta into submission failed, and their inability to invade that island meant the Allies increasingly choked the enemy supply lines to Libya with air and naval units. As German and Italian strength dwindled, the enormous potential of American military power came to be felt in the Mediterranean and the balance remained with the Allies from late 1942 until Mussolini's downfall in 1943. In September 1943, Italy concluded an armistice with the Allies, and the still-substantial Italian fleet sailed to Malta and ports in North Africa for surrender.

Even then, the Mediterranean campaign continued to exert an important influence elsewhere. The importance of Operation Dragoon, the Allied landings on France's Mediterranean coast, has often been downplayed by historians, but Douglas Porch argues that the amphibious landings on the French Riviera, made possible by Allied sea power and airpower during August 1944, were significant. The attack tied up between eight and ten German divisions that would have been more usefully employed elsewhere and cost Hitler more troops than were lost at either Stalingrad or Tunis. It also eased chronic Allied supply problems caused by the inadequacy of Channel ports, to the extent southern France was eventually handling one-third of supplies and reinforcements destined for the European continent. Finally, it lengthened the German frontline and absorbed those German divisions taken from Greece and Yugoslavia in October 1944.[49]

All this meant that events in the Mediterranean Sea and the decisions taken during 1940 relating to that campaign had shaped the continuing survival of Britain as an independent power throughout the Battle of Britain and beyond. In the shorter term, it was clear for anyone with eyes to see that sinking warships at sea with land-based airpower was not as straightforward as some of the airpower theorists had stated. By contrast, the carrier action at Taranto had demonstrated what could be achieved with naval airpower in the future.

CHAPTER 10

Conclusion

Let him who desires peace prepare for war.

—Vegetius, fourth century

We are agreed that the first duty of government is to safeguard our national security . . . and we will fulfill that duty.

—Prime Minister David Cameron and
Deputy Prime Minister Nick Clegg, 2010

D espite intense propagandizing efforts by Lord Northcliffe, no direct causal link is readily apparent between the success of Bleriot's epic cross-Channel flight in 1909 and the sudden official interest in heavier-than-air flight. But that year had witnessed the foundation of British military aviation, and Northcliffe and his supporters doubtless played a small part in pushing the politicians into action. This bore fruit in 1912 when the Royal Flying Corps was born. It was only unified in the sense of having army and naval wings under a single organizational umbrella, but it still lacked a coherent aircraft procurement policy. Even this fragile unity was shattered when the Royal Naval Air Service was formed in 1914, shortly before the outbreak of war. A few years later there was an abrupt return to unification, and although the new Royal Air Force supported the older services as its predecessors had done before, it now embodied a controversial new bombing philosophy that was to deflect British defense policy in the wrong direction. Great Britain had now established the largest air force in the world. By the armistice in 1918 Britain's air force had grown to 22,647 aircraft of all types and 291,170 officers and men. The RAF was not only the largest but the only "independent" air force in the world.[1] This came about because the Germans had shown what might be accomplished with just a small number of Gotha and Giant bombers; because their air raids took place when the war's out-come seemed to hang in the balance, the politicians were panicked into an ill-considered reorganization based upon extraordinary assumptions.

The creation of an independent Royal Air Force was justified on the exaggerated claim of damage caused by competition for resources between the RNAS and the RFC, and the aphorism of "attack being the best form of defense." This was further bolstered by a not altogether accurate intelligence report about German battle plans and an inflated estimate of British aero-engine production. Later, the interwar period would show that interservice friction had not been eliminated, and now there were *three* service competi-tors for the meager defense budget. But having gained control of naval avia-tion in 1918, the new ministry could pursue its doctrinal objective of strategic bombing without having to worry very much about the requirements of the other services. Consequently, the Royal Navy's carrier development and sup-porting air units lost their leading position and fell behind the United States and Japan between the wars, though the navy still remained a force to be reckoned with. Neither would the BEF of 1939–40 have the sort of ground-attack capability enjoyed by the Germans. There is little doubt that the air-craft of the RNAS deployed around the coasts were not being deployed to maximum effect by 1917, but the Admiralty was continuing to experiment and remained at the cutting edge of British military aviation. By contrast, the war in the air over land was little more than a private war with very limited impact on the ground situation

Back in 1909, the Royal Navy was still enjoying widespread support amongst the British public but also had to endure criticism within Parliament for the enormous costs of battleship construction. The criticism failed to pre-vent escalating naval expenditure, but the pressure to give more value for money over the next few years drove the Admiralty to make increased use of aircraft, airships, and submarines. Disappointing operations at Jutland and the Dardanelles did nothing to enhance the Royal Navy's reputation during World War I, and those with relatives who fought and died in the trenches were in no position to appreciate the overall maritime effort—crucial though it was to the war's outcome. It could not have helped to see the unedify-ing public spectacle of recriminations between the Jellicoe and Beatty fac-tions over the conduct of the Battle of Jutland in the postwar period. Neither could the publication of Lloyd George's *War Memoirs*, publicizing his self-aggrandizing and slanted version of the convoying issue, have inspired any public confidence in naval leadership.[2]

The Royal Navy's success in winning the first Battle of the Atlantic, with the help of aircraft and airships, enabled the American army to be transported to Europe and to tip the battlefield pressure against the Central Powers. At the same time, British naval power turned the logistical screws on the German armed forces and upon the home front. With German civilians dying of starvation, revolution was in the offing. By fall 1918, there was no longer any reasonable prospect of a German victory. The contribution of Britain's armed services to ultimate victory had been immense, but this achievement counted for little against the postwar demand for defense cuts in order to finance education and housing expectations and build on the success of the People's Budget of 1909.

Despite the Allied victory it is sometimes claimed that only the aviators emerged from this conflict flying high in the public's affections; however, precise evidence on this point remains scarce. Yet, in contrast to the squalid horror of the trenches where millions died for small tangible gains, this new air war harked back to a lost age, as the writers of the day created the knights-of-the-air mythology from genuine acts of chivalry by individual airmen. Inevitably perhaps, chivalry declined as the air combats intensified, but the memories lived on for future generations in the adventures of fictional heroes such as Captain W. E. Johns' character James Bigglesworth (or "Biggles") clearly demonstrated.[3]

Despite his opposition to a new Air Ministry and his late conversion to the merits of strategic bombing, Chief of Air Staff Sir Hugh Trenchard was faced with huge cuts to the RAF and needed a new role to justify its continued existence. Severe operational limitations in mountainous territory and heavy dependence on ground forces did not prevent the portrayal of imperial air policing as a successful and necessary policy during the interwar years. Aircraft alone were incapable of resolving conflicts beyond the realms of tax-compliance, the prevention of caravan raiding, and tribal bickering. But the experience doubtless hardened the future bomber barons to casually accept the suffering of innocents as a necessary part of war. Furthermore, imperial air policing did not assist RAF Bomber Command to meet its raison d'être of bombing in the early stages of World War II. The Air Ministry had also failed to invest in essential technical research until a very late stage, having spent the limited funds on creating an independent "air spirit." Trenchard officially retired as CAS in 1929 without having the chance to substantiate his airpower vision, but his influence remained powerful because he was an exceptionally forceful personality, retaining the ears of politicians and making frequent pronouncements in the House of Lords on airpower. Arthur "Bomber" Harris would later put Trenchard's theories into practice over Germany during World War II.

Sadly, the older services suffered as a result of Trenchard's retention of their airpower, though it would not be until 1940 and a string of defeats that the full extent of the problems would become painfully apparent. Trenchard failed to secure the massive air expansion demanded by the air lobby during his tenure as CAS, but it was certainly not for want of trying. He saved the RAF from dismemberment in the 1920s and received full acknowledgment from his peers for this remarkable achievement, but in fighting for the survival of the RAF as an independent service he trampled roughshod over the requirements of the other services.

The post-Trenchard period of 1929–33 began with the Royal Navy and Royal Air Force each continuing the struggle to maintain its position against powerful political pressures, which sought to preserve world peace through the pursuit of international disarmament. Air Ministry PR continued to popularize the new service, but it was still not enough to loosen the government's purse strings. With hindsight, the goal of complete international disarmament was hopelessly optimistic, but prior to 1933 it would have taken an extraordinary prophet to have read the signs accurately. Rearmament began in 1934, and the Baldwin and Chamberlain governments acted responsibly by gearing it to the nation's ability to pay. As more money became available for aeronautical research, better designs emerged from the drawing board, and if aircraft development kept pace with other technologically advanced nations it was largely thanks to the foresight and determination of British aircraft manufacturers rather than the encumbrance of Air Ministry bureaucracy. The financial shackles were removed from the RAF after the Munich Crisis of 1938, because the air lobby had sown the seeds of panic over the state of British air defenses and because aircraft could be built more quickly than warships, with quantifiable results shown within a relatively short time. Whilst this caused some jealous resentment in naval circles, Lord Chatfield credited Lord Rothermere's "one-sided campaign for the Air Force" with finally pushing the government into action on behalf of all the services.[4] However, the problems faced by the armed services and the governments of the 1930s were no more attributable to the supposed apathetic and naïve attitudes of British politicians of the 1930s than those of the previous decade. The unfortunate chiefs of staff were therefore placed in impossible positions between the wars and have subsequently sustained unfair criticism from frustrated service colleagues. While it is tempting to blame the decisions of the "Guilty Men" of the 1920s even more than those of the 1930s for the necessity of making up so much ground, to apportion guilt in this way is far too simplistic. It is nevertheless ironic that Winston Churchill's reputation—as a vociferous critic of appeasement during the 1930s and as an inspirational war leader in the 1940s—continues to prevent the wider public from under-standing his earlier role in creating the conditions that made British rearma-ment so difficult.

Contrary to many firm perceptions, the early phases of World War II showed that land-based airpower had not demonstrated an ascendancy over traditional sea power in terms of frustrating naval forces from achieving their objectives. While heavy casualties could sometimes be inflicted by land-based aircraft upon smaller ships, the Royal Navy, assisted by the Merchant Navy and their allies, demonstrated its ability to land and evacuate troops where required. In other words, it conferred a high degree of mobility upon the land forces in many situations. But in the Norway campaign, German airpower was able to decisively influence the land fighting in a way the naval forces could not. The success of German airpower in the Scandinavian and European theaters was not reflected by Allied airpower, because faulty doc-trine and neglect of army cooperation made it impossible for the RAF to make an effective contribution at this stage of the war. The requirement, as correctly recognized by the Luftwaffe, was to provide airborne and logistical support for the Wehrmacht—a policy that paid off handsomely. By contrast, bombing raids on the Ruhr, no matter how gallantly executed, could do noth-ing to influence the local situation in favor of the Allies. However, the Royal Navy helped preserve the BEF as a deterrent against Operation Sea Lion, and both survived sufficiently intact to deter Hitler's invasion planners after Dunkirk. Unfortunately, the naval successes were not always clear-cut, the most difficult operations being evacuations, and as Churchill said at the time, "We must be very careful not to assign to this deliverance [at Dunkirk] the attributes of victory." Instead of paying adequate tribute to the naval per-sonnel responsible for the "deliverance," Churchill seemed more concerned about quelling the soldiers' rancor toward the airmen and praising the air force, whose contribution to the operation's success was relatively small. In reality, the Luftwaffe's failure to prevent the evacuation was attributable to a combination of factors such as bad flying weather, the inherent limitations of the Luftwaffe in an anti-maritime role, sound naval organization, and the determination of exhausted sailors under murderous fire.

Mention the Battle of Britain and the Blitz to anyone and his or her mind will probably turn to Churchill's inspirational "Finest Hour" speech, iconic images of swooping Spitfires, and the spirited defiance of British civil-ians who knew "they could take it" and carry on fighting alone. The Finest Hour is now indelibly linked to the British sense of identity, and the RAF has achieved heroic status as a result. Unfortunately, this makes it hard to question, criticize, or even comment on the role of independent airpower within national defense. It is a magnificent story of which the British are understandably proud—a story of gallant knights of the air and the ultimate justification of independent airpower. Many still say, "Where would we have been in 1940 without the Royal Air Force?"

Indeed, the fighter pilots of all the nationalities that served with the British fought with tremendous determination and self-sacrifice, and would undoubtedly have done so even if the RAF had been tied more closely to the other services. Playing second fiddle to the needs of Bomber Command for so many years had done nothing to enhance the effectiveness of Fighter Command anyway. There were also countless acts of civilian bravery, and morale did not collapse even if it was occasionally shaken. While most Americans were still not prepared to send soldiers to Europe, they were keen to increase logistical support. Pro-British sentiments rose throughout the air battles, perhaps because of the pilot's exertions and the efforts made to publicize them. By the close of the 1940–41 air campaigns over England the Germans had yet to invade, but the reasons why the invasion fleet never sailed was more wide-ranging than a straightforward fight for supremacy of the air.

The truth concerning the German failure to invade is far more complex than the media is ever likely to allow. Massive German naval inferiority in the English Channel, a hastily improvised, unseaworthy invasion fleet of converted Rhine barges towed in trains by tugboats, and the decision to sail at night were just a few of the reasons why the German plan for Operation Sea Lion was unworkable. The main reason was the Luftwaffe's inability to overcome the enormous British naval superiority in the English Channel. These were all good reasons, brought to Hitler's attention in the summer of 1940. In my opinion, it was convenient for Hitler and the German Naval Staff to seize upon the Luftwaffe's bomber losses of 15 September as an excuse to postpone the invasion, rather than admitting the operation never had a chance from the outset. Planning for the invasion of Russia had already started the previous month, and the Kriegsmarine's *War Diary* entry for 10 September shows clearly that all German hopes were already pinned on bringing down Churchill's coalition by bombing and U-boat blockade rather than having to launch an invasion.[5] The bombing offensive continued by night from mid-September, and despite the experience of fighting a night blitz during an earlier conflict, the RAF could do little to prevent it.

But for all the operational difficulties that surrounded Sea Lion in 1940, there is still enough justification for the British to remain proud of their finest hour. The legend retains its potency because it works at many levels. For populist writers, the Battle of Britain is part of the lucrative World War

II genre and a literary well that never seems to run dry. For the Royal Air Force (and probably the independent air forces of other nations), it helps justify the existence (and expense) of its organization. The campaigns of RAF Bomber Command over Germany were many times fiercer than the Battle of Britain and resulted in horrific aircrew casualties, but they have proved far harder to present in a clear-cut light. Nobody seriously denies that the tremendous efforts of Bomber Command contributed to ultimate victory, but the full extent of that contribution remains unclear and a definitive balance sheet seemingly unattainable. Enormous damage was inflicted on the Reich, especially between 1943 and 1945, but the campaigns also absorbed vast British resources at the expense of the other armed services and made the crucial Battle of the Atlantic more costly than it might otherwise have been. Furthermore, the moral arguments surrounding area bombing, de-housing, and "soft targets" such as Dresden tend to spoil the narrative. Only after much campaigning by veterans' groups was the statue of Bomber Harris finally allowed to stand alongside that of Hugh Dowding at St. Clement Dane, London. Len Deighton's view of the Battle of Britain as a "gentlemen's war," or Adolf Galland's similar concept of a "fair war and without politics," may not be altogether accurate, but such noble sentiments are far easier to project onto the 1940 air campaigns than onto the British bomber offensive against Germany.[6]

Nobody who saw fighter pilots at the forefront of newsreel coverage during the summer of 1940 would have doubted the primacy of airpower, but in reality it was far less important than retaining command of the sea. But having fought for its existence during the interwar period, the Air Ministry developed sound PR skills that were put to good use in collaborating with the Ministry of Information, Crown Film Unit, and Anglo-American media agencies. A major naval contribution to survival was the dramatic action at Mers-el-Kébir, a tragedy that was politically and operationally necessary. Unfortunately, the fierce controversy and loss of life make it an achievement impossible to celebrate. The incident was internationally reported and a propaganda gift for Germany, but there could be no British PR mileage in this attack on a former ally. By contrast, little was said at the time about the less-visible maritime contribution to British survival—the enormous Merchant Navy effort to bring in essential war matériel, the collier's heroism in transporting coal along the coast to keep the power stations operating, and the successful destroyer raids on invasion shipping. The reasons for this lack of balance are easily discernible and were largely political and diplomatic. These can be summed up as the need to persuade the British people to carry on the fight and to encourage the United States to increase its support.

As British and German fighter pilots disputed the skies over England, another kind of Battle of Britain was being fought in the Mediterranean. Expectations that the Italian air force, nurtured on the doctrines of the internationally renowned Giulio Douhet, would sink the British Mediterranean fleet were dashed within weeks of Mussolini's declaration of war. Calabria quickly underlined the failure of land-based aircraft to sink warships en masse, and the significance of this was unlikely to have been lost on the planners of Operation Sea Lion. Taranto was also the harbinger of fundamental changes to the landscape of modern warfare. The importance of this transcends the debate as to whether Taranto represented a temporary local tactical success or a solid strategic victory, because it showed the world what might be achieved with just a handful of carrier-based biplanes, providing there was determination and a willingness to improvise solutions. The lessons were quickly absorbed by Japan and the United States, and the great sea battles centered around aircraft carriers in the Pacific were about to eclipse the primacy of the battleship. Just as the Gotha raid on London in June 1917 had triggered a sequence of changes that altered attitudes to national defense, Taranto was to ensure that a fleet based around the aircraft carrier would soon be internationally recognized as the most effective instrument for projecting power on distant shores. Indeed, in three of the six major wars that Britain has been involved in since 1945—Korea, Suez, and the Falklands—aircraft carriers have been the main provider of British airpower.[7] Predictably, perhaps, the main critic of the aircraft carrier since the end of World War II has been the Royal Air Force.[8]

Looking back on this period of 1909 to 1940, the moment of destiny occurred in the summer of 1917. By then, Britain was no longer an island, in the sense that British civilians could not be isolated from the perils associated with fighting on the European battlefield. But in neither 1917 nor 1940 had Germany's airpower developed to the extent it could allow its invading army to land in and occupy Great Britain. The hasty decisions taken in 1917 as a result of the Smuts Report changed the course of Britain's defense policy, and as others later imitated the British example, other nations may have been similarly adversely affected. The vital principle of maintaining unity of command was also undermined by the introduction of a third player into operational planning, but whether this has ever been adequately offset by the supposed "jointery" of the Chiefs of Staff Committee is debatable. Despite the service chief's undoubted high level of integrity, one wonders how these officers can be absolutely sure that loyalty to one's service will not interfere with the wider national interest. It is also easy to see how a divided Chiefs of

Staff Committee might create tempting opportunities for the "divide-and-rule" politician with his/her own agenda.

Today, the worrying economic climate of the early twenty-first century has reinvigorated interservice rivalry and pushed Western politicians into the same cost-driven policy mindset of 1920s contemporaries that preserved the RAF but neglected national defense as a whole.[9] Looking at some of today's defense problems, British politicians might do well to heed Lord Chatfield's warning made shortly after World War II: "It might happen again." Some say it already has, and at the very least, a national debate about the possibility of forcing the warring services into relinquishing their separate identities in order to create a new single unified service is surely long overdue.[10] Sadly, the fortress mentality of the individual services, combined with public apathy, suggests this is unlikely to happen. Such radicalism may be too strong a medicine for some, but the dissolution of the RAF would be a vital first step in the direction of armed services unification. Another desirable but equally unlikely development might be reversing government procurement policies that, since the end of World War II, saw the disappearance of so many famous aircraft names. Almost all of the truly great British aircraft that saw service in the two world wars came from private firms such as Sopwith, AVRO, and Hawker. These one-time household names have disappeared in the series of corporate mergers that eventually became BAE Systems plc. Technically part of the private sector, BAE Systems is so dependent on government contracts for military aircraft that it resembles a branch of the Ministry of Defense itself, and with many similarities to the discredited Royal Aircraft Factory of World War I. As already discussed, a major problem for the Royal Flying Corps in the early part of World War I was obtaining adequate equipment when it was saddled with the generally unsatisfactory products of the state-run Royal Aircraft Factory. Only by unshackling the creativity of private-sector aircraft designers can the nation hope to lead the way (or at least keep pace) with technological advances abroad.

The events of 1917 therefore have ramifications nearly one hundred years later and beg a long list of uncomfortable questions and might have beens. One wonders what might have happened had Churchill still been at the Admiralty during the Gotha raids of 1917. A better unification outcome in the form of a dynamic RNAS absorbing the moribund RFC may have been one possibility. This could still have been branded as the Royal Air Force but, under Churchill's energetic leadership, developed with emphasis on much-needed battlefield integration over land and sea. But beyond the realms of pipe dreams and counterfactual history, politicians of all stripes have proved reluctant to engage with a more serious and fundamental question that needs to be debated. The use of aircraft in war is now indispensable, but given the continuing and overriding importance of "unity of command" in an age of joint operations and small wars, one key question needs a convincing answer. What is the purpose of *independent* airpower?

NOTES

Chapter 1. A Defense Revolution

Epigraph: Daniel Boorstin, *The Image: A Guide to Pseudo-Events in America,* as quoted by Rockport Institute, http://www.rockportinstitute.com/transform ational-quotes (accessed 15 August 2012).

1. R. K. Massie, *Castles of Steel: Britain, Germany, and the Winning of the Great War at Sea* (London: Vintage, 2007).

2. D. Porch, *The Path to Victory: The Mediterranean Theater in World War II* (New York: Farrar, Straus & Giroux, 2004).

3. G. Hewitt, *Hitler's Armada: The Royal Navy and the Defence of Great Britain, April–October 1940* (Barnsley, South Yorkshire, UK: Pen & Sword Maritime, 2008); J. Mallman Showell, *Fuehrer Conferences on Naval Affairs 1939–1945* (London: Chatham, 2005).

4. D. Robinson, *Invasion 1940: The Truth about the Battle of Britain and What Stopped Hitler* (London: Constable, 2005).

5. J. Holland, *The Battle of Britain: Five Months that Changed History, May–October 1940* (New York: Bantam, 2010).

6. Roger Freeman and Neville Trotter, "Royal Air Force," 4 May 1995, Hansard, http://hansard.millbanksystems.com/commons/1995/may/04/royal -air-force#S6CV0259P0_19950504_HOC_291 (accessed 19 October 2012).

Chapter 2. The Road to War

Epigraph: L. Owen, *The Real Lord Northcliffe: Some Personal Recollections of a Private Secretary, 1902–1922* (London: Cassell, 1922), cited at http://www .archive.org/stream/reallordnorthcli00oweniala reallordnorthcli00oweniala_ djvu.txt (accessed 12 September 2012).

1. J. M. Bruce, "The Military Background—The British Aces," in *Air Aces of the 1914–1918 War*, ed. B. Robertson (Letchworth, Hertfordshire, UK: Harleyford Publications, 1959), 9.

2. Owen, *The Real Lord Northcliffe*.

3. B. Holman, "Of a Cross-Channel Passage," *AIRMINDED Airpower and British Society (mostly) 1908–1909*, http://airminded.org/2009/07/25/of-a-cross-channel-passage/ (accessed 3 February 2012).

4. Erskine Childers, *The Riddle of the Sands* (London: Dent, 1979; first published by Smith, Elder & Co., 1903).

5. I. F. Clarke, "Future War Fiction: The First Main Phase, 1871–1900," *Science Fiction Studies* 24, Part 3 (November 1993), http://www.depauw.edu/sfs/clarkeess.htm (accessed 21 August 2012).

6. H. G. Wells, as quoted by H. G. Castle, *Fire Over England: The German Air Raids in World War I* (London: Leo Cooper, 1982), 6.

7. H. G. Wells, *The War in the Air* (London: George Bell and Sons, 1908); and *Anticipations of the Reaction of Mechanical and Scientific Progress upon Human Life and Thought* (London: Chapman & Hall, 1902), 121, 125.

8. "Our Mission," The Air League, http://www.airleague.co.uk/about/our-mission/ (accessed 21 March 2012).

9. H. G. Wells, "Aeronautics," *Time*, 11 June 1923, http://www.time.com/time/magazine/article/0,9171,736150,00.html (accessed 5 August 2013).

10. P. Kennedy, *The Rise and Fall of British Naval Mastery* (New York: Penguin, 2001), 229. According to a newspaper report, Major Anstruther-Gray was told by Prime Minister Asquith that his assumption that the standard had been abandoned was incorrect. "Parliament: House of Commons," *Times* (London), 7 May 1909, p. 6.

11. H. Mackinder, "The Geographical Pivot of History," paper presented to the Royal Geographical Society, 25 January 1904, as quoted by Kennedy, *Mastery*, 183.

12. J. T. Sumida, *In Defence of Naval Supremacy: Finance, Technology, and British Naval Policy 1884–1914* (Boston, Massachusetts, and London: Unwin Hyman, 1989), 23.

13. Ibid., 14.

14. One hundred years later the figures were £40,987 million on defence dwarfed by £208,063 million on welfare and pensions. Data from "Total Public Spending Expenditure, 1909 and 2009," UKPublicSpending.co.uk, http://www.ukpublicspending.co.uk/total_spending_2009UKmn and http://www.ukpublicspending.co.uk/year_spending_1909UKmn_14mc1n_3031#ukgs30 (accessed 24 February 2012).

15. A. Wood, *Nineteenth Century Britain, 1815–1914* (London: Longman, 1996), 419.

16. Sumida, *Naval Supremacy*, 51–55; N. A. Lambert, *Sir John Fisher's Naval Revolution* (Columbia, SC: University of South Carolina Press, 1999), 15, 133–154, 243–245.

17. P. Hore, *The World Encyclopedia of Battleships* (London: Hermes House, 2010), 24.

18. P. Caddick-Adams, "Fisher, Adm. Sir John Arbuthnot, 1st Baron of Kilverstone (1841–1920)," in *Oxford Companion to Military History*, ed. R. Holmes (Oxford: Oxford University Press, 2001), 303.

19. Lambert, *Sir John Fisher's Naval Revolution*, 243–245. Also see WSC to the King (Royal Archives), 17 March 1910, as quoted by R. S. Churchill, *Winston S. Churchill: Companion*, vol. 2, Part 2, *1907–1911* (London: Heinemann, 1969), 997.

20. Kennedy, *Mastery*, 235.

21. Memorandum from Churchill, "Navy Estimates 1914–15," 5 December 1913, in R. S. Churchill, *Winston S. Churchill: Companion*, vol. 2, Part 3, *1911–1914* (London: Heinemann, 1969), 1822.

22. Memorandum from Churchill, 11 May 1914, in ibid., 1962–1964.

23. A. Temple Patterson. ed., *The Jellicoe Papers*, vol. 1 (London: Navy Records Society, 1966), 26–27.

24. A. Danchev and D. Todman, eds., *War Diaries, 1939–1945: The Diaries of Field Marshal Lord Alanbrooke* (London: Weidenfeld and Nicolson, 2001), 318, 401, 409–410, 444–446, 450–451, 456, 458–459, 472, 483, 515, 528, 532, and 568. Churchill's C-in-C Home Forces and later chief of the Imperial General Staff made many scathing references to Churchill's inability to grasp details, to relate one front to another, or to think in the strategic long term.

25. H. C. G. Matthew, "Haldane, Richard Burdon (1856–1928)," *Oxford Dictionary of National Biography* (DNB), cited at http://www.oxforddnb .com/view/article/33643?docPos=12 (accessed 1 March 2011); Kennedy, *Mastery*, 236.

26. Kennedy, *Mastery*, 234–236.

27. "Otto Eduard Leopold von Bismarck," in *Gale Encyclopaedia of Biography*, http://www.answers.com/topic/otto-von-bismarck (accessed 21 May 2014).

28. G. Sheffield, Entry for British Army, in *Oxford Companion to Military History*, ed. Holmes, 151.

29. Special cable to *New York Times*, "Two War Clouds Menace Europe," *New York Times*, 6 July 1911, pp. 1–3.

30. D. Yergin, *The Prize: The Epic Quest for Oil, Money, and Power* (New York: Simon & Schuster, 1991), 11–12.

31. Parliament: "Supply: War Airships," *Times* (London), 3 August 1909, p. 6.

32. From our Correspondent, "Aeronautics: Mr Haldane and Aerial Navigation," *Times* (London), 8 March 1909, p. 19.

33. Captain M. Sueter's speech to a subcommittee of the Committee of Imperial Defence, 5 February 1912, as quoted by T. R. Funderburk, *The Fighters: The Men and Machines of the First Air War* (London: Arthur Barker Ltd., 1966), i. The same wording is attributed to Captain Bertram Dickson in a memorandum to this subcommittee in Bruce, "The Military Background—The British Aces."

34. T. Funderburk, *The Early Birds of War: The Daring Pilots and Fighter Aeroplanes of World War I* (London: Arthur Barker Ltd., 1968), 26–27.

35. P. Hart, "Part I: Our First World War—Oral Account of Dolly Shepherd," *BBC History Magazine*, June 2014, p. 61.

36. W. Raleigh, *The War in the Air: Being the Story of the Part Played in the Great War by the Royal Air Force*, vol. 1 (Uckfield, East Sussex, UK: The Naval and Military Press Ltd., 1922), 137–138.

37. Bruce, "The Military Background—The British Aces," in Robertson, *Air Aces*, 12.

38. Figures given include both dreadnoughts and pre-dreadnoughts owing to disputes about what constituted a dreadnought. See C. Cook and J. Stevenson, "Naval Strength of Major European Powers in 1914," in *The Longman Handbook of Modern European History, 1763–1991* (London: Longman, 1992), 136.

39. Massie, *Castles*, 716, 302.

40. Ibid., 381, 418, 666.

Chapter 3. The Key to Victory

Epigraphs: (1) A. J. Balfour, letter to Mrs. Drew, 1918, as quoted in *The Penguin Dictionary of Quotations*, ed. J. Cohen and M. Cohen (Penguin Books, 1983), 19. (2) D. Lloyd George, *War Memoirs of Lloyd George* (London: Odhams Press Ltd., 1934), 649.

1. Raleigh, *War in the Air*, 471.

2. Arch Whitehouse, "The Zeppelin Raiders," in *The Years of the Sky Kings*" (New York: Doubleday, 1964), cited at Acepilots.com (updated 16 April 2012), http://acepilots.com/wwi/zeppelin.html (accessed 19 September 2013).

3. Massie, *Castles*, 364–365.

4. H. A. Jones, *The War in the Air: Being the Story of the Part Played in the War by the Royal Air Force* (Uckfield, East Sussex, UK: The Naval & Military Press, 1931), 3:243–244.

5. D. Divine, *The Broken Wing: A Study in the British Exercise of Air Power* (London: Hutchinson, 1966), 136.

6. A. Clark, *Aces High: The War in the Air Over the Western Front, 1914–18* (London: Fontana, 1974), 122–123.

7. Funderburk, *Fighters*, 41–43.

8. Jones, "Notes on Aeroplane Fighting in Single Seater Scouts, November 1916," Appendix X in *The War in the Air*, 3:396.

9. B. Robertson, ed., *Von Richthofen and the Flying Circus* (Letchworth, Hertfordshire, UK: Harleyford Publications, 1964), 30.

10. Ibid., 11.

11. D. A. Daso, "The Red Baron," *The Journal of the Air Force Association*, http://www.airforce-magazine.com/MagazineArchive/Pages/2012/March%202012/0312baron.aspx (accessed 13 March 2012).

12. Raleigh, *War in the Air*, 261. Also see Funderburk, *Fighters*, 43.

13. Funderburk, *Fighters*, 66.

14. Ibid., 160.

15. Jones, *The War in the Air*, 3:339–341. This official historian points out that most RFC officers supported Trenchard's offensive strategy.

16. Funderburk, *Fighters*, 57–58.

17. A. Boyle, *Trenchard* (London: Collins, 1962), 152–156, 184, 186–187.

18. Ibid., 184.

19. Funderburk, *Fighters*, 88.

20. Ibid., 65.

21. Divine, *Wing*, 38.

22. Tractor aircraft are pulled along by a front-mounted, engine-driven propeller, and "pushers" are pushed along by an engine and propeller mounted behind the crew. In the days when the RFC had no reliable interrupter gear for firing between the blades of a front-mounted propeller, this configuration allowed the pilot/crew to fire ahead in the line of flight. Unfortunately, this layout meant there was more chance of death or serious injury in the event of a forced landing because the weight of the engine behind the crew could push them into the ground.

23. Clark, *Aces High*, 131–133.

24. "8 Naval Squadron," *The Aerodrome: Aces and Aircraft of World War I*, http://www.theaerodrome.com/services/gbritain/raf/208.php (accessed 9 August 2012). Also see J. M. Bruce, "R. A. Little," in Robertson, *Air Aces*, 39–40.

25. J. M. Bruce, "Part 1: The Military Background: The British Aces," in Robertson, *Air Aces*, 19.

26. Funderburk, *Early Birds*, 111–113. Collishaw was one of the great air aces of the 1914–18 war; he scored sixty victories, making him the third-highest British and Dominion ace.

27. Harry von Bülow-Bothkamp, *Die Luftwacht*, no. 5 (May 1927): 262, as quoted by R. Fredette, *The First Battle of Britain 1917–18* (London: Cassell, 1966), 37.

28. H. G. Castle, *Fire Over England: The German Air Raids in World War I* (London: Leo Cooper, 1982), 183.

29. S. Sassoon, *Memoirs of an Infantry Officer* (London: Faber & Faber, 1930), 208.

30. Fredette, *First Battle*, 59.

31. Ibid., 56–58.

32. Ibid., 62.

33. Ibid., 58.

34. Castle, *Fire*, 185.

35. N. Longmate, *Island Fortress: The Defence of Great Britain 1603–1945* (London: Pimlico, 2001), 449-450.

36. Ibid., 450.

37. Castle, *Fire*, 58–66.

38. Divine, *Wing*, 105.

39. So unimportant did Lloyd George seem to consider the air situation of 1917–18 by the 1930s that his published memoirs barely allude to the air situation at all.

40. Editorial/Leader, "Lessons of the Air Attack," *Times*, 28 May 1917, p. 7.

41. Editorial/Leader, "The Bombing of London," *Times*, 9 July 1917, p. 7.

42. Fredette, *First Battle*, 112.

43. Ibid., 113.

44. "War Cabinet Committee on Air Organisation and Home Defence Against Air Raids," First Report, GT. 1451, TNA CAB 24/22, The National Archives, Kew, London.

45. Divine, *Wing*, 109.

46. Castle, *Fire*, 205–208; Fredette, *First Battle*, "Summary of the Gotha and Giant Raids on England," 263–264.

47. Divine, *Wing*, 110.

48. Ibid., 110.

49. Ibid., 111.

50. H. R. Allen, *Legacy of Lord Trenchard* (London: Cassell, 1972), 14.

51. Divine, *Wing*, 112–113. The author has quoted at length from documents written by Henderson and Cowdray, but presumably because of the referencing conventions used in the 1960s has given no specific details as to where they were obtained. In all probability they were read at the former Public Record Office, London.

52. Ibid., 114.

53. D. Edgerton, *England and the Aeroplane: An Essay on a Militant and Technological Nation* (London: Macmillan, 1991), 32; and M. Kerr, *Land, Sea, and Air: Reminiscences* (London: Longman & Co., 1927), 290–1, as quoted by N. Hanson, *First Blitz: The Secret German Plan to Raze London to the Ground in 1918* (New York: Doubleday, 2008), 322.

54. "Air Organisation and Home Defence," Second Report, TNA CAB 24/20.

55. W. K. Hancock, *Smuts*, vol. 1, *The Sanguine Years* (Cambridge: Cambridge University Press, 1962), 438–442.

56. Allen, *Legacy of Lord Trenchard*, 22.

57. "Distance from Nancy to . . . ," TimeandDate.com, http://www.timeanddate .com/worldclock/distances.html?n=1288&sort=1 (accessed 9 June 2014).

58. Divine, *Wing*, 119–20.

59. R. Davenport-Hines, "Weir, William Douglas, first Viscount Weir (1877–1959)," DNB, http://www.oxforddnb.com/view/article/36818?docPos=3 (accessed 14 January 2011).

60. M. Campbell, *The Peril from the Air* (London: Hutchinson, 1937), 64–65.

61. Hanson, *First Blitz*, 207–208.

62. Ibid., 235.

63. J. H. Morrow Jr., "Defeat of the German and Austro-Hungarian Air Forces," in *Why Air Forces Fail: An Anatomy of Defeat*, ed. R. Higham and S. J. Harris (Lexington, KY: The University Press of Kentucky, 2006), 120.

64. "The Great Air Fight," *Flight and the Aircraft Engineer*, 14 November 1918, p. 1299, Flightglobal/Archive, http://www.flightglobal.com/pdfarchive/view/ 1918/1918%20 %201298.html (accessed 24 September 2013); Clark, *Aces*, 179–180.

65. Divine, *Wing*, 140.

66. Morrow, "Defeat of the German and Austro-Hungarian Air Forces," in *Why Air Forces Fail*, ed. Higham and Harris, 121.

67. Funderburk, *Fighters*, 178.

68. Fredette, *First Battle*, "Summary of the Gotha and Giant Raids on England," 266.

69. Ibid., 231.

70. Massie, *Castles*, 57, 72–73, 97.

71. Ibid., 245.

72. Ibid., 716

73. R. H. S. Bacon, *The Dover Patrol, 1915–1917* (New York: George H. Doran Company, 1919), 2:117.

74. Eric Grove, interview by Tony Robinson, "The Lost Submarine of World War I," *Time Team Special*, Channel 4, broadcast 31 August 2013.

75. Massie, *Castles*, 667–668.

76. Jellicoe to Admiralty, 30 October 1914, as quoted by Massie, *Castles*, 632, 675.

77. Massie, *Castles*, 665.

78. B. Ranft, "Beatty, David, 1st Earl Beatty," DNB, http://www.oxforddnb.com/view/article/30661?docPos=2 (accessed 23 October 2013).

79. A. Lambert, "Jellicoe, John Rushworth, First Earl Jellicoe (1859–1935)," DNB, http://www.oxforddnb.com/view/article/34171?docPoss=3 (accessed 23 October 2013).

80. Massie, *Castles*, 682–684.

81. Ibid., 662.

82. R. Rhodes-James, "Gallipoli Campaign," in *Oxford Companion to Military History*, ed. Holmes, 343–344.

83. Massie, *Castles*, 716–717.

84. Ibid., 701.

85. R. Compton Hall, *Submarines and the War at Sea 1914–18* (London: Macmillan, 1991), 260–261, and memorandum from Department BIII of the Naval staff to the Kaiser, 6 January 1916, as quoted on p. 281; Lloyd George, *War Memoirs*, 692–693; Longmate, *Island Fortress*, 448, repeats Lloyd George's assertion that he forced convoying upon the Admiralty, but Sir John Jellicoe stated that convoying had already been adopted in principle as a result of the United States entering the war. Furthermore, Lloyd George's famous visit to the Admiralty on 30 April 1917 was about anti-submarine work and not about the convoy system. Also see R. H. Bacon, *The Life of John Rushworth Jellicoe* (London: Cassell, 1936), 360–361.

86. Divine, *Wing*, 138.

87. Ibid., 136–137.

88. Entry for UC.36 (+1917), WRECKSITE, http://www.wrecksite.eu/wreck.aspx?1685 (accessed 22 August 2012). In recent years a question has arisen as to whether the identity of submarine UC.36 has been confused with submarine UB.36. It is possible that UC.36 was rammed and sunk by the French steamer *Moliére*.

89. Massie, *Castles*, 737–738.

90. Ibid., 738.

91. Divine, *Wing*, 138; J. Terraine, *Business in Great Waters: The U-boat Wars, 1916–45* (London: Mandarin Paperbacks, 1990), 48.

92. Massie, *Castles*, 506.

93. Ibid., 696–697.

94. Ibid., 509.

95. Ibid., 734–736.

96. R. Spector, *At War at Sea: Sailors and Warfare in the Twentieth Century* (London: Allen Lane, 2001), 122–124.

97. D. Hobbs, "The First Pearl Harbor: The Attack by British Torpedo Planes in the German High Seas Fleet Planned for 1918," in *Warship 2007*, ed. J. Jordan (London: Conway, 2007), 29–34.

Chapter 4. The Savior of the Royal Air Force

Epigraph: Sir Hugh Trenchard's speech to the Cambridge University Aeronautical Society, April 1925, in Boyle, *Trenchard*, 519.

1. V. Orange, "Trenchard, Hugh Montague, first Viscount Trenchard (1873–1956)," DNB, http://www.oxforddnb.com/view/article/36552?docPos=2 (accessed 27 June 2013).

2. H. Montgomery Hyde, *British Air Policy between the Wars 1918–1939* (London: Heinemann, 1976), 57.

3. J. Slessor, "An Afterword," in Fredette, *First Battle*, 253.

4. Orange, "Trenchard," 3.

5. Hyde, *Air Policy*, 44.

6. Jones, *The War in the Air*, 6:135–152; and appendices in separate volumes: Appendix XII, "Statistics of work of squadrons of the Inter-Allied Independent Air Force," 41; Appendix XIII, "Industrial targets bombed by squadrons of the Independent Air Force incurring wastage, June–November 1918," 41; Appendix XXXII, "Price list of various British wartime airframes and engines," 155. Also see Divine, *Wing*, 142–143.

7. Orange, "Trenchard," 4.

8. The National Archives, Kew, TNA AIR 1/460/15/312/99, as quoted by Hanson, *First Blitz*, 326.

9. Hanson, *First Blitz*, 327.

10. J. Slessor, *Air Power and Armies* (London: Oxford University Press, 1936) as quoted by A. D. Harvey, "The Royal Air Force and Close Support, 1918–1940," *War in History* 15, no. 4 (2008): 462–486.

11. Slessor in Fredette, *First Battle*, 253.

12. *Blackadder Goes Forth*, 1989, Internet Movie Database, http://www.imdb.com/title/tt0096548/ (accessed 17 October 2013).

13. Divine, *Wing*, 148.

14. Siegfried Sassoon, "Editorial Impressions," from *Counter-Attack and Other Poems* (New York: E. P. Dutton, 1918); Divine, *Wing*, 143.

15. Divine, *Wing*, 148–150.

16. B. Holman, "The Shadow of the Airliner: Commercial Bombers and the Rhetorical Destruction of Britain 1917–35," *Twentieth Century British History* (published online 10 December 2012), p. 4, http://tcbh.oxfordjournals.org/content/early/2012/12/09/tcbh.hws042.full?keytype=ref&ijkey=zoFEF12YV5XswPg (accessed, 6 September 2013).

17. W. Churchill, *The World Crisis*, vol. 4, *The Aftermath* (London: Odhams, 1950), as quoted by Divine, *Wing*, 150.

18. Divine, *Wing*, 150–151.

19. Ibid., 153–154.

20. Winston Churchill, speech, 15 December 1919, Hansard, http://hansard.millbanksystems.com/commons/1919/dec/15/pay-etc-of-the-air-force#S5CV0123P0_19191215_HOC_385 (accessed 22 July 2012).

21. Entry for 2 December 1919, *Diary of Field Marshal Sir Henry Wilson*, as quoted by C. Callwell, *Field Marshal Sir Henry Wilson: His Life and Diaries* (London: Cassell, 1927), 2:216.

22. L. Amery, *My Political Life* (London: Hutchinson, 1953) as quoted by Boyle, *Trenchard*, 369.

23. Trenchard to Beatty, 22 November 1919, TNA AIR 8/17/2A, in *The Beatty Papers*, vol. 2, *1916–1927*, ed. B. Ranft (Leicester, UK: Scolar Press, 1993), 82–85.

24. S. Roskill, *Admiral of the Fleet Earl Beatty: The Last Naval Hero* (London: Collins, 1981), 305.

25. Boyle, *Trenchard*, 348–349.

26. A. Lambert, *Admirals* (London: Faber and Faber, 2008), 373. It should be understood that the Chiefs of Staff Committee began as a subcommittee of the Committee of Imperial Defence (CID) in 1923. The CID's chief limitation was in being an advisory body for the army and navy without executive power.

27. Boyle, *Trenchard*, 349.

28. Lambert, *Admirals*, 372.

29. Allen, *Legacy*, 38–39.

30. Boyle, *Trenchard*, 350.

31. Government White Paper tabled in the House of Commons, 11 December 1919, as quoted by Divine, *Wing*, 155–156. Also quoted by Boyle, *Trenchard*, 351–352.

32. Divine, *Wing*, 158.

33. Entry for 13 December 1920, *Diary of Field Marshal Sir Henry Wilson*, as quoted by Callwell, *Henry Wilson: Diaries*, 273.

34. S. Hoare, *Empire of the Air: The Advent of the Air Age, 1922–1928* (London: Collins, 1957), 265; R. J. Q. Adams, "Hoare, Samuel John Gurney, Viscount Templewood (1880–1959)," DNB, http://www.oxforddnb.com/view/article/33898?docPos=1 (accessed 14 July 2011).

35. Boyle, *Trenchard*, 508–511.

36. M. Marqusee, "Imperial Whitewash: Feelgood versions of British history are blinding us to the ways in which we are even now repeating it," *Guardian*, 31 July 2006, http://www.guardian.co.uk/commentisfree/2006/jul/31/whitewashingtheempire, (accessed 26 July 2011).

37. R. M. Douglas, "Did Britain Use Chemical Weapons in Mandatory Iraq?" *The Journal of Modern History* 81, no. 4 (December 2009): 859–887.

38. Marqusee, "Imperial Whitewash."

39. Allen, *Legacy*, 49–51.

40. Divine, *Wing*, 157.

41. TNA AIR 5/552, as quoted by Harvey, "The Royal Air Force and Close Support, 1918–1940," 470.

42. T. Hughes, *Overlord: General Pete Quesada and the Triumph of Tactical Air Power in World War II* (New York and London: Free Press,1995), 61, as quoted by Harvey, "The Royal Air Force and Close Support, 1918–1940," 470.

43. Allen, *Legacy*, 135–136.

44. Boyle, *Trenchard*, 467–471.

45. Holman, "The Shadow of the Airliner," 5.

46. Boyle, *Trenchard*, 471–475.

47. Ibid., 472.

48. Ibid., 373.

49. Ibid., 374.

50. H. R. Allen, *Who Won the Battle of Britain?* (Frogmore, St. Albans, Hertfordshire, UK: Panther, 1976), 88–90, 92.

51. Boyle, *Trenchard*, 504.

52. P. G. Halpern, "Keyes, Roger John Brownlow (1872–1945)," DNB, http://www.oxforddnb.com/view/article/34309?docPos=2 (accessed 21 July 2011).

53. W. James, "Keyes, Roger John Brownlow (1872–1945)," in *Military Lives: Intimate Biographies of the Famous by the Famous*, ed. B. Harrison and H. Strachan (Oxford: Oxford University Press, 2002), 265.

54. Boyle, *Trenchard*, 544–566.

55. Speech by Sir Samuel Hoare, 25 February 1926, Hansard, http://hansard.millbanksystems.com/commons/1926/feb/25/sir-samuel-hoares-statement#S5CV0192P0_19260225_HOC_345 (accessed 22 July 2011).

56. C. Webster and N. Frankland, *The Strategic Air Offensive against Germany 1939–1945* (London: HMSO, 1961), 4:72–73, as quoted by Allen, *Legacy*, 53–54.

57. Allen, *Legacy*, 54–57.

58. Ibid., 58; Boyle, *Trenchard*, 576–578. For a good summary of the history of airpower up to the end of World War II, see: D. Moran, "Strategic History and the History of War," Naval Postgraduate School, http://www.clausewitz.com/readings/Moran-StrategicTheory.pdf (accessed 22 July 2011).

59. Webster and Frankland, *Strategic Air Offensive*, 4:81–82, as quoted by Allen, *Legacy*, 58.

60. Webster and Frankland, *Strategic Air Offensive*, 4:81, as quoted by Allen, *Legacy*, 59.

61. The Ten Year Rule was introduced in August 1919. This mandate instructed the armed forces to draft their financial estimates on the assumption there would not be a major war within ten years. In 1928, Churchill successfully had this renewed and self-perpetuating, but it was finally abolished in 1932.
62. Boyle, *Trenchard*, 552–553, 570.
63. Allen, *Legacy*, 58–59.

Chapter 5. Imperial Policing

Epigraph: War Office Minutes of 12 May 1919 as quoted by M. Gilbert, *Winston S. Churchill* (London: Heinemann, 1976), 4:230.

1. J. Corum, "The Myth of Air Control: Reassessing the History," *Aerospace Power Journal*, Winter 2000, http://www.academia.edu/1295387/The_Myth _of_Air_Control_Reassessing_the_History (accessed 24 August 2011).
2. D. Beatty, "Lord Beatty on Air Control: Relations with other Services: A Reply to Lord Trenchard," *Times*, 2 May 1930, p. 15.
3. T. Wilson and R. Prior, "Maurice, Sir Frederick Barton," DNB, http://www .oxforddnb.com/view/article/34948?docPos=1 (accessed 19 August 2010).
4. F. Maurice, "The Air Weapon: Function in War and Peace: 'Independence' and its Limits," *Times*, 16 April 1930, p. 15.
5. H. Trenchard, "Police of the Air: The RAF's Duties in Peace: Lord Trenchard's Faith," *Times*, 25 April 1930, p. 13.
6. "The Air Campaign in Waziristan: Official Dispatches," *Times*, 21 November 1925, p. 11.
7. Corum's views are in favor of an integrated approach to airpower.
8. Editorial abstract in Corum, "The Myth of Air Control," p. 1.
9. Ibid.
10. M. Dippold, "Air Occupation: Asking the Right Questions," *Airpower Journal* 11, no. 4 (Winter 1997): 78; N. Naastad, "Policing the British Empire from the Air," in *Use of Air Power in Peace Operations*, ed. C. Rønnfelt (Oslo: Norwegian Institute of International Affairs, 1997), 19–3; and various other sources quoted by Corum, "The Myth of Air Control," p. 2.
11. F. A. Skoulding, "With 'Z' Unit in Somaliland," *The RAF Quarterly* 2, no. 3 (July 1931): 387–396.
12. Corum, "The Myth of Air Control," p. 2.
13. Boyle, *Trenchard*, 380–384.
14. Ibid., 383.
15. Ibid., 382–384.
16. Captain Guest's Statement, 21 March 1922, Hansard, http://hansard.mill banksystems.com/commons/1922/mar/21/captain-guests-statement (accessed 5 September 2011).
17. Ibid.

18. Ibid.
19. C. F. A. Portal, "Air Force Co-operation in Policing the Empire," *Journal of the Royal United Service Institution*, May 1937, p. 348.
20. D. Omissi, *Air Power and Colonial Control: The Royal Air Force, 1919–1939* (Manchester, UK: Manchester University Press, 1990), 123.
21. Corum, "The Myth of Air Control," p. 3.
22. Ibid., p. 4.
23. P. A. Towle, *Pilots and Rebels: The Use of Aircraft in Unconventional Warfare, 1918–1988* (Sterling, VA: Brassey's, 1989), 19.
24. Corum, "The Myth of Air Control," p. 6.
25. Allen, *Legacy*, 40.
26. D. W. Parsons, "British Air Control: A Model for the Application of Air Power in Low-Intensity Conflict?" *Airpower Journal*, Summer 1994, p. 2.
27. Ibid., p. 4.
28. Corum, "The Myth of Air Control," p. 4.
29. J. A. Chamier, "The Use of Air Power for Replacing Military Garrisons," *RUSI Journal* 66 (February–November 1921): 205–12.
30. "Notes on the Method of Employment of the Air Arm," as quoted by Towle, *Pilots and Rebels*, 20.
31. Despatch from the Government of India (No. 11 of 1925) to Secretary of State, India, 15 October 1925, TNA CAB 24/179.
32. Corum, "The Myth of Air Control," p. 5.
33. B. Liddell Hart, *The British Way of Warfare* (London: Faber and Faber, 1923), 114, as quoted by Corum, "The Myth of Air Control," p. 5.
34. R. Cross, *The Bombers: The Illustrated Story of Offensive Strategy and Tactics in the Twentieth Century* (London. Macmillan, 1987), as quoted by Corum, "The Myth of Air Control," p. 5.
35. Omissi, *Air Power*, 193–196.
36. Corum, "The Myth of Air Control," p. 8.
37. "Gas Warfare," from M. A. Hankey, Secretary of Cabinet to the Prime Minister, 4 May 1920, p. 96, TNA CAB 24/105 Draft Memorandum.
38. Memorandum by the President of the Board of Education, "Gas Warfare," 17 May 1920, p. 8, TNA CAB 44/106.
39. Conclusions of a Meeting of the Cabinet held at 10 Downing Street, SW1, on 12 May 1920 at 11 a.m., pp. 104–106, TNA CAB 23/21 Cabinet 27 (207).
40. Memorandum from Secretary of State for War, 7 August 1920, TNA CAB 24/110. The "other source" was claimed to be *Des Moines Register*, 22 March 1920.
41. Douglas, "Did Britain Use Chemical Weapons in Mandatory Iraq?" 859–887.

Chapter 6. The Locust Years

Epigraph: E. Chatfield, *It Might Happen Again*, vol. 2, *The Navy and Defence: The Autobiography of Admiral of the Fleet Lord Chatfield* (London: William Heinemann Ltd., 1947), 10.

1. Allen, *Legacy*, 63.
2. S. Baldwin, Statement by the Lord President of the Council, International Affairs HC 10 November 1932,Vol. 270 cc525 –641, Hansard, http://hansard.millbanksystems.com/commons/1932/nov/10/international-affairs#S5CV0270P0_19321110_HOC_284 (accessed 15 August 2012).
3. Ibid.
4. R. Lamb, *The Drift to War* (London: Bloomsbury, 1989), as quoted by P. Mason, *One in the Eye for Harold* (London: Robson Press, 2011), 135–136.
5. R. Overy, "The Dangers of the Blitz Spirit: The History Essay," *BBC History Magazine*, October 2013, pp. 29–32.
6. Viscount Rothermere, speech to the House of Lords, "The Defence Services: Policy and Supply," HL Deb, 15 May 1935, Vol. 96, cc866–910, Hansard, http://hansard.millbanksystems.com/lords/1935/may/15/the-defence-services-policy-and-supply#S5LV0096P0_19350515_HOL_46 (accessed 15 August 2012).
7. Allen, *Legacy*, 63.
8. Holman, "The Shadow of the Airliner."
9. "Rebuilding the Fw 200 Condor is one of the most significant aircraft restoration projects in Europe," *Deutsche Lufthansa Berlin Stiftung*, http://www.dlbs.de/en/Projects/Focke-Wulf-Condor/index.php (accessed 9 September 2013); "The Sunderland I," *Flight and the Aircraft Engineer*, Flightglobal/Archive, 26 January 1939, pp. 75–80, http://www.flightglobal.com/pdfarchive/view/1939/1939%20-%200185.html (accessed 9 September 2013).
10. Morrow, "Defeat of the German and Austro-Hungarian Air Forces," 128.
11. Holman, "The Shadow of the Airliner."
12. W. S. Churchill, "The Locust Years," speech to House of Commons, 12 November 1936, The Churchill Society, London, http://www.churchill-society-London.org.uk (accessed 6 December 2011). This suggests a period beginning in 1932 or "certainly from the beginning of 1933."
13. E. Chatfield, A. Montgomery Massingbird, E. Ellington, Committee of Imperial Defence, "Re-Orientation of the Air Defence System of Great Britain," 14 May 1935, TNA CAB 24/256.
14. C. Ponting, *1940: Myth & Reality* (London: Hamish Hamilton Ltd., 1990), 30–32.
15. M. M. Postan, *British War Production: History of the Second World War* (London: HMSO, 1952), 9–10.

16. Lord McIntosh of Haringey, First World War Debt, "Written Answer to Lord Laird," 23 October 2002, Hansard, http://hansard.millbanksystems .com/written_answers/2002/oct/23/first-world-war-debt (accessed 15 May 2009).

17. C. Whitham, "Seeing the Wood for the Trees: The British Foreign Office and the Anglo American Trade Agreement of 1938," *Twentieth Century British History* 16, no. 1 (2005): 29–51, http://tcbh.oupjournals .org/cgi/content/abstract/16/1/29 (accessed 25 April 2005).

18. Ponting, *1940*, 30–32.

19. A. Crozier, "(Arthur) Neville Chamberlain, 1896–1940," DNB, http:// www.oxforddnb.com/view/printable/32347 (accessed 4 January 2012).

20. Parliamentary Archives, London, House of Commons Parliamentary Papers Online, "Statistical Abstract for the United Kingdom 1924–1938" (CD-Rom). Data from "National Revenue, Expenditure, etc., No. 151— Amount of the National Expenditure (Exchequer Issues) of the United Kingdom under the Principal Heads thereof, in each Year ended 31st March," Columns 1924-5–1938-9 (inc.) (Ann Arbor, MI: ProQuest Information and Learning Company, 2006), pp. 176–177.

21. J. F. Dunnigan and A. A. Nofi, *Dirty Little Secrets of World War II* (New York: Quill, William Morrow, 1994), 46.

22. Parliamentary Archives, "Statistical Abstract for the United Kingdom 1924–1938."

23. G. Peden, "The Treasury and the Defence of Empire: Table 4.1, Distribution of Expenses by Defence Departments," in *In Imperial Defence 1856–1956: The Old World Order*, ed. G. Kennedy (Oxford: Routledge, 2008), 80.

24. Lambert, *Sir John Fisher's Naval Revolution*, 145, 147–151.

25. R. Hough, *Bless Our Ship: Mountbatten and the Kelly* (London: Coronet Books, 1991), 49.

26. Hewitt, *Hitler's Armada*, 79.

27. C. M. Bell, "Great Britain and the London Naval Conference," in *At the Crossroad between Peace and War: The London Naval Conference in 1930*, ed. J. H. Maurer and C. M. Bell (Annapolis, MD: Naval Institute Press, 2014), 55–56, 60–66; D. Howell, "Alexander, Albert Victor," DNB, http://www.oxforddnb.com/view/article/30368?docPos=1 (accessed 6 December 2011).

28. Rev. N. Tracy, "Field, Sir Frederick Laurence (1871–1945)," DNB, http://www.oxforddnb.com/view/article/33123 (accessed 27 June 2014). Much of the criticism over Field's ability to represent naval interests seems to have come from Admirals Beatty, Keyes, and Kelly, but his biographer warns that the criticism must be seen in context and suggests it "perhaps reveals more about the critics themselves than it does about Field."

29. Dunnigan and Nofi, *Secrets*, 65.

30. Kennedy, *Mastery*, 288.

31. Sir H. Dowding, "The Great Lesson of this War: Sea-Air Power is the Key to Victory," *Sunday Chronicle* (London), 29 November 1942, Liddell Hart Archives, London, LH1/245/32.

32. W. S. Churchill, *The Gathering Storm*, vol. 1 of *The Second World War* (London: Penguin Classics, 2005), 125–126; J. Maiolo, *The Royal Navy and Nazi Germany, 1933–1939: A Study in Appeasement and the Origins of the Second World War* (London: Macmillan, 1998), 73.

33. "Essay by Vice Admiral H. Haye for British Naval Intelligence Division, 15 October 1945," TNA ADM 223/690.

34. M. M. Postan, *History of the Second World War: Design and Development of Weapons: Studies on Government and Industrial Organisation* (London: HMSO, 1964), 23.

35. Ibid., 23–27.

36. E. Grove, "It Has Happened Again: Lord Chatfield and his Critique of British Defence Policy Making," 1–9, Phoenix Think Tank, October 2012 http://www.phoenixthinktank.org/2012/10/lord-chatfield-and-his-critique-of-british-defence-policy-making/ (accessed 13 September 2013).

37. Minute from G. N. Oliver, Director of Training and Staff Duties, 13 October 1939, and Minute from Director of Naval Intelligence, 9 November 1939, TNA ADM 1/9920.

38. Papers of Captain S. W. Roskill, Letter from Captain Bonatz to Roskill, 12 February 1975, CA ROSK 6/30, Churchill Archives, Cambridge; R. Bennett, *Behind the Battle: Intelligence in the War with Germany, 1939–45,* (London: Sinclair-Stevenson, 1994), 176; F. H. Hinsley et al., *British Intelligence in the Second World War*, vol. 1, *Its Influence on Strategy and Operations* (London: HMSO, 1979), 103.

39. W. Hollingsworth, "British Lord was Spy for Japan," http://www.japantimes.co.jp/news/2002/01/05/news/british-lord-was-spy-for-japan/#.U60_ufldUsQ (accessed 27 June 2014).

40. C. Barnett, *Engage the Enemy More Closely: The Royal Navy and the Second World War* (London: Hodder and Stoughton, 1991); E. Ranson, *British Defence Policy and Appeasement between the Wars, 1919–1939* (London: The Historical Association, 1993).

41. Dunnigan and Nofi, *Secrets*, 66.

42. J. T. Sumida, "The Best Laid Plans: The Development of British Battle-Fleet Tactics, 1919–1942," *International History Review* 14, no. 4 (1992): 681–700.

43. "Captain's Confidential Reports," Report by Admiral de Roebeck on Forbes, June 23–August 1924; TNA ADM 196/90.

44. Great Britain, Admiralty, Naval Staff, Tactical Division, P[rogress in] T[actics], October 1935, pp. 66–68, as quoted by Sumida, "The Best Laid Plans," 690.

45. G. Till, *Air Power and the Royal Navy, 1914–45,* as quoted by Sumida, "The Best Laid Plans," 691.

46. Minute from Director of Naval Ordnance, 11 December 1939, TNA ADM 1/9920.

47. J. Roberts, "Call for Fire!" *Warships International Fleet Review,* June 2012, pp. 39–41.

48. Hewitt, *Hitler's Armada,* 83.

49. Cato, *Guilty Men* (London: V. Gollancz, 1940), 70.

50. Committee of Imperial Defence: Report by a Sub-Committee, "Vulnerability of Capital Ships to Air Attack," Para 60(1), TNA CAB 24/264.

51. Ibid., Para 16, 60(3).

52. Ibid., Para 54.

53. Ibid., Para 57.

54. Hewitt, *Hitler's Armada,* 81.

55. Hough, *Bless Our Ship,* 49.

56. From Forbes to Roskill, 22 February 1955, Papers of Captain S. W. Roskill, CA ROSK 6/30, Churchill Archives, Cambridge. The German torpedo dropped from aircraft was fragile and necessitated slow and straight approaches, making the bomber vulnerable to AA fire. These torpedoes were mainly used against merchant ships.

57. "Vulnerability of Capital Ships," paras 13 and 18, CAB 24/264.

58. G. D. Franklin, "A Breakdown in Communication: Britain's Over-estimation of Asdic's Capabilities in the 1930s," *The Mariner's Mirror* 84, no. 2 (1988): 202–214. Also see G. D. Franklin, *Britain's Anti-Submarine Capability, 1919–1939* (London: Frank Cass & Co., 2003), 190.

59. J. Terraine, *The Right of the Line: The Royal Air Force in the European War, 1939–1945* (Ware, Hertfordshire, UK: Wordsworth, 1997), 226–227, 232–233.

60. D. Divine, *The Blunted Sword* (London: Hutchinson, 1964), 168–169.

61. W. S. Churchill, *The Gathering Storm,* 453.

62. Churchill, *The Gathering Storm,* 453–455, Appendix M, 638–641.

63. Hewitt, *Hitler's Armada,* 36–38. .

64. *C.B. 3001/36—Progress in Naval Gunnery—Part VII: Gunnery in Foreign Navies* (internal Admiralty publication, 1936), 96, TNA ADM 186/338. Also see A. Raven and J. Roberts, *British Battleships of World War II* (London: Arms and Armour Press, 1976), 276–277.

65. S. Brownrigg, "Gunnery in the Royal Navy," in *Britain's Glorious Navy,* by R. H. S. Bacon (London: Odham's, ca. 1942), 221–222.

66. B. Lavery, *Churchill's Navy: The Ships, Men, and Organisation, 1939–1945* (London: Conway, 2006), 50.

67. R. Brodhurst, *Churchill's Anchor* (London: Leo Cooper, 1991), 167, 129. This incident is dealt with in detail by G. S. Snyder, *The Royal Oak Disaster* (London: William Kimber, 1976).

68. C. Cook, "The Myth of the Aviator and the Flight to Fascism," *History Today* 53, no. 12 (2003): 41.

69. P. S. Meilinger, "Salmond, Sir John Maitland (1881–1968)," DNB, http://www.oxforddnb.com/view/printable/35915 (accessed 11 November 2011).

70. Ibid., p. 4.

71. TNA CAB 27/648, "Appendix, Air Ministry Programme, CP.218(83), Minute by the Chancellor of the Exchequer."

72. TNA CAB 27/648 CP247 (38), Minute by the Chancellor of the Exchequer.

73. Divine, *Wing*, 214–215.

74. Sir Kingsley Wood's Statement, HC Deb, 09 March 1939, Vol. 344, cc2379–5082379, Hansard, http://hansard.millbanksystems.com/commons/1939/mar/09/sir-kingsley-woods-statement#S5CV0344P0_19390309_HOC_328 (accessed 5 January 2012).

75. Terraine, *The Right of the Line*, 44.

76. Boyle, *Trenchard*, 701.

77. J. Sweetman, "Ellington, Sir Edward Leonard (1877–1967)," DNB, http://www.oxforddnb.com/view/printable/67138 (accessed 11 November 2011).

78. Terraine, *The Right of the Line*, 44.

79. J. Ferris, "Achieving Air Ascendency: Challenge and Response in British Strategic Air Defence, 1915–40," in *Air Power History: Turning Points from Kitty Hawk to Kosovo*, ed. S. Cox and P. Gray (London: Routledge, 2002), 25.

80. Divine, *Wing*, 194.

81. K. Robbins, "Lister, Philip Cunliffe (1884–1972)," DNB, http://www.oxforddnb.com/view/article/30990?docPos=1; The Prime Minister, HC Deb, 25 May 1938, Vol. 336, cc1233–3531233, Hansard, http://hansard.millbanksystems.com/commons/1938/may/25/air-defences#S5CV0336P0_19380525_HOC_326 (accessed 10 January 2012).

82. Sir Kingsley Wood's Statement, 09 March 1939, Hansard.

83. Divine, *Wing*, 190–191.

84. Terraine, *The Right of the Line*, 233.

85. Divine, *Wing*, 207.

86. Dunnigan and Nofi, *Secrets*, 47.

87. L. McKinstry, "How the Spitfire Nearly Missed Its Finest Hour," *BBC History Magazine* 8, no. 11 (2007): 17–20.

88. Allen, *Who Won*, 44–45.

89. J. D. Scott, *History of Vickers* (London: Weidenfeld & Nicolson, 1962), 12.

90. Divine, *Wing*, 184–188.

91. Ibid., 188–189.

92. Allen, *Who Won*, 50.

93. V. Orange, "Newall, Cyril Norton (1886–1963)," DNB, http://www.ox forddnb.com/view/article/35208?docPos=2 (accessed 9 December 2011).

94. D. Zimmerman, *Britain's Shield: Radar and the Defeat of the Luftwaffe* (Stroud, Gloucestershire, UK: Sutton Publishing Ltd., 2001), 226.

95. E. C. Williams, "Height Measurement by RDF," 3 June 1940, AIR 16/877; "Minutes of a Meeting Held at Air Ministry on 19 October 1940 to Discuss the Calibration of RDF. Stations," TNA AVIA 7/183.

96. A. J. Cumming, *The Royal Navy and the Battle of Britain* (Annapolis, MD: Naval Institute Press, 2010), 74; S. Cox, Part 2, "The RAF's Response," in *The Burning Blue*, ed. P. Addison and J. Crang (London: Pimlico, 2000), 60.

97. Loose minute sheet from Air Marshal Joubert, 14 January 1941, TNA AIR 8/577; Unsigned and undated note, headed Present Filtering Organisation, TNA AVIA 7/183; J. A. J. Tester to Air Ministry, 9 October 1939, TNA AVIA 7/410; E. C. Williams to Signals 1, Air Ministry, dated 6 August 1940, TNA AVIA 7/410; From R. Watson Watt to Air Ministry, dated 21 December 1940, TNA AIR 20/2268.

98. Robinson, *Invasion 1940*, 148–150.

99. "Report No. 11. Visit to Sutton Bridge on 3 May 1940. Notes by the Inspector General," dated 14 May 1940, signed Ludlow Hewitt, Air Chief Marshal, Inspector General, TNA AIR 33/10.

100. Minutes of Meeting of Air Fighting Committee and Gun Sub Committee, 1934–1940, TNA AIR 5/1126.

101. J. Klinkowitz, *Pacific Skies: American Flyers in World War II* (Jackson, MS: University Press of Mississippi, 2004), 40.

102. L. Deighton, *Battle of Britain* (London: Book Club Associates, 1980), 192.

103. Sir Kingsley Wood's Statement, 09 March 1939, Hansard.

104. Various sources quoted in "Table 2: Air Strengths (Metropolitan air strengths only are given), Column for August 1939," in *The Making of the Second World War*, ed. A. Adamthwaite (London: Routledge, 1979), 227. It should be noted that on the eve of the German offensive in the west in May 1940, the Luftwaffe could only muster some 4,050 aircraft of all

types; A. Price, *Pictorial History of the Luftwaffe, 1933–1945* (London: Ian Allan, 1969), 22. This was approximately 160 less than they possessed at the outbreak of war, doubtless a consequence of having to fight the Polish campaign.

105. *Jane's Fighting Ships* (London, 1939), data as quoted by Adamthwaite, *The Making of the Second World War*, "Table 4: The Naval Strengths of the Leading Powers, Column for August 1939," 228.

Chapter 7. The Air War

Epigraphs: (1) Archive footage of Bader speaking on *Heroes of the Skies*, Channel 5, broadcast 25 September 2012. (2) Allen, *Who Won*, 191. (3) From Kennedy to Roosevelt, Diary, 31 July 1940, Joseph P. Kennedy Papers, John F. Kennedy Presidential Library, Boston, Massachusetts, as quoted by Holland, *Battle*, 410.

1. R. Higham and S. J. Harris, "Defeats of the Royal Air Force: Norway, France, Greece, and Malaya, 1940–1942," in *Why Air Forces Fail*, ed. Higham and Harris, 315.

2. C. Goulter, A. Gordon, and G. Sheffield, "The Royal Navy did not win the 'Battle of Britain': But we need a holistic view of Britain's defences in 1940," *RUSI Journal*, 20 October 2006, https://www.rusi.org/analysis/com mentary/)/ref:C4538D604EF124/#.U0J2g_ldWVI.

3. Diary entry for 1 March 1941 in H. Knocke, *I Flew for the Fuhrer* (London: Evans Brothers, 1953), 95.

4. "Dowding's Despatch on the Battle of Britain," TNA PREM 4/39 and AIR 20/502, par. 1.

5. Dowding to Air Ministry, 16 May 1940, TNA AIR 2/7068.

6. W. S. Churchill, *Their Finest Hour*, vol. 2 of *The Second World War* (London: Cassell, 1949), 91. Churchill praised the operation as a "glorious victory of the Royal Air Force," but also emphasized the bombs plunging into "the soft sand, which muffled their explosions," leading to the dubious statement "Presently the soldiers regarded the air attacks with contempt."

7. Holland, *Battle*, 242.

8. Ibid., 264; Churchill, *Their Finest Hour*, 91–92, 102.

9. R. Hough and D. Richards, *The Battle of Britain: The Jubilee History* (London: Hodder and Stoughton, 1989), 95.

10. Papers of Sir Henry Tizard, Dowding to Tizard, 24 November 1939, IWM HTT 26; From Fighter Command HQ to Air Ministry, "Fighter Tactics," 30 June 1940, TNA AIR 2/3146; Letter from RAF Staff College, Andover to Dowding, 3 October 1940, TNA AIR 16/659.

11. Holland, *Battle*, 510.

12. Higham and Harris, "Defeats of the Royal Air Force," in *Why Air Forces Fail*, ed. Higham and Harris, 325.

13. W. S. Churchill, "Their Finest Hour," speech to Parliament at Westminster, 18 June 1940, The Churchill Centre and Museum at Cabinet War Rooms, London, http://www.winstonchurchill.org/learn/speeches/speeches-of-winston-churchill/1940-finest-hour/122-their-finest-hour (accessed 3 March 2010).

14. Prime Minister to Secretary of State for Air, in Churchill, *Their Finest Hour*, 561.

15. Loose draft, "Fighter Strength," dated ca. 24 May 1940, TNA AIR 10/5556.

16. Churchill, *Their Finest Hour*, 144.

17. E. Edwards, "The Battle of Britain Celebrations: Is it Over?" Fleet Air Arm Association, http://www.faaa.org.uk/?p=328 (accessed 23 June 2014).

18. Holland, *Battle*, 362–363.

19. Ibid., 442.

20. R. Wright, *Dowding and the Battle of Britain* (London: McDonald & Co., 1969), 160–167.

21. A. Galland, *The First and the Last* (London: Cerberus Publishing Co., 2001), 100.

22. Allen, *Who Won*, 137.

23. E. Thomas, "The Intelligence Aspect," in *The Battle Re-Thought: A Symposium on the Battle of Britain*, ed. H. Probert and S. Cox, 42–46. Shrewsbury, UK: Airlife Publishing Ltd., 1991. http://www.rafmuseum.org.uk/documents/Research/RAF-Historical-Society-Journals/Bracknell-No-1-Battle-of-Britain.pdf (accessed 1 May 2012). RAF Intelligence initially believed the Luftwaffe's frontline strength to be around five thousand aircraft when it was closer to three thousand.

24. P. Bishop, *Fighter Boys: Saving Britain 1940* (New York: Harper Perennial, 2003), 314–315.

25. *The Air Historical Branch Narrative*, pp. 395–397, TNA AIR 41/15; Churchill, *Their Finest Hour*, 291–292.

26. *Narrative*, p. 396, TNA Air 41/15.

27. Data from Single-engine Fighter Pilot Strength, RAF and German Air Force: Tables 1 & 2, in *The Battle of Britain: The Myth and the Reality*, R. Overy (London: Penguin, 2000), 162.

28. J. Corum, "Defeat of the Luftwaffe, 1939–45," in *Why Air Forces Fail*, ed. Higham and Harris, 219.

29. *Narrative*, pp. 395–397, TNA AIR 41/15. However, Bishop, *Fighter Boys*, 218, asserts that "promising pilots" were sometimes posted directly from their flying schools to their squadrons without passing through the operational stage at all.

30. "Minutes of Conference on Training held at Headquarters, Fighter Command, at 11.00 hrs on 23 October 1940," TNA AIR 16/636.

31. Peter Brothers, interviewed by Nigel Lewis, "The Fewer," *BBC History Magazine* 1, no. 2 (2000): 16.

32. Hough and Richards, *The Battle of Britain: The Jubilee History*, 156.

33. Hopkinson to Ministry of Information, 17 August 1940, TNA FO 371/24231, A3961/26/45, as quoted by N. Cull, *Selling War: The British Propaganda Campaign Against American Neutrality in World War II* (Oxford: Oxford University Press, 1995), 89.

34. A. Price, "Myth and Legend," *Aeroplane Monthly* 25, no. 10, iss. 294 (1997): 23.

35. Park to Dowding, "German Air Attacks on England, 6 August to 10 September," par. 18, TNA AIR 2/7355.

36. J. E. Johnson and P. B. Lucas, *Glorious Summer* (London: Stanley Paul & Co., Ltd., 1990), 3. This is a reference to the Messerschmitt Me.109E's strong performance at high altitude.

37. Park, "German Air Attacks," TNA AIR 2/7355.

38. Cumming, *Royal Navy*, 92–94.

39. P. B. Lucas, *Flying Colours: The Epic Story of Douglas Bader* (London: Hutchinson, 1981), 135–136.

40. Allen, *Who Won*, 118.

41. Appendix B to "Notes on Air Defence of Great Britain," TNA ADM 199/64. This document gives official response times and indicates that filtering could be done in fifty-five seconds—i.e., the time taken between detection and the appearance of the raid in visual form at the operations room. But if the raid had been detected by the Royal Observer Corps, it could be one minute and forty-five seconds. Allen suggests that in practice it could be much longer and gives a built-in delay of four minutes. Allen, *Who Won*, 58.

42. Allen, *Who Won*, 117–118.

43. Dunnigan and Nofi, *Secrets*, 134.

44. Park, "German Air Attacks," TNA AIR2/7355.

45. Price, "Myth and Legend," 23.

46. An average of data from various sources individually quoted by Terraine, *The Right of the Line*, 119–120, as calculated by Cumming, *Royal Navy*, Appendix II, 157.

47. Cumming, *Royal Navy*, 157.

48. Holland, *Battle*, 530. This does not appear to be a verbatim quote from Dowding.

49. A. Zamoyski, *The Forgotten Few: The Polish Air Force in the Second World War* (London: John Murray Publishers, Ltd., 1995), 91.

50. Allen, *Who Won*, 194. Also see data in "Roll of Honour of the Few," Battle of Britain Historical Society, http://battleofbritain1940.net/bobhsoc/index.html (accessed 22 September 2014).

51. Dunnigan and Nofi, *Secrets*, 202.

52. Allen, *Who Won*, 192.

53. "Dowding's Despatch on the Battle of Britain," par. 106, TNA PREM 4/39 and AIR 20/502; "Minutes of Conference on Training held at Headquarters, Fighter Command at 11.00 hrs on 23 October 1940," TNA AIR 16/636. At this date, 440 RAF pilots were nonoperational, representing one-third of all Fighter Command pilots. Some twenty "C" class squadrons with approximately sixteen nonoperational pilots located in quieter areas were effectively nonoperational.

54. Robinson, *Invasion 1940*, 232.

55. Hewitt, *Hitler's Armada*, 50–51.

56. J. Corum, "The Luftwaffe and the Lessons Learned in the Spanish Civil War," in *Air Power History*, ed. Cox and Gray, 80.

57. R. Overy, "The Dangers of the Blitz Spirit: The History Essay," *BBC History Magazine*, October 2013, pp. 29–32.

58. Viscount Caldecote, Emergency Powers (Defence) Bill 1939, HL Deb, 22 May 1940, Vol. 116, cc381–8, Hansard, http://hansard.millbanksystems .com/lords/1940/may/22/emergency-powers-defence-bill (accessed 31 January 2012).

59. Allen, *Who Won*, 58.

60. Price, *Pictorial History of the Luftwaffe*, 27–28.

61. J. Corum, "Defeat of the Luftwaffe, 1939–45," in *Why Air Forces Fail*, ed. Higham and Harris, 204–207.

62. J. Ray, *The Battle of Britain: New Perspectives: Behind the Scenes of the Great Air War* (London: Arms and Armour Press, 1994), 160–167.

63. Churchill, *Their Finest Hour*, 281.

64. Broadcast to the nation on 11 September 1940, in Churchill, *Their Finest Hour*, 290–291.

65. There can be little doubt that Kennedy's political views were colored by pro-German sympathies and anti-Semitism but this does not necessarily invalidate his assessment of British foreign policy motives.

66. Churchill, *Their Finest Hour*, 405; Letter from Admiral Charles Forbes to Godfrey Style, 6 February 1947, CA ROSK 4/49; Entry for 12 July 1940, J. Colville, *The Fringes of Power: The Ten Downing Street Diaries, 1939–1955* (New York: W. W. Norton, 1985), 192.

67. Memo from W. S. Churchill to C-in-C Home Forces, 10 July 1940, TNA CAB 120/438, REF: 95419.

68. R. Toye, "Untold Stories of Churchill's World War II Speeches," 19 August 2013, University of Exeter Research News, www.exeter.ac.uk/news/re search/title_313389_en.html (accessed 13 September 2013).

69. W. Lippmann, "Today and Tomorrow: Havana and the Battle of Britain," *Washington Post*, 30 July 1940, p. 7.

70. From Morris Wilson to Ministry of Aircraft Production, BRINY 1763, 4 December 1940, TNA AIR 75/63. Text includes message from Slessor to Chief of Air Staff, 2 December 1940.

71. "Rise of Aid-to-Britain Sentiment," *Washington Post*, 29 December 1940, p. 11. This graph is imprecisely drawn, but the figure of 88 percent seems reasonable. Also see G. Gallup, "The Gallup Poll: 60% Favor Greater Aid to England," *Washington Post*, p. 11; "Sectional Vote on U.S. Entering War, Giving Greater Aid to Britain," *Washington Post*, p. 11.

72. Interview with Barry Cornwell, as quoted by P. Knightley, *The First Casualty: The War Correspondent as Hero and Myth-Maker from the Crimea to Kosovo* (London: Prion Books, 2001), 258.

73. Cull, *Selling War*, 90.

74. Halifax to Sinclair, 19 August 1940, TNA FO 371/24321, A3799/26/45, as quoted by Cull, *Selling War*, 90.

75. Hopkinson to MoI, 17 August 1940, TNA FO 371/24231, A3961/26/45, as quoted by Cull, *Selling War*, 89.

76. Cull, *Selling War*, 47.

77. H. R. J. Pilott, interview by henryjean, "A South East Londoner's Story—Chapter 1," *WW2 People's War: An archive of World War II memories - written by the public, gathered by the BBC*, 14 November 2003, http://www.bbc.co.uk/history/ww2peopleswar/stories/18/a2043118.shtml; various stories in the *Washington Post*, 1940–1941.

78. Overy, "Blitz Spirit," p. 29.

79. Minutes of MoI Policy Committee, 22 July 1940, TNA INF 1/849.

80. D. Stafford, *Roosevelt & Churchill: Men of Secrets* (London: Abacus, 2000), 49, 123.

81. F. Capra, *The Name above the Title* (London: W. H, Allen, 1972), 326.

82. Press Release from MoI Films Division in Imperial War Museum, as quoted by A. Calder, *The Myth of the Blitz* (London: Pimlico, 1997), 248.

83. *The Battle of Britain*, ADM 10, Imperial War Museum, Film and Video Archive.

84. From J. M. Parrish, MoI, to C. Plumbley, HMSO, 28 March 1941, TNA STAT 14/226; Air Ministry, *The Battle of Britain: 8 August–31 August 1940* (London: HMSO, 1941), 7.

85. Cook, "The Myth of the Aviator and the Flight to Fascism," 41; A. J. Cumming, "We'll get by with a little help from our friends: The Battle of Britain and the Pilot in Anglo-American Relations, 1940–45," *European Journal of American Culture* 26, no. 1 (2007): pp. 11–26.

Chapter 8. The Naval War

Epigraph: Letter from Admiral Charles Forbes to Godfrey Style, 6 February 1947, CA ROSK 4/49. These remarks were made at a Navy Club dinner.

1. Minute from G. M. B Langley for Director of Naval Air Division, 18 October 1939, TNA ADM 1/9920. Also see P. C. Smith, *Skua! The Royal Navy's Dive-Bomber* (Barnsley, South Yorkshire, UK: Pen & Sword Aviation, 2006); P. C. Smith, *The History of Dive Bombing: A Comprehensive History from 1911 Onward* (Barnsley, South Yorkshire, UK: Pen & Sword Aviation, 2007).

2. Divine, *The Blunted Sword*, 159–160.

3. A. D. Harvey, "The Stuka Myth," *BBC History Magazine Second World War Special: Britain's Year of Defiance* (2010), p. 52.

4. G. Paust and M. Lancelot, *Fighting Wings* (New York: Essential Books, 1944), 136, 145.

5. "Tactical Summary of Bombing Attacks by German Aircraft on HM Ships and Shipping, September 1939 to February 1941," TNA ADM 199/1189/A/NAD326/41.

6. Essay by Grand Admiral K. Dönitz, 24 September 1945, TNA ADM 223/668.

7. Churchill, *The Gathering Storm*, 537; G. B. Mason, "HMS *Rodney*—Nelson-class 16inch Gun Battleship," *Service Histories of Royal Navy Warships in World War 2*, Naval History.net, http://www.naval-history.net/xGM-Chrono-01BB-Rodney.htm (accessed 23 February 2012).

8. M. Griehl, *Junkers Ju.87 Stuka* (Shrewsbury, UK: Airlife Publishing Ltd., 2001), 69, 71–72, 137.

9. Ibid., 201.

10. Tactical Summary, TNA ADM 199/1189/ A/NAD326/41.

11. Letter from Dowding to Wing Commander J. Whitworth Jones, Air Ministry, 25 November 1939, IWM HTT 226, Tizard Papers FC/S.18093.

12. P. Schenk, *Invasion of England, 1940* (London: Conway Maritime Press, 1990), 246.

13. Translation of Vice Admiral W. Wegener, *Seestrategie des Weltkrieges* (The Naval Strategy of the World War), p. 1, submitted by British Naval Attaché, Berlin, 1939, TNA ADM 1/9956.

14. Hinsley et al., *British Intelligence in the Second World War*, vol. 1, *Its Influence on Strategy and Operations*, 103.

15. Cumming, *The Royal Navy and the Battle of Britain*, 111; Hewitt, *Hitler's Armada*, 98–101.

16. J. Levy, "Lost Leader: Admiral of the Fleet, Sir Charles Forbes," *The Mariner's Mirror* 88, no. 2 (2002): p. 190.

17. Conjunct Expeditions to Norway, April–June 1940, pp. 31–32, ADM 234/332 No.17. Also see Levy, "Lost Leader," p. 191.

18. Churchill, *The Gathering Storm*, 563–564.

19. G. B. Mason, "HMS *Gurkha*—Tribal Class Destroyer," *Service Histories of Royal Navy Warships in World War 2*, Naval History.net, http://www

.naval-history.net/xGM-Chrono-10DD-34Tribal-Gurkha1.htm (accessed 10 May 2009).

20. Churchill, *The Gathering Storm*, 560–561, 563; F. Kersoudy, *Norway, 1940* (London: Collins, 1990), 135–136.

21. "On this day, 10 April 1940," Fleet Air Arm Officers Association, http:// www.fleetairarmoa.org/news/on-this-day-10-april-1940 (accessed 12 June 2014).

22. A. Thomas, *Royal Navy Aces of World War II* (Oxford: Osprey, 2007), 90.

23. "W. P. Lucy, RN," Fleet Air Arm Archive 1939–1945, http://www.fleet airarmarchive.net/rollofhonour/COs/CommandingOfficers-l.htm.

24. Hewitt, *Hitler's Armada*, 102–106.

25. Forbes to Admiralty, 15 June 1940, as quoted by S. Roskill, *The War at Sea, 1939–45*, vol. 1 (London: HMSO, 1954), 267–268.

26. Roskill, *The War at Sea*, 198.

27. Levy, "Lost Leader," 190.

28. V. Howland, "The Loss of the *Glorious*: An Analysis of the Action," *International Naval Research Organization*, http://www.warship.org/no119 94.htm (accessed 29 August 2013).

29. P. Caddick-Adams, Entry for Norway campaign (1940), in *Oxford Companion to Military History*, ed. Holmes, 664.

30. Churchill, *The Gathering Storm*, 537.

31. E. A. Seal, Ministry of Works, to Vice Admiral Sir Ralph Edwards, "Draft Minute to the Prime Minister," CA ROSK 4/75.

32. Danchev and Todman, *Alanbrooke*, 318, 401, 409–410, 444–446, 450–451, 456, 458–459, 472, 483, 515, 528, 532, and 586. Brooke was Churchill's C-in-C Home Forces and later chief of Imperial General Staff. His diary made many scathing references to Churchill's inept meddling, including, for example, his inability to grasp details, to relate one front to another, or to think in the strategic long term.

33. Letter from Controller of the Navy Ralph Edwards to Stephen Roskill, 28 July 1954, CA ROSK 5/124. Also see "Admiralty Reply," *Times* (London), 8 November 1940, p. 9. Edwards may have been among the group of younger naval officers on the operations staff that approached Lieutenant-Commander Robert Bower, MP, about the conditions of excessive secrecy surrounding the Norway campaign, expressing "grave disquiet" regarding the "whole conduct of naval operations" by senior officers.

34. Forbes to Roskill, 28 January 1950, CA ROSK 6/30.

35. Danchev and Todman, *Alanbrooke*, 400; "Pound, Sir Alfred Dudley Pickman Rogers (1877–1943)," in *Who's Who in Military History From 1453*, ed. J. Keegan and A. Wheatcroft (Leicester, UK: Promotional Reprint Company, 1987), 259.

36. From "Turtle" Hamilton to Forbes from HMS *Aurora*, 27 May 1940, CA ROSK 4/42.

37. Page 2 of Enclosure No. II to Commanding Officer, HMS *Curacoa's* letter No. 0307/191 of 5 May 1940," par 12–13, TNA ADM 199/66.

38. Ron Babb, interview by author, 7 April 2004.

39. F. W. Winterbotham, *The Ultra Secret* (London: Weidenfeld & Nicolson, 1999), 68.

40. A. Hezlet, *Aircraft and Sea Power* (London: Peter Davies, 1970), 155–156.

41. Hewitt, *Hitler's Armada*, 107–108.

42. Higham and Harris, "Defeats of the Royal Air Force," 319.

43. Churchill, *The Gathering Storm*, 537, and Appendix R.

44. Churchill, *The Gathering Storm*, Appendix R.

45. E. Raeder, *My Life* (Annapolis, MD: Naval Institute Press, 1960), 311.

46. Churchill, *The Gathering Storm*, p.592.

47. Hewitt, *Hitler's Armada*, 112–113.

48. Ibid., 131–132.

49. L. Rees, "Hitler's Greatest Gamble," *BBC History Magazine Second World War Special: Britain's Year of Defiance* (2010), pp. 27–28.

50. Hewitt, *Hitler's Armada*, 117–118.

51. Ibid., 120–126.

52. David Divine, Obituary, *Times* (London), 2 May 1987, p. 72.

53. Professor Geoffrey Wawro, director of Military History Center, University of North Texas, as quoted by Rees, "Hitler's Greatest Gamble," p. 29.

54. Churchill, *Their Finest Hour*, 89–90. These British shipping losses do not include more than 170 miscellaneous small craft.

55. Roberts, "Call for Fire," p. 40.

56. Hewitt, *Hitler's Armada*, 127.

57. Ibid., 129.

58. G. Letchford, "Kent (Fortress) Royal Engineers in France," *WW2 People's War: An archive of World War Two memories - written by the public, gathered by the BBC*, http://www.bbc.co.uk/ww2peopleswar/stories/39/a4034639.shtml (accessed 15 February 2012); Major Peter Keeble, Obituary, *The Telegraph* (London), 15 February 2004, http://www.telegraph.co.uk/news/obituaries/1475298/Major-Peter-Keeble.html (accessed 15 February 2012).

59. "Operations XD and XDA: Recognition of Officers and Men" and Appendix III, "Demolitions Carried Out," TNA ADM 1/11397.

60. Essay by General Admiral O. Schniewind and Admiral K. Schuster, 26 November 1945, TNA ADM 223/696.

61. M. Portillo, D. Keen, P. Brothers, A. Lambert, V. Bailey, C. Barnett, and A. Fishlock, "The Battles of Britain—Transcript," *The Things We Forgot to Remember*, BBC Radio 4, broadcast 2005, made available on The Open University, 17 May 2005, http://www.open.edu/openlearn/history-the-arts/history/the-battles-britain-transcript (accessed 15 February 2012).

62. Hewitt, *Hitler's Armada*, x. Also see G. B. Mason, "HMS *Prince of Wales King George* V-class 14inch Gun Battleship," *Service Histories of Royal Navy Warships in World War 2*, Naval History.net, http://www.naval-history.net/xGM-Chrono-01BB-Prince%20of%20Wales.htm (accessed 27 February 2012).

63. Churchill, *Their Finest Hour*, 206–211.

64. M. Simpson, "Somerville, Sir James Fownes," DNB, http://www.oxforddnb.com/view/article/36191 (accessed 27 June 2012).

65. "The First Pictures from Oran! The Gratitude of the Comrade-in-Arms," in *Signal: Hitler's Wartime Picture Magazine*, ed. S. L. Mayer (London: Bison Books, 1978).

66. R. Jenkins, *Churchill* (London: Pan, 2002), 623–625.

67. G. Gallup, "U.S. Public Favors Occupation of Islands in Caribbean if Hitler Wins, Poll Shows: 87% Would Take Over Foreign Holdings Near Canal," *Washington Post*, 21 July 1940, p. 2; Lippmann, "Today and Tomorrow, p. 7.

68. "Report of the C-in-C Navy to the Fuehrer in the afternoon of 6 September 1940," as quoted by Showell, *Fuehrer Conferences*, 134; "U.S. Acts Swiftly to Start Bases: Britons Hail America as Ally; Leaders of Congress Favor Deal," and "British Pledge Never to Sink or Surrender Fleet," *Washington Post*, 4 September 1940, pp. 1, 4.

69. Churchill, *Their Finest Hour*, 494–450, 212.

70. A. Hague, Convoy HX.79, *Arnold Hague Convoy Database*, http://www.convoyweb.org.uk/hx/index.html (accessed 13 May 2014).

71. Churchill, "Table II: Monthly Totals of Shipping Losses, British Allied and Neutral," in *Their Finest Hour*, 639.

72. J. Ellis, "Table 74," in *The World War II Databook: The Essential Facts and Figures for all the Combatants* (London: Aurum Press, 1993). This source gives 5,553 Merchant Navy crewmen casualties in British registered ships in 1940. I have divided this by 366 days to reach a daily figure of 15.172 and multiplied this by the 114 days of the Battle of Britain to reach a total of 1,730. The resulting figure cannot be an exact comparison, but I believe it to be a reasonable estimate.

73. Terraine, *The Right of the Line*, 234.

74. B. Ireland, *Battle of the Atlantic* (London: Leo Cooper, 2003), 220–221.

75. Terraine, *The Right of the Line*, 240–242.

76. Ibid., 436–438.

77. From Forbes to Admiralty, 4 June 1940, TNA ADM 1/10556. The "fleet-in being" is a term generally associated with the theories of Admiral A. T. Mahan of the U.S. Navy, though it was not originally coined by him. In essence, it means avoiding potential losses from offensive action when more might be gained by conserving the fleet in harbor as a deterrent.

78. Holland, *Battle*, 576–577.

79. Hewitt, *Hitler's Armada*, 141–142.

80. Longmate, *Island Fortress*, 517–517.

81. Ibid., 519.

82. Showell, "Report of the Naval Staff, 10 September 1940," in *Fuehrer Conferences*, 136.

83. Churchill, "Prime Minister to Secretary of State for Air, 23 September 1940," in *Their Finest Hour*, 405.

84. Showell, "Report of the Naval Staff, 10 September 1940," in *Fuehrer Conferences*, 136.

85. Ministry of Defence, Naval Historical Branch, Naval Intelligence Division, "German Plans for the Invasion of England in 1940: Operation "Sea Lion," MoD NID 24, GHS/1, p. 51. Also see K. Assmann, "Operation Sea Lion," U.S. Naval Institute *Proceedings* 76, no. 1 (1950): 1–13.

86. Longmate, *Island Fortress*, 502–503.

87. Hewitt, *Hitler's Armada*, 8–11.

88. Ibid., 42–43.

89. F. Ruge, *Sea Warfare 1939–1945* (London: Cassell, 1957), 85.

90. G. Blumentritt, Extract from "An Cosantóir," trans. T. B. Dunne, British Intelligence Section, *The Irish Defence Journal* 1, no. 1 (1949): 10–14; Ruge, *Sea Warfare*, 85.

91. "Sixty Years Ago: 'The Channel Dash,'" Ministry of Defence, cited on the National Archives website, http://webarchive.nationalarchives.gov .uk/+/http://www.operations.mod.uk/onthisday/newsItem_id=1451.htm (accessed 18 September 2012).

92. From Forbes to Admiralty, 4 June 1940 TNA ADM 1/10556. For the opinions of Forbes' reporting officers, see "Captain's Confidential Reports," Entries by Chatfield, July 1925–July 1928 and 6 December 1931, TNA ADM 196/90.

93. Roskill, *The War at Sea*, 257.

94. From Forbes to Admiralty, 4 June 1940, TNA ADM 1/10556.

Chapter 9. The Vital Mediterranean

Epigraph: R. Langsworth, *Churchill by Himself: The Definitive Collection of Quotations* (New York: PublicAffairs, 2008), 176. This is a famous Churchill witticism allegedly made at a 1937 conference with the German ambassador to Great Britain. However, there is no attribution to this remark.

1. Porch, *Path*, 80–81.
2. "Origins," Schneider Trophy website, http://www.hydroretro.net/coupeen/coupeeng.htm (accessed 25 July 2012).
3. B. Gunston, *World Encyclopaedia of Aero Engines* (Wellingborough, Northampton, UK: Patrick Stephens Limited, 1989), 58.
4. R. P. Hallion, foreword to *The Command of the Air*, by G. Douhet (Washington, DC: New imprint by Air Force History and Museums Program, 1998; first published: New York: Coward-McCann, 1942), http://permanent.access.gpo.gov/airforcehistory/www.airforcehistory.hq.af.mil/Publications/fulltext/command_of_the_air.pdf (accessed 25 July 2012).
5. Foreword to *The Command of the Air*, by Douhet, viii.
6. J. Greene and A. Massignani, *The Naval War in the Mediterranean 1940–1943* (Annapolis, MD: Naval Institute Press, 2011), 17.
7. G. Gallup, "The Gallup Poll: 60% Favor Greater Aid to England" and "Rise of Aid-to-Britain Sentiment," *Washington Post*, 29 December 1940, p. 11.
8. Lippmann, "Today and Tomorrow," p. 7.
9. Roosevelt's stance became less unambiguously pro-British as the war progressed: he was constantly suspicious of British foreign policy motives regarding the British Empire, and he sided with Soviet leader Joseph Stalin in discussions over the postwar future of Europe. However, in 1940–41, it would be hard to imagine how the British could have continued the war for long without Roosevelt's assistance in securing the Lend-Lease Bill.
10. Porch, *Path*, 666–667.
11. War Cabinet, "Military Policy in the Middle East—Report by the Minister for Co-Ordination of Defence," 13 January 1940, pp. 1–9, TNA CAB 66/4/48.
12. Memorandum from Churchill to C-in-C Home Forces, 10 July 1940, TNA CAB 120/438, REF:95419.
13. War Cabinet Weekly Resume (86), "Naval, Military and Air Situation 30 January 1941–24 April 1941," p. 102, TNA CAB 66/16/15.
14. S. David, *Military Blunders: The How and Why of Military Failure* (London: Robinson, 1997), 187.
15. Greene and Massignani, *Naval War*, 11.
16. Porch, *Path*, 8.
17. J. Piekalkiewicz, *Sea War: 1939–1945* (London and New York: Blandford Press, 1987), 82.
18. A. Iachino, *Tramonto di Una Grande Marina* (Milan: Mondadori, 1961) as quoted by Greene and Massignani, *Naval War*, 39.
19. Porch, *Path*, 49.
20. Greene and Massignani, *Naval War*, 14–15, 52.

21. Ibid., 35–36.

22. Ibid., 32–34.

23. Ibid., 37.

24. H. T. Lenton, *British and Empire Warships of the Second World War* (London: Greenhill Books, 1998), 32.

25. A. B. Cunningham, "Report of an Action with the Italian Fleet off Calabria, 9 July 1940" (Cunningham's Despatch), *Supplement to the London Gazette*, 28 April 1948, 2643–2649, https://www.thegazette.co.uk/London/issue/38273/page/2643 (accessed 24 September 2014).

26. Ibid., 2646–2648.

27. P. C. Smith, *Critical Conflict: The Royal Navy's Mediterranean Campaign in 1940* (Barnsley, South Yorkshire, UK: Pen & Sword Maritime, 2011), 90–91.

28. A. B. Cunningham, *A Sailor's Odyssey* (London: Hutchinson, 1951), 201.

29. Greene and Massignani, *Naval War*, 65.

30. Ibid., 66.

31. M. Muggeridge, ed., *Ciano's Diary 1939–43* (London: Heinemann, 1947), 276–277.

32. Smith, *Critical Conflict*, 87–88.

33. R. Farley, "Attack on Taranto," *Warships International Fleet Review*, January 2011, pp. 42–43.

34. Greene and Massignani, *Naval War*, 82–85.

35. Ibid., 104–105; R. Gannon, *Hellions of the Deep: The Development of American Torpedoes in World War II* (University Park, PA: Penn State University Press, 1996), 49.

36. A. B. Cunningham, "Fleet Air Arm Operations against Taranto, on 11 November 1940" (Cunningham's Despatch), *Supplement to the London Gazette*, 24 July 1947, 3471–3472. https://www.thegazette.co.uk/London/issue/38023/supplement/3473 (accessed 24 September 2014).

37. Cunningham, "Fleet Air Arm Operations against Taranto," pp. 3473–3475.

38. Ibid., pp. 3475–3477.

39. Ibid., p. 3476.

40. W. S. Churchill, speech to House of Commons, "Fleet Air Arm Success," Hansard, 13 November 1940, http://hansard.millbanksystems.com/commons/1940/nov/13/fleet-air-arm-success (accessed 1 August 2012).

41. Smith, *Critical Conflict*, 259.

42. Farley, "Attack on Taranto," p. 42.

43. Ibid., pp. 42–43.

44. Churchill, *Their Finest Hour*, 544–545.

45. V. Orange, "Collishaw, Raymond (1893–1976)," DNB, http://www.oxford dnb.com/view/article/72029 (accessed 27 June 2014; A. B. Cunningham and R. Collishaw, *The London Gazette*, 4 March 1941, https://www .thegazette.co.uk/London/issue/35094/page/1303 (accessed 8 August 2012).

46. From Forbes to Admiralty, 4 June 1940, TNA ADM 1/10556.

47. David, *Military Blunders*, 196.

48. Porch, *Path*, 142–143.

49. Ibid., 664–665.

Chapter 10. Conclusion

Epigraphs: (1) Cohen and Cohen, eds., *Penguin Dictionary of Quotations*, 403. (2) Foreword to "The Coalition: Our Programme for Government," as quoted in "The Strategic Defence and Security Review," 10 September 2010, UK Parliament website, http://www.publications.parliament.uk/pa/ cm201011/cmselect/cmdfence/writev/hc345/ucm0102.htm (accessed 23 October 2013).

1. Royal Air Force, "The Early Years of Flight," chapter 1 in *A Short History of the Royal Air Force*, http://www.raf.mod.uk/rafcms/mediafiles/ F21BE44E_EE18_2A21_DE9200FADAA9DB6E.pdf (accessed 27 June 2014).

2. Lloyd George, *War Memoirs*, 692–693, 733.

3. W. E. Johns, *Biggles of 266* (London: Dean, 1962) and *The Camels are Coming* (London: Red Fox, 1993).

4. Chatfield, *It Might Happen Again*, 83.

5. War Diary entry for 10 September 1940, in Showell, *Fuehrer Conferences*, 136.

6. L. Deighton, *Fighter: The Story of the Battle of Britain* (London: Jonathan Cape Ltd., 1977), ii; L. Mosley, *Battle of Britain* (London: Pan Books, 1969), 196–197.

7. A. Velicogna et al., "Naval Aviation: A Historical Perspective," Phoenix Think Tank, July 2011, http://www.phoenixthinktank.org/2011/07/naval- aviation-a-historical-perspective-2/ (accessed 13 September 2013).

8. M. Clapp, "Commanding Carrier Aviation," Phoenix Think Tank, October 2010, http://www.phoenixthinktank.org/2011/05/commanding- carrier-aviation/ (accessed 13 September 2013).

9. A. J. Cumming, "Rivalry and Retreat: The Royal Navy and Royal Air Force in the Missile Age 1945–1970," Phoenix Think Tank, June 2013, http://www .phoenixthinktank.org/2013/06/history-of-airpower-series-paper-4-rivalry- and-retreat-the-royal-navy-and-royal-air-force-in-the-missile-age-1945–1 (accessed 13 September 2013).

10. Grove, "It Has Happened Again: Lord Chatfield and his Critique of British Defence Policy Making."

BIBLIOGRAPHY

Archives

Churchill Archives, Cambridge
> CA ROSK The Papers of Captain S. W. Roskill

Imperial War Museum, London
> IWM HTT 226, The Papers of Sir Henry Tizard
> Film and Video Archive, ADM 10, *The Battle of Britain*

Liddell Hart Centre for Military Archives, London
> The Papers of Sir Basil Liddell Hart.

Ministry of Defence, Naval Historical Branch, London
> MoD NID 24 Naval Intelligence Division

The National Archives, Kew
> ADM 1 Admiralty and Ministry of Defence, Navy Department.
> ADM 186 Admiralty Publications, Correspondence and Papers 1660–1976, 1827–1970
> ADM 196 Officers' Service Records (Series III)
> ADM 199 Admiralty: War History Cases and Papers, Second World War 1922–1968
> ADM 223 Admiralty: Naval Intelligence Reports and Papers 1914–1978
> ADM 234/332 Admiralty, and Ministry of Defence, Navy Department: Reference Books (BR Series)
> AIR 2 Air Ministry and Ministry of Defence: Registered Files 1887–1985
> AIR 5 Air Ministry: Air Historical Branch: Papers (Series II)
> AIR 6 Air Board and Air Ministry, Air Council, Minutes and Memoranda 1916–1976

AIR 10 Ministry of Defence and Predecessors: Air Publications and Reports 1913–1979

AIR 16 Air Ministry: Fighter Command: Registered Files 1925–1988

AIR 20 Air Ministry and Ministry of Defence: Papers Accumulated in the Air Historical Branch

AIR 33 Air Ministry: Royal Air Force Inspectorate General: Reports and Papers 1938–1977

AIR 41 Air Ministry and Ministry of Defence: Air Historical Branch: Narratives and Monographs 1942–1991

AVIA 7 Ministry of Aviation and Predecessors: Royal Radar Establishment and Predecessors: Registered Files 1917– 1969

CAB 16 Committee of Imperial Defence: Ad Hoc-Sub-Committees: Minutes, Memoranda and Reports, 1905–1939

CAB 23 War Cabinet and Cabinet Minutes 1916–1939

CAB 24 War Cabinet and Cabinet Memoranda (GT CP and G War Series) 1915–1939

CAB 27/648 (38) Defence Programmes and their Acceleration

CAB 44 Committee of Imperial Defence, Historical Branch and Cabinet Office, Historical Section: War Histories: Draft Chapters and Narratives,

CAB 66 War Cabinet Military 1914–1965

CAB 120 Ministry of Defence Secretariat

PREM 4/39 Prime Minister's Office: Confidential Correspondence and Papers 1934–1946

The National Newspaper Library, London

MA 78 *Washington Post*, 1940–1941

Books

Adamthwaite, A. *The Making of the Second World War.* London: Routledge, 1979.

Addison, P., and J. Crang. *The Burning Blue.* London: Pimlico, 2000.

Air Ministry. *The Battle of Britain: 8 August–31 August 1940.* London: His Majesty's Stationery Office (HMSO), 1941.

Allen, H. R. *The Legacy of Lord Trenchard.* London: Cassell, 1972.

———. *Who Won the Battle of Britain?* Frogmore, St. Albans, Hertfordshire, UK: Panther, 1976.

Bacon, R. H. *The Life of John Rushworth Jellicoe.* London: Cassell, 1936.

Bacon, R. H. S. *Britain's Glorious Navy.* London: Odhams, ca.1942.

———. *The Dover Patrol 1915–1917.* Vol. 2. New York: George H. Doran Company, 1919.

Barnett, C. *Engage the Enemy More Closely: The Royal Navy and the Second World War.* London: Hodder and Stoughton, 1991.

Bennett, R. *Behind the Battle: Intelligence in the War with Germany.* London: Sinclair-Stevenson, 1994.

Bishop, P. *Fighter Boys: Saving Britain 1940.* London: Harper Perennial, 2003.

Blake, R., ed. *The Private Papers of Douglas Haig, 1914–1919.* London: Eyre & Spottiswood, 1952.

Boyle, A. *Trenchard.* London: Collins, 1962.

Brodhurst, R. *Churchill's Anchor.* London: Leo Cooper, 1991.

Calder, A. *The Myth of the Blitz.* London: Pimlico, 1997.

Callwell, C. *Field Marshal Sir Henry Wilson: His Life and Diaries.* Vol. 2. London: Cassell, 1927.

Campbell, M. *The Peril from the Air.* London: Hutchinson, 1937.

Capra, F. *The Name above the Title.* New York: W. H. Allen, 1972.

Castle, H. G. *Fire Over England: The German Air Raids in World War I.* London: Leo Cooper, 1982.

Cato. *Guilty Men.* London: V. Gollancz, 1940.

Chatfield, E. *It Might Happen Again.* Vol. 2, *The Navy and Defence: The Autobiography of Admiral of the Fleet Lord Chatfield.* London: William Heinemann Ltd., 1947.

Childers, Erskine. *The Riddle of the Sands.* London: Dent, 1979. First published by Smith, Elder & Co., 1903.

Churchill, R. S. *Winston S. Churchill: Companion.* Vol. 2, Part 2, *1907–1911.* London: Heinemann, 1969.

———. *Winston S. Churchill: Companion.* Vol. 2, Part 3, *1911–1914.* London: Heinemann, 1969.

Churchill, W. S. *The Gathering Storm.* Vol. 1 of *The Second World War.* London: Penguin Classics, 2005.

———. *Their Finest Hour.* Vol. 2 of *The Second World War.* London: Cassell, 1949.

Clark, A. *Aces High: The War in the Air over the Western Front 1914–18.* London: Fontana, 1974.

Cohen, J., and M. Cohen, eds. *The Penguin Dictionary of Quotations.* London: Penguin Books, 1983.

Colville, J. *The Fringes of Power: The Ten Downing Street Diaries, 1939–1955.* New York: W. W. Norton, 1985.

Compton Hall, R. *Submarines and the War at Sea 1914–18.* London: Macmillan, 1991.

Cook, C., and J. Stevenson. *The Longman Handbook of Modern European History, 1763–1991.* London: Longman, 1992.

Cox, S., and P. Gray, eds. *Air Power History: Turning Points from Kitty Hawk to Kosovo.* Oxford: Routledge, 2002.

Cull, N. *Selling War: The British Propaganda Campaign against American Neutrality in World War II*. Oxford: Oxford University Press, 1996.

Cumming, A. J. *The Royal Navy and the Battle of Britain*. Annapolis, MD: Naval Institute Press, 2010.

Cunningham, A. B. *A Sailor's Odyssey*. London: Hutchinson, 1951.

Danchev, A., and D. Todman, eds., *War Diaries 1939–1945: The Diaries of Field Marshal Lord Alanbrooke*. London: Weidenfeld and Nicolson, 2001.

David, S. *Military Blunders: The How and Why of Military Failure*. London: Robinson, 1997.

Deighton, L. *Fighter: The Story of the Battle of Britain*. London: Jonathan Cape Ltd., 1977.

———. *Battle of Britain*. London: Book Club Associates, 1980.

Divine, D. *The Blunted Sword*. London: Hutchinson, 1964.

———. *The Broken Wing: A Study in the British Exercise of Air Power*. London: Hutchinson, 1966.

Douhet, G. *The Command of the Air*. Washington, DC: New imprint by Air Force and Museums Program, 1998. First published 1942 by Coward McGann Inc.

Dunnigan, F., and A. A. Nofi. *Dirty Little Secrets of World War II*. New York: Quill, William Morrow, 1994.

Ellis, J. *The World War II Databook: The Essential Facts and Figures for all the Combatants*. London: Aurum Press, 1993.

Franklin, G. D. *Britain's Anti-Submarine Capability, 1919–1939*. London: Frank Cass & Co., 2003.

Fredette, R. *The First Battle of Britain 1917–18*. London: Cassell, 1966.

Funderburk, T. *The Early Birds of War: The Daring Pilots and Fighter Aeroplanes of World War I*. London: Arthur Barker Ltd., 1968.

———. *The Fighters: The Men and Machines of the First Air War*. London: Arthur Barker Ltd., 1966.

Galland, A. *The First and the Last*. London: Cerberus Publishing Co., 2001.

Gannon, R. *Hellions of the Deep: The Development of American Torpedoes in World War II*. University Park, PA: Penn State University Press, 1996.

Gilbert, M. *Winston S. Churchill*. London: Heinemann, 1976.

Greene, J., and A. Massignani. *The Naval War in the Mediterranean, 1940–1943*. Annapolis, MD: Naval Institute Press, 2011.

Griehl, M. *Junkers Ju.87 Stuka*. Shrewsbury, UK: Airlife Publishing Ltd., 2001.

Gunston, B. *World Encyclopaedia of Aero Engines*. Wellingborough, Northampton, UK: Patrick Stephens Limited, 1989.

Hancock, W. K. *Smuts: The Sanguine Years*. Vol. 1. Cambridge: Cambridge University Press, 1962.

Hanson, N. *First Blitz: The Secret German Plan to Raze London to the Ground in 1918*. New York: Doubleday, 2008.

Harrison, B., and H. Strachan, eds. *Military Lives: Intimate Biographies of the Famous by the Famous*. Oxford: Oxford University Press, 2002.

Hewitt, G. *Hitler's Armada: The Royal Navy and the Defence of Great Britain, April–October 1940*. Barnsley, South Yorkshire, UK: Pen & Sword Maritime, 2008.

Hezlet, A. *Aircraft and Sea Power*. London: Peter Davies, 1970.

Higham, R., and S. J. Harris, eds. *Why Air Forces Fail: An Anatomy of Defeat*. Lexington, KY: The University Press of Kentucky, 2006.

Hinsley, F. H., E. E. Thomas, C. F. G. Ransom, and R. C. Knight. *British Intelligence in the Second World War*. Vol. 1, *Its Influence on Strategy and Operations*. London: HMSO, 1979.

Hoare, S. *Empire of the Air: The Advent of the Air Age, 1922–1928*. London: Collins, 1957.

Holland, J. *The Battle of Britain: Five Months That Changed History, May–October 1940*. New York: Bantam, 2010.

Holmes, R., ed. *Oxford Companion to Military History*. Oxford: Oxford University Press, 2001.

Hore, P. *The World Encyclopedia of Battleships*. London: Hermes House, 2010.

Hough, R. *Bless Our Ship: Mountbatten and the Kelly*. London: Coronet Books, 1991.

Hough, R., and D. Richards. *The Battle of Britain: The Jubilee History*. London: Hodder and Stoughton, 1989.

Ireland, B. *Battle of the Atlantic*. London: Leo Cooper, 2003.

Jenkins, R. *Churchill*. London: Pan, 2002.

Johns, W. E. *Biggles of 266*. London: Dean, 1962.

———. *The Camels are Coming*. London: Red Fox, 1993.

Johnson, J. E., and P. B. Lucas. *Glorious Summer*. London: Stanley Paul & Co., Ltd., 1990.

Jones, H. A. *The War in the Air: Being the Story of the Part Played in the War by the Royal Air Force*. Vols. 3 and 6. Uckfield, East Sussex, UK: The Naval & Military Press, 1931.

Jordan, J., ed. *Warship 2007*. London: Conway, 2007.

Keegan, J., and A. Wheatcroft, eds. *Who's Who in Military History from 1453*. Leicester, UK: Promotional Reprint Company, 1987.

Kennedy, G., ed. *In Imperial Defence 1856–1956: The Old World Order*. Oxford: Routledge, 2008.

Kennedy, P. *The Rise and Fall of British Naval Mastery*. New York: Penguin, 2001.

Kersoudy, F. *Norway, 1940*. London: Collins, 1990.

Klinkowitz, J. *Pacific Skies: American Flyers in World War II*. Jackson, MS: University Press of Mississippi, 2004.

Knightley, P. *The First Casualty: The War Correspondent as Hero and Myth-Maker from the Crimea to Kosovo*. London: Prion Books, 2001.

Knocke, H. *I Flew for the Fuhrer*. London: Evans Brothers, 1953.

Lambert, A. *Admirals*. London: Faber and Faber, 2008.

Lambert, N. *Sir John Fisher's Naval Revolution*. Columbia, SC: University of South Carolina Press, 1999.

Langsworth, R. *Churchill by Himself: The Definitive Collection of Quotations*. New York: PublicAffairs, 2008.

Lavery, B. *Churchill's Navy: The Ships, Men, and Organisation, 1939–1945*. London: Conway, 2006.

Lenton, H. T. *British and Empire Warships of the Second World War*. London: Greenhill Books, 1998.

Lloyd George, D. *War Memoirs of David Lloyd George*. Vol. 1. London: Odhams Press Ltd., 1934.

Longmate, N. *Island Fortress: The Defence of Great Britain 1603–1945*. London: Pimlico, 2001.

Lucas, P. B. *Flying Colours: The Epic Story of Douglas Bader*. London: Hutchinson, 1981.

Maiolo, J. *The Royal Navy and Nazi Germany, 1933–1939: A Study in Appeasement and the Origins of the Second World War*. London: Macmillan, 1998.

Mallman Showell, J. *Fuehrer Conferences on Naval Affairs 1939–1945*. London: Chatham, 2005.

Mason, P. *One in the Eye for Harold*. London: Robson Press, 2011.

Massie, R. K. *Castles of Steel: Britain, Germany, and the Winning of the Great War at Sea*. London: Vintage, 2007.

Maurer, J. H., and C. M. Bell, eds. *At the Crossroads between Peace and War: The London Naval Conference in 1930*. Annapolis, MD: Naval Institute Press, 2014.

Mayer, S. L., ed. *Signal: Hitler's Wartime Picture Magazine*. London: Bison Books, 1978.

Montgomery Hyde, H. *British Air Policy between the Wars 1918–1939*. London: Heinemann, 1976.

Mosley, L. *Battle of Britain*. London: Pan Books, 1969.

Muggeridge, M., ed. *Ciano's Diary 1939–43*. London: Heinemann, 1947.

Omissi, D. *Air Power and Colonial Control: The Royal Air Force, 1919–1939*. Manchester, UK: Manchester University Press, 1990.

Overy, R. *The Battle of Britain: The Myth and the Reality*. London: Penguin, 2000.

Owen, L. *The Real Lord Northcliffe: Some Personal Recollections of a Private Secretary, 1902–1922.* London: Cassell, 1922.

Paust, G., and M. Lancelot. *Fighting Wings.* New York: Essential Books, 1944.

Piekalkiewicz, J. *Sea War: 1939–1945.* London and New York: Blandford Press, 1987.

Ponting, C. *1940: Myth & Reality.* London: Hamish Hamilton Ltd., 1990.

Porch, D. *The Path to Victory: The Mediterranean Theater in World War II.* New York: Farrar, Straus & Giroux, 2004.

Postan, M. M. *British War Production: History of the Second World War.* London: HMSO, 1952.

———. *History of the Second World War: Design and Development of Weapons: Studies on Government and Industrial Organisation.* London: HMSO, 1964.

Price, A. *Pictorial History of the Luftwaffe, 1933–1945.* London: Ian Allan, 1969.

Raeder, E. *My Life.* Annapolis, MD: Naval Institute Press, 1960.

Raleigh, W. *The War in the Air: Being the Story of the Part Played in the Great War by the Royal Air Force.* Vol. 1. Uckfield, East Sussex, UK: The Naval and Military Press Ltd., 1922.

Ranft, B. *The Beatty Papers.* Vol. 2, *1916–1927.* Leicester, UK: Scolar Press, 1993.

Ranson, E. *British Defence Policy and Appeasement between the Wars 1919–1939.* London: The Historical Association, 1993.

Raven, A., and J. Roberts. *British Battleships of World War II.* London: Arms and Armour Press, 1976.

Ray, J. *The Battle of Britain: New Perspectives: Behind the Scenes of the Great Air War.* London: Arms and Armour Press, 1994.

Robertson, B., ed. *Air Aces of the 1914–1918 War.* Letchworth, Hertfordshire, UK: Harleyford Publications, 1959.

———. *Von Richthofen and the Flying Circus.* Letchworth, Hertfordshire, UK: Harleyford Publications, 1964.

Robinson, D. *Invasion 1940: The Truth about the Battle of Britain and What Stopped Hitler.* London: Constable, 2005.

Roskill, S. *Admiral of the Fleet Earl Beatty: The Last Naval Hero.* London: Collins, 1981.

———. *The War at Sea, 1939–45.* Vol. 1. London: HMSO, 1954.

Ruge, F. *Sea Warfare 1939–1945.* London: Cassell, 1957.

Sassoon, S. *Memoirs of an Infantry Officer.* London: Faber & Faber, 1930.

Schenk, P. *Invasion of England, 1940.* London: Conway Maritime Press, 1990.

Scott, J. D. *History of Vickers.* London: Weidenfeld & Nicolson, 1962.

Smith, P. C. *Critical Conflict: The Royal Navy's Mediterranean Campaign in 1940.* Barnsley, South Yorkshire, UK: Pen & Sword Maritime, 2011.

————. *The History of Dive Bombing: A Comprehensive History from 1911 Onward*. Barnsley, South Yorkshire, UK: Pen & Sword Aviation, 2007.

————. *Skua! The Royal Navy's Dive-Bomber*. Barnsley, South Yorkshire, UK: Pen & Sword Aviation, 2006.

Snyder, G. S. *The Royal Oak Disaster*. London: William Kimber, 1976.

Spector, R. *At War at Sea: Sailors and Warfare in the Twentieth Century*. London: Allen Lane, 2001.

Stafford, D. *Roosevelt & Churchill: Men of Secrets*. London: Abacus, 2000.

Sumida, J. T. *In Defence of Naval Supremacy: Finance, Technology, and British Naval Policy 1884–1914*. Boston, Massachusetts and London: Unwin Hyman, 1989.

Temple Patterson, A., ed. *The Jellicoe Papers*. Vol. 1. London: Navy Records Society, 1966.

Terraine, J. *Business in Great Waters: The U-boat Wars, 1916–45* London: Mandarin Paperbacks, 1990.

————. *The Right of the Line: The Royal Air Force in the European War, 1939–1945*. Ware, Hertfordshire, UK: Wordsworth, 1997.

Thomas, A. *Royal Navy Aces of World War II*. Oxford: Osprey, 2007.

Towle, P. A. *Pilots and Rebels: The Use of Aircraft in Unconventional Warfare, 1918–1988*. London: Brassey's, 1989.

Webster, C., and N. Frankland. *The Strategic Air Offensive against Germany 1939–1945*. Vol. 4. London: HMSO, 1961.

Wells, H. G. *Anticipations of the Reaction of Mechanical and Scientific Progress upon Human Life and Thought*. London: Chapman & Hall, 1902.

————. *The War in the Air*. London: George Bell and Sons, 1908.

Winterbotham, F. W. *The Ultra Secret*. London: Weidenfeld & Nicolson, 1999.

Wood, A. *Nineteenth Century Britain, 1815–1914* London: Longman, 1996.

Wright, R. *Dowding and the Battle of Britain*. London: McDonald and Co., 1969.

Yergin, D. *The Prize: The Epic Quest for Oil, Money, and Power*. New York: Simon & Schuster, 1991.

Zamoyski, A. *The Forgotten Few: The Polish Air Force in the Second World War*. London: John Murray Publishers, Ltd., 1995.

Zimmerman, D. *Britain's Shield: Radar and the Defeat of the Luftwaffe*. Stroud, Gloucestershire, UK: Sutton Publishing Ltd., 2001.

Websites

Hansard

Baldwin, S. Statement by the Lord President of the Council. International Affairs HC, on 10 November 1932, Vol. 270, cc525–641, Hansard. http://hansard.millbanksystems.com/commons/1932/nov/10/international-affairs#S5CV0270P0_19321110_HOC_284 (accessed 15 August 2012).

Caldecote, Viscount. Emergency Powers (Defence) Bill 1939. HL Deb, 22 May 1940, Vol. 116, cc381–8, Hansard. http://hansard.millbanksystems.com/lords/1940/may/22/emergency-powers-defence-bill (accessed 31 January 2012).

Churchill, W. S. Speech. 15 December 1919, Hansard. http://hansard.mill banksystems.com/commons/1919/dec/15/pay-etc-of-the-air-force #S5CV0123P0_19191215_HOC_385 (accessed 22 July 2012).

Churchill, W. S. Speech to House of Commons, "Fleet Air Arm Success." 13 November 1940, Hansard. http://hansard.millbanksystems.com/commons/1940/nov/13/fleet-air-arm-success (accessed 1 August 2012).

Freeman, R., and N. Trotter. "Royal Air Force." 4 May1995, Hansard. http://hansard.millbanksystems.com/commons/1995/may/04/royal-air-force #S6CV0259P0_19950504_HOC_291 (accessed 19 October 2012).

Guest, Captain. Statement. 21 March 1922, Hansard. http://hansard.millbank systems.com/commons/1922/mar/21/captain-guests-statement (accessed 5 September 2011).

Hoare, Sir Samuel. Speech. 25 February 1926, Hansard. http://hansard.millbank systems.com/commons/1926/feb/25/sir-samuel-hoares-statement #S5CV0192P0_19260225_HOC_345 (accessed 22 July 2011).

McIntosh, Lord, of Haringey. First World War Debt. "Written Answer to Lord Laird." 23 October 2002, Hansard. http://hansard.millbanksystems.com/written_answers/2002/oct/23/first-world-war-debt (accessed 15 May 2009).

The Prime Minister. HC Deb, 25 May 1938, Vol. 336, cc1233–3531233, Hansard. http://hansard.millbanksystems.com/commons/1938/may/25/air-defenc es#S5CV0336P0_19380525_HOC_326 (accessed 10 January 2012).

Rothermere, Viscount. Speech to the House of Lords. "The Defence Services: Policy and Supply." HL Deb, 15 May 1935, Vol. 96, cc866–910, Hansard. http://hansard.millbanksystems.com/lords/1935/may/15/the-defence-services-policy-and-supply#S5LV0096P0_19350515_HOL_46 (accessed 15 August 2012).

Wood, Sir Kingsley. Statement. HC Deb, 09 March 1939, Vol. 344, cc2379–5082379, Hansard. http://hansard.millbanksystems.com/commons/1939/mar/09/sir-kingsley-woods-statement#S5CV0344P0_19390309_HOC_328 (accessed 5 January 2012).

Oxford Dictionary of National Biography

Various biographical entries, http://www.oxforddnb.com/

UK Ministry of Defence

"The Early Years of Flight." Chapter 1 in *A Short History of the Royal Air Force.* Royal Air Force. http://www.raf.mod.uk/rafcms/mediafiles/F21BE44E_ EE18_2A21_DE9200FADAA9DB6E.pdf (accessed 27 June 2014).

"Sixty Years Ago: 'The Channel Dash.'" Ministry of Defence, February 2002. Cited on the National Archives website: http://webarchive.nationalarchives.

gov.uk/+/http://www.operations.mod.uk/onthisday/newsItem_id=1451.htm (accessed 18 September 2012).

Thomas, E. "The Intelligence Aspect," in *The Battle Re-Thought: A Symposium on the Battle of Britain*, ed. H. Probert and S. Cox, 42– 46. Shrewsbury, UK: Airlife Publishing Ltd., 1991. http://www.rafmuseum.org .uk/documents/Research/RAF-Historical-Society-Journals/Bracknell-No-1-Battle-of-Britain.pdf (accessed 1 May 2012).

Phoenix Think Tank

Clapp, M. "Commanding Carrier Aviation." October 2010. http://www.phoenix thinktank.org/2011/05/commanding-carrier-aviation/ (accessed 13 September 2013).

Cumming, A. J. "Rivalry and Retreat: The Royal Navy and Royal Air Force in the Missile Age 1945–1970." June 2013, http://www.phoenixthinktank.org/ 2013/06/history-of-airpower-series-paper-4-rivalry-and-retreat-the-royal-navy-and-royal-air-force-in-the-missile-age-1945–1 (accessed 13 September 2013).

Grove, E. "It Has Happened Again: Lord Chatfield and his Critique of British Defence Policy Making." October 2012, http://www.phoenixthinktank.org/ 2012/10/lord-chatfield-and-his-critique-of-british-defence-policy-making/, (accessed 13 September 2013).

Velicogna, A., Clarke, A., Ward, S., Thomas, N., Gedge, T., Jermy, S., Clapp, M., Hobbs, D. "Naval Aviation: A Historical Perspective." http://www .phoenixthinktank.org/2011/07/naval-aviation-a-historical-perspective-2/ (accessed 13 September 2013).

***Time* Magazine Archive**

http://www.time.com/time/archive

The *Times* Digital Archive 1785–1985

http://infotrac.galegroup.com/

Other Websites, Including Other Newspapers

"8 Naval Squadron." *The Aerodrome: Aces and Aircraft of World War I.* http:// www.theaerodrome.com/services/gbritain/raf/208.php (accessed 9 August 2012).

Boorstin, D. Quote from *The Image: A Guide to Pseudo-Events in America.* Rockport Institute. http://www.rockportinstitute.com/transformational-quotes (accessed 15 August 2012).

Churchill, W. S. "Their Finest Hour." Speech to Parliament at Westminster, 18 June 1940. The Churchill Centre and Museum at Cabinet War Rooms, London. http://winstonchurchill.org/learn/speeches-of-winston-churchill/1940-finest-hour/122-their-finest-hour (accessed 3 March 2010).

———. "The Locust Years." Speech to House of Commons, 12 November 1936. The Churchill Society, London. http://www.churchill-society-London.org. uk (accessed 6 December 2011).

Clarke, I. F. "Future War Fiction: The First Main Phase, 1871–1900." *Science Fiction Studies* 24, Part 3 (November 1993). http://www.depauw.edu/sfs/clarkeess.htm (accessed 21 August 2012).

Cunningham, A. B., and R. Collishaw. *The London Gazette*, 4 March 1941. https://www.thegazette.co.uk/London/issue/35094/page/1303 (accessed 8 August 2012).

"Distance from Nancy to . . . ." TimeandDate.com. http://www.timeanddate.com/worldclock/distances.html?n=1288&sort=1 (accessed 9 June 2014).

Edwards, E. "The Battle of Britain Celebrations: Is it Over?" *Fleet Air Arm Association*. http://www.faaa.org.uk/?p=328 (accessed 23 June 2014).

Entry for UC-36 (+1917). WRECKSITE. http://www.wrecksite.eu/wreck.aspx?1685 (accessed 22 August 2012).

Foreword to "The Coalition: Our Programme for Government." As quoted in "The Strategic Defence and Security Review," 10 September 2010, UK Parliament Website, Parliamentary Business, Publications and Records. http://www.publications.parliament.uk/pa/cm201011/cmselect/cmdfence/writev/hc345/ucm0102.htm (accessed 23 October 2013).

Hague, A. "Convoy HX.79." *Arnold Hague Convoy Database*. http://www.convoyweb.org.uk/hx/index.html (accessed 13 May 2014).

Hollingsworth, W. "British Lord was Spy for Japan," http://www.japantimes.co.jp/news/2002/01/05/news/british-lord-was-spy-for-japan/#.U60_ufldUsQ (accessed 27 June 2014).

Holman, B. "Of a Cross-Channel Passage." *AIRMINDED: Airpower and British Society (mostly) 1908–1909*. http://airminded.org/2009/07/25/of-a-cross-channel-passage/ (accessed 3 February 2012).

Keeble, Major Peter. Obituary. *The Telegraph*, 15 February 2004. http://www.telegraph.co.uk/news/obituaries/1475298/Major-Peter-Keeble.html (accessed 15 February 2012).

Letchford, G. "Kent (Fortress) Royal Engineers in France." *WW2 People's War: An archive of World War Two memories - written by the public, gathered by the BBC*. http://www.bbc.co.uk/ww2peopleswar/stories/39/a4034639.shtml (accessed 15 February 2012).

Marqusee, M. "Imperial Whitewash: Feelgood versions of British history are blinding us to the ways in which we are even now repeating it." *Guardian*, 31 July 2006. http://www.guardian.co.uk/commentisfree/2006/jul/31/whitewashingtheempire, (accessed 26 July 2011).

Mason, G. B. "HMS *Rodney*—Nelson-class 16inch Gun Battleship." *Service Histories of Royal Navy Warships in World War 2*. Naval-History.net. http://www.naval-history.net/xGM-Chrono-01BB-Rodney.htm (accessed 23 February 2012).

———. "HMS *Gurkha*—Tribal Class Destroyer." *Service Histories of Royal Navy Warships in World War 2*. Naval-History.net. http://www.naval-history.net/xGM-Chrono-10DD-34Tribal-Gurkha1.htm (accessed 10 May 2009).

————. "HMS *Prince of Wales King George V*-class 14inch Gun Battleship." *Service Histories of Royal Navy Warships in World War 2*. Naval-His tory.net. http://www.naval-history.net/xGM-Chrono-01BB-Prince%20of% 20Wales.htm (accessed 27 February 2012).

Moran, D. "Strategic History and the History of War." Naval Postgraduate School. http://www.clausewitz.com/readings/Moran-StrategicTheory.pdf (accessed 22 July 2011).

"On this day, 10 April 1940." Fleet Air Arm Officers' Association. http://www .fleetairarmoa.org/news/on-this-day-10-april-1940 (accessed 12 June 2014).

"Origins." Schneider Trophy Website. http://www.hydroretro.net/coupeen/coupe eng.htm (accessed 25 July 2012).

"Our Mission." The Air League. http://www.airleague.co.uk/about/our-mission/ (accessed 21 March 2012).

Pilott, H. R. J. "A South East Londoner's Story—Chapter 1." Interview by henryjean. *WW2 People's War: An archive of World War Two memories - written by the public, gathered by the BBC*. 14 November 2003. http://www .bbc.co.uk/history/ww2peopleswar/stories/18/a2043118.shtml (accessed 2 December 2013).

"Rebuilding the Fw200 Condor is one of the most significant aircraft restoration projects in Europe." *Deutsche Lufthansa Berlin Stiftung*. http://www.dlbs.de/ en/Projects/Focke-Wulf-Condor/index.php (accessed 9 September 2013).

Sassoon, Siegfried. "Editorial Impressions" from *Counter-Attack and Other Poems*. New York: E. P. Dutton, 1918.

"Total Public Spending Expenditure, 1909 and 2009." UKPublicSpending.co.uk. http://www.ukpublicspending.co.uk/total_spending_2009UKmn (accessed 24 February 2012).

Toye, R. "Untold Stories of Churchill's World War II Speeches." University of Exeter Research News, 19 August 2013. http://www.exeter.ac.uk/news/ research/title_313389_en.html (accessed 13 September 2013).

"W. P. Lucy, RN," Fleet Air Arm Archive 1939–1945, http://www.fleetair armarchive.net/rollofhonour/COs/CommandingOfficers-l.htm.

Whitehouse, Arch. "The Zeppelin Raiders: An Excerpt from *The Years of the Sky Kings*." New York: Doubleday, 1964. Acepilots.com. Updated 16 April 2012. http://acepilots.com/wwi/zeppelin.html (accessed 19 September 2013).

Periodicals

Assmann, K. "Operation Sea Lion." U.S. Naval Institute *Proceedings* 76, no. 1 (January 1950).

Blumentritt, G. Extract from "An Cosantóir," trans. T. B. Dunne, British Intelligence Section, *The Irish Defence Journal* 1, no. 1 (1949): 10–14.

Brothers, Peter. "The Fewer." Interview by Nigel Lewis. *BBC History Magazine* 1, no. 2 (2000): 16.

Chamier, J. A. "The Use of Air Power for Replacing Military Garrisons." *RUSI Journal* 66 (February–November 1921).

Cook, C. "The Myth of the Aviator and the Flight to Fascism." *History Today* 53, no. 12 (2003): 41.

Corum, J. "The Myth of Air Control: Reassessing the History." *Aerospace Power Journal* (Winter 2000).

Cumming, A. J. "We'll get by with a little help from our friends: The Battle of Britain and the pilot in Anglo-American Relations, 1940–45." *European Journal of American Culture* 26, no. 1 (2007): 11–26.

Daso, D. A. "The Red Baron." *The Journal of the Air Force Association*. http://www.airforce-magazine.com/MagazineArchive/Pages/2012/March%20 2012/0312baron.aspx. (accessed 13 March 2012).

Douglas, R. M. "Did Britain Use Chemical Weapons in Mandatory Iraq?" *The Journal of Modern History* 81, no. 4 (December 2009): 859–887.

Farley, R. "Attack on Taranto." *Warships International Fleet Review* (January 2011): 42–43.

Franklin, G. D. "A Breakdown in Communication: Britain's Over-estimation of Asdic's Capabilities in the 1930s." *The Mariner's Mirror* 84, no. 2 (1988): 202–214.

Goulter, C., A. Gordon, and G. Sheffield. "The Royal Navy did not win the 'Battle of Britain': But we need a holistic view of Britain's defences in 1940." *RUSI Journal*, 20 October 2006, https://www.rusi.org/analysis/commentary/)/ ref:C4538D604EF124/#.U0J2g_ldWVI.

"The Great Air Fight." *Flight and the Aircraft Engineer*. Flightglobal/Archive, 14 November 1918, 1299. http://www.flightglobal.com/pdfarchive/view/ 1918/1918%20-%201298.html (accessed 24 September 2013).

Hart, P. "Part I: Our First World War—Oral Account of Dolly Shepherd." *BBC History Magazine*, June 2014, p. 61.

Harvey, A. D. "The Royal Air Force and Close Support, 1918–1940." *War in History* 15, no. 4 (2008): 475–476.

———. "The Stuka Myth." *BBC History Magazine Second World War Special: Britain's Year of Defiance* (2010): 52.

Holman, B. "The Shadow of the Airliner: Commercial Bombers and the Rhetorical Destruction of Britain, 1917–35." *Twentieth Century British History*, first published online: 10 December 2012. http://tcbh.oxfordjournals.org/ content/early/2012/12/09/tcbh.hws042.full?keytype=ref&ijkey=zoFEF12Y V5XswPg (accessed 22 August 2013).

Howland, V. "The Loss of the *Glorious*: An Analysis of the Action." *International Naval Research Organization*. http://www.warship.org/no11994.htm (accessed 29 August 2013).

Levy, J. "Lost Leader: Admiral of the Fleet, Sir Charles Forbes." *The Mariner's Mirror* 88, no. 2 (2002): 190.

McKinstry, L. "How the Spitfire Nearly Missed Its Finest Hour." *BBC History Magazine* 8, no. 11 (2007): 17–20.

Overy, R. "The Dangers of the Blitz Spirit: The History Essay." *BBC History Magazine*, October 2013, pp. 29–32.

Parsons, D. W. "British Air Control: A Model for the Application of Air Power in Low-Intensity Conflict?" *Airpower Journal*, Summer 1994.

Portal, C. F. A. "Air Force Co-operation in Policing the Empire." *Journal of the Royal United Service Institution*, May 1937.

Price, A. "Myth and Legend." *Aeroplane Monthly* 25, no. 10, iss. 294 (1997): 23.

Rees, L. "Hitler's Greatest Gamble." *BBC History Magazine Second World War Special: Britain's Year of Defiance*, 2010, pp. 27–28.

Roberts, J. "Call for Fire!" *Warships International Fleet Review*, June 2012, 39–41.

Skoulding, F. A."With 'Z' Unit in Somaliland." *The RAF Quarterly* 2, no. 3 (July 1931): 387–396.

Sumida, J. T. "The Best Laid Plans: The Development of British Battle-Fleet Tactics, 1919–1942." *International History Review* 14, no. 4 (1992): 681–700.

"The Sunderland I." *Flight and the Aircraft Engineer.* Flightglobal/Archive, 26 January 1939, 75–80. http://www.flightglobal.com/pdfarchive/view/1939/1939%20-%200185.html (accessed 9 September 2013).

Wells, H. G. "Aeronautics," *Time*, 11 June 1923, http://www.time.com/time/magazine/article/0,9171,736150,00.html (accessed 5 August 2013).

Whitham, C. "Seeing the Wood for the Trees: The British Foreign Office and the Anglo American Trade Agreement of 1938." *Twentieth Century British History* 16, no. 1 (2005): 29–51. http://tcbh.oupjournals.org/cgi/content/abstract/16/1/29 (accessed 25 April 2005).

Audiovisual Sources

Bader, D. Archive footage of Bader speaking on *Heroes of the Skies*. Channel 5, broadcast 25 September 2012.

Grove, Eric. "The Lost Submarine of World War I." Interview by Tony Robinson. *Time Team Special*, Channel 4, broadcast 31 August 2013.

Parliamentary Archives, London, House of Commons Parliamentary Papers Online. "Statistical Abstract for the United Kingdom 1924–1938" (CD Rom). Data from "National Revenue, Expenditure, etc., No. 151—Amount of the National Expenditure (Exchequer Issues) of the United Kingdom under the Principal Heads thereof, in each Year ended 31st March," Columns 1924-5–1938-9 (inc.). Ann Arbor, MI: ProQuest Information and Learning Company, 2006.

Portillo, M., D. Keen, P. Brothers, A. Lambert, V. Bailey, C. Barnett, and A. Fishlock. "The Battles of Britain—Transcript." *The Things We Forgot to Remember.* BBC Radio 4, broadcast 2005. The Open University, 17 May 2005. http://www.open.edu/openlearn/history-the-arts/history/the-battles-britain-transcript., (accessed 15 February 2012).

INDEX

ABOUT THE AUTHOR

Anthony J. Cumming, after a career in the British civil service, earned his PhD in history at the University of Plymouth in 2006. That year, he also won the University of London's Julian Corbett Prize for Research in Modern Naval History. He lives in Devon, UK, with his wife and pet greyhound.

The Naval Institute Press is the book-publishing arm of the U.S. Naval Institute, a private, nonprofit, membership society for sea service professionals and others who share an interest in naval and maritime affairs. Established in 1873 at the U.S. Naval Academy in Annapolis, Maryland, where its offices remain today, the Naval Institute has members worldwide.

Members of the Naval Institute support the education programs of the society and receive the influential monthly magazine *Proceedings* or the colorful bimonthly magazine *Naval History* and discounts on fine nautical prints and on ship and aircraft photos. They also have access to the transcripts of the Institute's Oral History Program and get discounted admission to any of the Institute-sponsored seminars offered around the country.

The Naval Institute's book-publishing program, begun in 1898 with basic guides to naval practices, has broadened its scope to include books of more general interest. Now the Naval Institute Press publishes about seventy titles each year, ranging from how-to books on boating and navigation to battle histories, biographies, ship and aircraft guides, and novels. Institute members receive significant discounts on the Press's more than eight hundred books in print.

Full-time students are eligible for special half-price membership rates. Life memberships are also available.

For a free catalog describing Naval Institute Press books currently available, and for further information about joining the U.S. Naval Institute, please write to:

Member Services
U.S. Naval Institute
291 Wood Road
Annapolis, MD 21402-5034
Telephone: (800) 233-8764
Fax: (410) 571-1703
Web address: www.usni.org